UCKINGHAM

HERTS

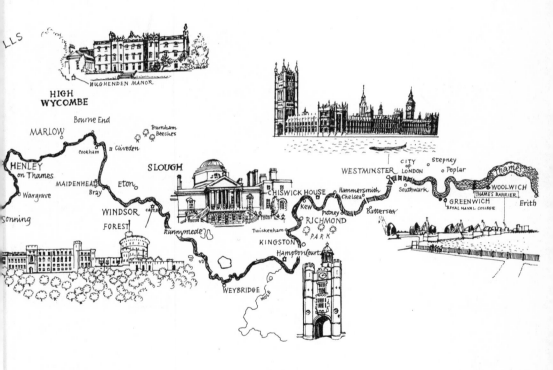

SURREY

A WALK ALONG THE THAMES PATH

Goring Gap: the view from downstream, near Streatley.

''Tis distance lends enchantment to the view.'

– *Pleasures of Hope*, Thomas Campbell

A WALK ALONG THE THAMES PATH

GARETH HUW DAVIES

Illustrated by Fiona Silver

MICHAEL JOSEPH
LONDON

MICHAEL JOSEPH LTD

Published by the Penguin Group
27 Wrights Lane, London W8 5TZ, England
Viking Penguin Inc., 40 West 23rd Street, New York, New York 10010, USA
Penguin Books Australia Ltd, Ringwood, Victoria, Australia
Penguin Books Canada Ltd, 2801 John Street, Markham, Ontario, Canada
L3R 1B4
Penguin Books (NZ) Ltd, 182–190 Wairau Road, Auckland 10, New Zealand

Penguin Books Ltd, Registered Offices: Harmondsworth, Middlesex, England

First published 1989

Photoset in 10½ on 12 pt Linotron Ehrhardt
by Wilmaset, Birkenhead, Wirral
Printed and bound in Great Britain by
Richard Clay Limited, Bungay, Suffolk

A CIP catalogue record for this book is available from the British Library

ISBN 0 7181 2969 5

The extracts from *Growltiger's Last Stand* and *Waste Land* are reproduced by
permission of Faber & Faber Ltd

To Avril, Laura and Timothy

Close to the source of the River Thames, near Kemble, Glos.

'Mighty things from small beginnings grow.'

– *Annus Mirabilis*, John Dryden

1

IT is wonderful how this walking through a country of a fine
summer's day heightens the heart.

— Charles Dickens, senior.

I DECIDED TO walk the bank of the river Thames, the 180 miles from its
source to the Thames Barrier at Woolwich, with no firmer purpose than to
watch an astonishing national institution unfold and to write an entirely
personal account of what I found upon its banks.

There is a cornucopia of writings on the Thames, from such sixteenth
century pioneer explorers of the lowlands as Leland to the consumer guides
that chart every inch of the navigable waterway, record every pub and lock
and bridge and ancient house. I will not attempt to emulate them. My
account will be incomplete and ought not to be used for navigation.

My plan is to steal upon an unsuspecting river and seek some of its
personality as it is reflected in the people who live and work beside it, or
upon it. And where it allows me, to tease out some of its secrets.

There are many grander and more testing walks than this in Britain. I
shall need neither heroism nor map reading skills. All previous long
distance footpaths, renamed national trails in 1989, had linked remote cast
out places. The Thames path is a masterstroke, a people's path, accessible
to the merest Sunday afternoon whim, or, over its full length, the mightiest
summer holiday ambition outside Britain's hills or coasts.

Three weeks should see the average walker through it. The Countryside
Commission expect it to be the best trudged of all their trails, exceeding
even the Pennine Way, with many thousands of users every year. For many
miles it runs exactly where it ought to, within inches of the water. Only
when it reaches London does its grip slip, like a badly printed overlay.

My route will be set with regular refreshment for body and spirit, in pub
and church and preserved building. There will be conversation and
diversion. There are many books to read.

1

Yet, too, there will be unexpected moments of bewildering isolation. And I shall learn that to be on the north bank when you require the south, or the other way round, is a rare frustration in an age that has declared the ferryman obsolete.

Victorian writers on my path could amble for many hours through river meadows where brown-armed hay makers looked up from their backbreaking toil. Many of the meadows are now subjected to a spiritless form of mechanised agriculture which extends to the very water's edge, evicting Ratty from his 'bijou riverside residence, above flood level and remote from noise and dust'*. Yet I will restore my spirits by recounting many a conservationist's bankside victory.

R.L.Stevenson found it astonishing what a river could do, 'all by following gravity in the innocence of its heart.' Veterans of upland treks find this river's inclines unexceptional. The Thames falls by only 600 feet from the source to London Bridge – 300 feet in the first nine miles; 100 feet in the next eleven; 100 in the next seventy-two miles to Great Marlow, 100 in the last forty-eight miles. But walkers will not find an easier long distance route.

So I set off, downhill all the way, to discover for myself the world's most illustrious river.

It is a slight beginning. A wide, low-shouldered valley and the faint memory of water, long ago flowed away. A thousand dandelion clocks marking time past, or time to come.

At the last stile, a scrum of Frisians loiter indifferently. 'Obstruct you? We always stand here.' An ash sprawls a branch out overhead, like a giant athlete straining for the tape.

But this is the beginning of the course. In the shelter of a high spinney of hawthorn and sycamore, stands a plain marble obelisk. 'The Conservators of the River Thames, 1857–1974. This stone was placed here to mark the source of the River Thames.'

It is marble, the material of high monuments, celebrating heroes and great moments in history. Formal enough for those places of official ceremonial, many miles downstream, it seems too grand for this pure, small corner. But it has served the purpose of those who put it here because it is unmarked by the vandal.

There is no water anywhere. No signs of a great river about to be born. I find signs of recent excavation. People come to find water, see none, so instinctively dig for it. Water diviners ply their sticks here and concentrate, unavailingly. Nothing gurgles from this shallow mark under its huge protective ash.

Wind in the Willows, Kenneth Grahame.

2

A rook probes for insects in this dry meadow. A chiff-chaff chimes noon in the spinney. A wren performing a sweet concerto for tiny voice, so rapid and complex it would defeat any human notation.

How did the river ever escape this quiet place deep in rural Gloucestershire? I have no doubt it was certainly here. Simple signs confirm it. An ancient line of tottering oak trees heads east: their roots may still find some refreshment in deep traces of the old river.

It is not only the river that has departed. On my left, Isambard Kingdom Brunel's navigators once leant on their spades. Their memorial, the London to Cheltenham railway passes within two hundred yards, and within view of this spot. Isambard's works will follow me all the way down to the sea, but his men never slaked their thirsts with such a pure draught as from the Thames' first clear bubblings here.

On my right great stones piled up for the Fosse Way, from Aquae Sulis to Corinium, its surveyor perfectly aware of the watery grove a few hundred paces to the north-west. His road, coming up from the south-west, is aimed straight at the very eye of the spring.

In the event he veered right and drove his road straight to Cirencester. This might be an astonishing coincidence in route making, or a matter of careful calculation, designed to bring good fortune to the road.

And so I follow a memory, on a morning in late spring, gently tipping into summer, along the fold of a deserted valley. Its route is so smoothed and softened by ploughing that there is now not the slightest sign that the River Thames ran here.

After a picnic lunch in a springy meadow and a detailed perusal of the 1:25,000 map, I get down to business and strike east to find water and the twentieth century.

The first firm evidence comes almost a mile to the east of the spring, across the screaming road, once the Fosse Way, now the A344, its spirit battered out by tarmac and the motor car. In the middle of a grass meadow I find a shattered stone footbridge, and beyond it, a defunct channel swaying across the field. It too is dry and empty in this year of downpour. But there is no question that this is the original course of the River Thames.

The channel snakes out of reach behind a fence. I stand on grazeable England. The fence excludes me from planted England. The dry channel strikes a straight line to the next bridge, a functional countryside arrangement of two pipes. It slips back under the fence and within a few yards this channel has drawn enough moisture out of the air or the land to accept the firm imprint of my boot.

As the Queen has two birthdays, so her greatest river has two beginnings, the actual and the ceremonial. In each case the ceremonial occasion is the grander. I stand now at the actual birthplace, the point where water first issues from the ground and after much adventure, will eventually find its way to the North Sea.

It is a witches cauldron, covered by a metal grill. It is encrusted with a residual chalky smear of vegetation, left from when the winter groundwater ebbed up. There is a foundation of stones about four feet down in the clear water. Through this courses the first undefiled waters of one of the world's greatest rivers.

Little dart-shaped creatures are its first inhabitants. I assume there are coins in there too, thrown in in hopeful first appeal to this water's magic. Their age will depend on when people first took this rival source seriously, and when the earlier source at Thameshead expired.

But there are no river gods in residence. This is not the Ganges or the Nile, and it bears none of the marks of people who venerate rivers. Father Thames has been bumped up and down the river in effigy: once, in a version made for the Great Exhibition, he reposed where the marble obelisk now stands, a powerless target for the vandal. He will reappear in this story in due time.

For a monument we have only a derilict agricultural relic, a wind pump croaking overhead, its irrelevant gyrations activated by the merest breeze.

I have found rising water. But methodical detective work requires more. Where is the *running* water to confirm that the river really is alive. A neat concrete channel is in place to usher any flow out of this moody place, but the River Thames tantalisingly refuses to run in it. A case of continuous maternity, beyond the womb.

This occasional river is green, heavily accompanied by hawthorn, oak and ash, but it is not yet wet. These trees were clearly once the custodians of something more important. For some yards, out of sight under their cover, the river continues to struggle for a viable existence. A thirsty cow could extinguish the Thames at this point.

I find circumstantial evidence of gathering wetness. A coot shoots upwards, on a Concorde-steep trajectory, the first water bird. Then another departure: two mallard beat up skywards, at the angle of lesser jets.

For the next two hundred yards, I cannot check the river's status. A dense carpet of marsh marigolds, smothers the channel. Then in a gap in this layer of green and yellow I see water, sharp and clear, six inches deep. The River Thames is flowing from a field in the parish of Kemble, Gloucestershire, bordered by the Roman road, the eighteenth century Thames and Severn Canal, nineteenth century railway and the A429. Essential England.

Set against the rivers of the world, the Thames is insignificant. A mere 250 miles long from source to estuary, it does not even make the list of the longest fifty. It could fit sixteen times into the Nile (4,160 miles). It would be an unimportant tributary to the Yellow River (3,010 miles), the Mekong (2,600), the Brahmaputra (1,840), the Danube (1,770), and even the Dnepr (1,420). In Europe it is outrun by the Rhine (820), the Elbe (720), and the Vistula (630).

The Thames trundles across six counties, four of which, Bucks, Oxfordshire, Wiltshire and Berkshire do not even possess first class cricket teams, and one of which, Middlesex, no longer exists as a local government entity. Its route is so tortuous that, unlike the Humber or the Trent or even the Severn, it carries no freight over much of its length, apart from the token coal boat, and probably never will again.

Yet the Thames, carving a silvery dividing line across southern England, stands above all other rivers as a historical focus. It has the most impeccable royal connections. It links palaces, dungeons, places of state execution, and Civil War battle sites. Thames bridges and embankments are named after royalty. Thames docks were royal docks.

Kings and queens drifted down the river in gilded barges until this century. For a time, when it was wider than it is today, the Thames in London inspired from Canaletto's brush the majestic, multi-coloured bustle of Venice. Its force and magic worked on one of the greatest of our landscape artists, Joseph Turner, until the hour of his death.

The Thames percolates through our finest literature, through Dickens and Shakespeare, T. S. Eliot and Wordsworth. It inspired one of the best remembered poems of the nineteenth century, 'Upon Westminster Bridge', and one of the most enchanting rural sagas of the twentieth, *The Wind in the Willows*.

The river is an indispensable servant, a national utility as both drain and provider of drinking water. The threat it once posed led men to build a wonder of the architectural world, and the public pay to admire the Thames Barrier, my finishing post.

The cleaning of the tidal Thames is one of this country's most spectacular acts of ecological improvement. That supreme arbiter of water purity, the salmon, swims again where only the Victorian utopians predicted it would ever return.

The transformation of London's deserted Docklands, once the world's grandest port, into a glittering, prosperous riverside community, is a remarkable achievement in urban renewal.

Its many famous associations are randomly bestowed. One of the world's most illustrious universities; certainly the most famous race on water between two craft; unquestionably the foreground to the most famous legislature; and the most important botanical gardens. Alone of our rivers it has a Father, a minor cousin of Neptune's, and its own police force.

In London, the river is a uniquely permanent force. London could be erased by planners or catastrophe, every blade of grass could be plucked out, but the river will flow on. Nothing short of terminal Northern Hemisphere drought could stop it.

When it all but dried up in 1976, the most searing summer for 250 years, its trickle in a muddy gash was the symbol of national crisis, not the baked fields of rural England. When it froze, as it frequently did until the nineteenth century, the Thames became an extension of London, a technicolour city of booths and marquees.

> THE best preparation for a walking holiday lies not in fine weather so much as in hard feet, and to get the feet hard there is but one way, and that is by walking. I have never found any other way effectual.
>
> – *With Knapsack and Notebook*, The Rev A. N. Cooper.

I had arrived at the Thames on an exuberant morning in late May, twenty miles south of Gloucester, thirty miles north-east of Bristol and closer still to the sea, the Severn Estuary. Yet my journey took little over an hour from Paddington Station on Brunel's swift railway.

This route, intertwined with the Thames for much of it its way, has much to enchant you. It passes one of southern England's most sensational mysteries, the Uffington White Horse, gouged from the turf of the Marlborough Downs by ancient man. It hangs this morning, mid-prance in the haze. I have passed it hundreds of times, yet each occasion this prehistoric vision is as thrilling as a child's first painting.

The train stops at Kemble. To reach Thameshead I strike north-west and within minutes out of the village pass stone walled fields. Turn right on to the Fosse Way for a few hundred yards, then left through an old railway goods yard near the site of the medieval village of Hillasey, back across the railway line on a public footpath and down to Trewsbury Mead to the river's original birthplace.

So in less than two hours from Paddington, I find the thread which shall guide me to the edge of the North Sea. Before long I am striding through the safe bosom of England, a place drenched in history, to the spot where I first saw running water.

From here I have a choice of destinations. The first is from here to Cricklade, eleven and a half miles away. The second is a further ten miles to Lechlade, where official boating begins, offering voyages to wherever your fancy and your vessel may take you, to the ends of the earth if you wish. The third is Oxford, an additional thirty miles from Lechlade, five days' walking from where I stand. Today my ambition is modest. Let the walk to Cricklade soften my boots and stiffen my calves.

A continuous drift of water crowfoot, like headlights in a long exposure night photograph, reforms to cover the river. On the north bank the discernible beginning of the river is celebrated, not by English oaks but with a line of alien conifers. Dry-stone walls, topped with vertical lines of stones stacked like books, parcel up the fields.

Before I have gone a mile, I hear news from downriver. The Thames is still flowing. John and Marie carry the tidings. They have cycled from London in three days and are sitting over their picnic at a point where the river, after its indecisive start, now has tangible form. They made high speed westwards to Windsor, 'where the river is civilised', then met a succession of stiles.

The cyclists set off to Bath, whence they will turn eastwards along the Kennet and Avon canal. It will be an easier, duller route, entirely dictated by man. In due course the River Thames will swallow the Kennet and welcome them back at Reading.

Here the Kemble to Cirencester railway steps over the river and the thundering A429. It is, of course, closed, like most of our discreet country railways. There is a profuse tangle on this silent highway, which still cuts straight and obliging into Kemble as if awaiting a second coming. The Thames, invigorated by the intermingling of two streams, squeezes under both road and railway like a wise old man walking past an argument.

For a few hundred yards the river is more vegetation than water, a dense buffer of water crowfoot overlying a sluggish drift. Then at last, just below Clayfurlong Farm, the River Thames is deep enough for me to tentatively and symbolically dip a toe.

In earlier days the river must have flowed strongly here and been capable of significant flooding. There is a stout barrier of oak and ash, waymarking, and helping to hold the water in. Now the river has an occasional status, rather like a desert stream activated by deluge, although after two days of rain there is no obvious sign of impending spate.

The Kemble to Ewen road crosses on Parker's Bridge, two low arches ample enough to admit a flood of water crowfoot, as a joyful alternative to water.

I am on the edge of Ewen. The parish notice board fixes its place in official England. It is in the parish of Kemble, in the district council ward of Thameshead, in the constituency of Tewkesbury and Cirencester, and in the European constituency of The Cotswolds.

It is also the first settlement on the Thames, about as close to the beginning of the river as, a curve of the Earth away, Southend-on-Sea is to its end.

Many of its stone houses have an intense creamy-golden beauty, highlighted with lichen. This original work was memorable. Some later imitators were less successful. The same raw materials are available in the hills to the north, but standards seem to have slipped. Could not any of those many layers of authority on the notice board have preserved such excellence?

There are incongruous touches throughout our landscape. I am not in the least surprised to find black Welsh mountain sheep cropping an Ewen meadow.

Like many villages, Ewen does not welcome hasty or disrespectful intruders. A freelance notice tries where many official thirty miles an hour speed limit signs have failed. 'Slow: cats and dogs.' Who could disobey? But if terrorising animals is wrong, so too is blighting the landscape. A monstrous snub-nosed silo rises in vulgar challenge to those fine houses.

I need no longer fear for the survival of the River Thames. Identity crisis overcome, it is flowing freely under the bridge at Home Farm. A heron rises languidly with the characteristic resistance to sudden departure of birds with big wings.

Where there are herons there must be fish. I muse inexpertly on a vast community of water life, exercising theoretical free passage from Gloucestershire to the North Sea.

Before it becomes tedious to record too many firsts, there is one more. On a slight fall below Ewen, I come upon what can only be described as a pride of swans, the archetypal family group. It is early summer, and the two cygnets are already the size of fluffy footballs. But at my sudden alien presence over a familiar horizon, the mother unleashes the sustained hiss of a high-pressure puncture in fearsome warning.

Now the young river can be credited with a temper. It is spririted enough to exceed its confines, so the dreary hand of the engineer has created a concrete weir. But he still tolerates playfulness and lets the Thames meander beyond with those full curves produced by wiggling a rope on a flat surface.

Ordered slabs of cereals border alternate sides of the river, where once there was meadowland. The river has already become a refuge to persecuted wildlife. It is a corridor in which plants and creatures may live and expand. Where else in Gloucestershire can the yellow flag iris, with its sword leaves and head as vivid as a traffic light, flower so securely?

A kestrel beats time over the warming afternoon land. The cygnets I passed upstream, we can be assured, are too big to be threatened. If a swan can break a man's arm, it can rout a kestrel.

At Upper Mill Farm, six hundred yards beyond Ewen, the river has been manipulated as an aesthetic feature. It has been bent to the right like a pipe

8

cleaner, and tamed to gush out of a stone wall. It scurries secretly down past the farm, away from the path. I walk over a field of newly cut hay into Somerford Keynes and experience that glorious refreshment of a summer afternoon after heavy rain.

Sunshine, high wind and newly cut field. The components of workaday rural England in summer. This was a flat and monochrome countryside when the sun was in. But the clouds have cleared and it is refreshed and brilliant. I look for the comforting certainties of the two and a half inch to the mile map. Everything in its place – wind pump, foot bridges, the footpath to All Saints, even though the scale is now 1:25,000.

'If church locked, phone the vicar on . . . ' says a note in the porch. Wonders. It is open, yielding to my tentative touch. This is the parish of Somerford Keynes. The parish is a wonderfully random subdivision, its boundaries known only to those who live in them, and to map readers. An uncountable succession of parishes interlock from here to London, each with a small group of elected citizens weighing their tiny concerns. I write as one: our deepest cares are nothing to the person living a mile away in the next parish.

I am inside that calm, serene space of the parish church. Suspended between Sundays, between centuries. It is Mrs G. Axe's week for flower duty. There is a note for the despairing from the Swindon Samaritans. John and Evelyn Ready, of Buffalo, New York, were the church's last visitors. They have added an explanatory note. It appears that Evelyn is descended from Thomas Gardner, born 1592, who emigrated to Massachusetts in 1632. How did the Thames flow then?

Five local Haywards died in the Great War. John Bowley expired in 1911, leaving £100, the interest of which is to keep in good order the graves of his father, mother and sisters. He also left £200 for 'four poor men and four poor women.' But Mr Bowley's charity came with a self-regarding condition, 'That a marble tablet be placed in the church to record these legacies.'

I return to the river and follow the path a mile or so east. The land between Somerford Keynes and Ashton Keynes has been hollowed out to serve the pre-mix concrete industry, spoiling the look of the Thames in its most agreeable youth. Vast seas of gravel, deposited aeons ago by a huge ancestor river, have been extracted in shallow pits the size of villages.

The river picks its way through big sheets of blue; on the map it is shown as a vulnerable hair-thin line. But there is the compensation of new habitat. I find an artificial lake with edges already softened by planted rushes, flickering with dragonflies.

At Lower Mill Farm, now the vital hub of the Cotswolds Water Sports Centre ('three lakes, 350 members') the Thames has acquired two enclosing walls, but the proprietors have not given it a name. I conduct a straw poll of patrons which confirms that many people do not know the identity of the gurgling flow they cross on their way from their cars to the shop which sells everything a windsurfer would need.

A lady in a black wet suit furls a rainbow sail and tells a typical story of the becalmed beginner. 'It took me about half an hour of very hard work to get anywhere near the shore.' It is a big lake. A man in gold-rimmed spectacles and an unnecessarily heavy blue anorak tells me they pray for wind, of not more than ten and not less than three knots.

The Thames, having nothing to do with sport at this point, squeezes through the heart of this place of wet-suited acolytes of the wind and sets off in perfect incongruity. I am walking along the top of a high cliff, which from the side looks like some cut-away geological model. Should one of the mechanical diggers, which are gouging and scraping the gravel beneath, stray too close and pierce the cliff's foundations the entire river Thames would spill on to the pit's rugged bottom like a child's bucket of water upset on the beach.

But the river runs safely on under heavy woodland cover, through Freeth's Wood and Flood Hatches Copse, to Ashton Keynes. A Thames Water Authority control room, built in 1939 in imitation of a GWR railway station, offers tantalising glimpses of gadgets and dials which now order the flow.

Ashton Keynes is a copywriter's village: a beehive in a back garden; a black cat asleep on a doormat; a memorial seat; 'presented by the Ashton Keynes and Leigh WI on the occasion of their jubilee, 1920-1970'. The Long House has been re-roofed in natural stone. Ducks waddle down the main road. Each house has its own bridge. A notice on a telegraph post advertises a classical guitar concert.

But I cannot cheat. The villagers know this is an alternative Thames, even if the estate agents might not volunteer the fact. One branch of the river has already slipped away south to meander around the back of the village. Nature never orders its lines as neatly as this. The branch I see was routed through Ashton to feed the mill in a distant century. But if Hollywood were making a film, set on the juvenile Thames, I'm sure they would bring their cameras into Ashton.

Ray Cooper, a twinkling man in his seventies, is busy with an old green mower on the wide fringe of grass which borders the new Thames. He is a Gloucestershire man; we are now in Wiltshire. He moved here more than half a century ago, in 1933, and has not yet fully come to terms with his new locality.

'When we moved here I said to Father "I won't stick it. Let's go back".'

'Father said "No, son. We'll wear them down." And we did.'

10

Ashton folk were very strange, he recalls. 'If Ashton lost a football match, the referee would be in the brook.'

He remembers floods: in 1936 a summer storm washed the hay crop away. Cows were confined to the barns. Children were passed over the school wall by a man on a bicycle who had pedalled them through the high waters. During the war American soldiers battered down fine old gateposts with their tanks.

Ray doesn't know many of the new Ashtonians who drive their bright company cars over the neat line of drawbridges to distant jobs every morning. I leave this good natured exile as he dreams still of Gloucestershire.

The lawn he has yet to cut comes to an end. In and out of the stone wall which wraps around the last house in Ashton, a busy provider is working. Every nine seconds, a ball of blue and yellow streaks out. A blue tit is raiding for its family a convenient larder, a gnarled old elm tree opposite.

Ashton is about as conventionally pretty a place as I shall find on the Thames. I leave it by wading through a rich meadow still drenched with the earlier rain. The river is becalmed, wandering quietly on behind a fence, twenty yards to my left. There is sweet spontaneous music: the sudden cascade of a chiff-chaff; the sad descending song of a willow warbler.

Clover flowers set a golden haze upon the meadow, like smeared butter. This effect is sustained over three fields. Squadrons of big black dragonflies dance and spurt from the river, which runs deep and slow. A common sandpiper sprints away on juddering wings. Cows slurp from the flow at a trodden-down drinking point.

Two miles out from Ashton on one of the many wiggles in the river at Waterhay, I make my picnic table on an ancient stone farm bridge, garlanded with yellow stonecrop, while intermittent war continues in the air under my feet. Dragonflies on four powerful translucent wings command their airspace. They swing across to repel bewildered insect intruders, engaging them in sudden dogfight.

The abuse of the river was an environmental scandal of the sixties and seventies. The blame can be pinned on the vast water authorities, distant and beyond democratic accountability. Banks were remoulded as cross sections from a geometry textbook; rivers were allowed to dry up through drainage and the lowering of the water table. It didn't matter that the river was a fundamental thread running through a community.

But the Thames has many friends, and it has suffered less than most. Here, swollen with the waters of Swill Brook, it is dignified on my map as two parallel lines enclosing a corridor of blue. I walk on for a mile or so, around the bottom of Hailstone Hill where the river flows clear and swift, water weed bent flat by the surge. Hailstone House peers into the far north.

11

The only thing to mar its perfect aspect is the regular passage of enormous military aircraft.

The course of the former and long defunct Midland and South Western Junction railway from Cheltenham to Andover crosses the river here. Old railways were ambitious in their choice of destinations: this simple little line unlocked the whole of southern England to the west Midlands.

Its silent route is marked by a wall of high trees. While most industrial remains subside into their landscape, disused railway lines flourish as luxuriant, growing relics.

Swindon Golden Carp Anglers Association asserts its rights to the river with a notice: 'Private Fishing, By Order, (signed S. Scott, Sec.)'. It is the first claim upon the river, which had been open to all up to this point.

The river is still small enough to allow sudden discoveries. A little crumbling wharf of lichen-encrusted stones; a party of eight ducklings bursting out from the sheltering bank like Olympic swimmers.

St Sampson church, Cricklade, appears in the east, the four pinnacles on its tower the shape of newly-sharpened pencils crammed into a holder. An elderly man, walking out of the town, says they don't look after the river as they used to. He has heard of evil substances flowing off farmed land. This is the common man's perception of the poisoning of the countryside.

I reach an official sign advertising a wonder of lowland Britain: 'One of the finest examples in Great Britain of ancient meadow, noted for rich plant life, which has been mantained by long and consistent management for hay-making and subsequent grazing. From August 1st to February 12th, the land is subject to common grazing rights.' This is how the Nature Conservancy Council records North Meadow, half a mile west of Cricklade.

It is as if I have chanced upon a great master in a provincial art gallery. Imagine an East Anglian prairie. Then replace the wheat in that huge unhedged sweep with a dozen types of meadow flower and thirty different grasses. This is the shock of North Meadow, a mile-long torrent of red and yellow, spreading, transmuting and dissolving from April until July.

My footpath runs directly alongside this, the finest flowerbed on the entire river, three feet of alluvium on a flat gravel base, the product of centuries of dousing by the Thames. Today, by comparison, the rest of the Thames valley is destitute.

North Meadow does two surprising things: it offers the abundant spread of the old hay meadow, through which those Victorian writers in whose path I follow waded half the way to London, kicking up clouds of seeds and perfume. And it contains a desperately rare flower, the snake's head fritillary, in glorious natural abundance.

If this meadow's fritillaries, with their melancholic hanging heads, chequered red and purple, were a crop, the EEC would have to seriously consider restraining their numbers. There are about three million in this 112 acres, an estimated three quarters of the British population.

Geoffrey Grigson, writing in his *Englishman's Flora* (Phoenix House, 1958), considers the snake's head fritillary to be a botanical aberration. He cannot believe that early sharp-eyed botanists could have missed it in the wild before its first official record in 1736, at a time when it was certainly grown in gardens. The botanist Lyte wrote in 1597 'Of the faculties of these pleasant flowers there is nothing set downe in the ancient or later writers, but they are greatly esteemed for the beautifieng of our gardens.' Grigson concludes that the fritillary escaped from Tudor and Jacobean gardens.

My guide, Keith Porter, of the Nature Conservancy Council, looks in vain for its seed heads – the fritillary is believed to multiply through its bulbs – and finds an adder's tongue fern instead. A chimney sweep moth grips a stem – small, jet black except for a tiny white fleck on the edge of its wings. A banded agrion, a dragonfly on dark wings, snipes in a limitless territory. I pick out a snail as tiny as a baby's toenail.

I have never found grasses particularly interesting. Here they are spaced out like exhibits at a show, some with thin streamlined heads erect, others flopping in the pose of a frozen firework on hair-thin stems. There is meadow barley, meadow brome, tufted hair grass, and a dozen others.

As we wander round the edge of the moor we pass, in the sea of yellow and white, little distinct islands of colour – the Burgundy-red heads of the great burnet, the soft creams of meadow rue, and pepper saxifrage.

Keith, whose pleasant job it is to patrol these tranquil acres, detects changes from year to year, caused by slight fluctuations in weather, favouring now the sorrel over the hay rattle, now the yellow of the buttercup over the blue of self-heal.

How did this miracle come about? Almost certainly through man's agency. Eight hundred years ago this marshy land might have been alder carr and willow. It seems the Saxon farmers tamed it, and turned their beasts on it.

Under the 1824 Enclosure Act, which abolished strip farming, it ought to have been parcelled into modest fields. This would surely have broken for ever this elegant sweep of flower and grass. By now those fields would in turn have been turned over to the various tedious expressions of modern agriculture.

But North Meadow was never enclosed. Instead it was divided into grazing plots, marked with hefty stones and imaginary lines. Rights were apportioned to townspeople. They were granted first vesture – anything that falls to the sweep of a scythe. Today the ancient Lammas system prevails on the meadow: anyone in the borough of Cricklade is allowed to graze their animals from Lammas, August 1st, to Lady Day, February 12th. So bizarre is the scope of official preservation, that the very marking stones, on which are chiselled the initials of their original tenants, are designated as listed buildings.

In 1974 North Meadow was declared one of the 240 or so national nature reserves. The Nature Conservancy Council licences the July hay harvest, but by tractor hauled mower not scythe. They have allowed North Meadow to spring up, in microcosm, across Britain. Part of the meadow is harvested for seed, which is sucked from the mown hay by a vacuum process.

Yet the defence of this exceptional habitat is not complete. The modern farmer prefers his cattle to dine on rich nitrogen-boosted grass, whereas this colourful mixture would be full of mysteries to the modern beast, like some exotic breakfast cereal set before a child raised on pap. 'They don't think it is productive enough,' says Keith.

Once a year the Thames pours out through a gap in the hedge at the north corner, flooding part of the meadow with a nitrogen and slurry-based cocktail. At this young stage of the river, the side-effects of this rich soaking are slight: perhaps it brings on the ladies smock at the expense of the creeping buttercup or the bulbous buttercup.

In one corner that lanky invader of the common roadside, the hogweed, is raising its umbrella head above the summering flowers. They don't want it here, but because the council cannot fix the exact time the meadow is cut, it cannot stop the hogweed setting seed. Careful husbandry will be required to eradicate it.

I leave this meadow with the thrill I might experience as the single member of the audience hearing one of the fine orchestras. Brilliant in its constituent parts, gloriously drawn together. The neglect and abuse of the countryside shames us all.

In the dimming evening I trudge into Cricklade. I shall carry away the image of this miraculously surviving tapestry as far as the sea.

> TWILL surely rain, I see with sorrow
> Our jaunt must be put off tomorrow.
> – Edward Jenner.

The next morning I pick up my tracks by North Meadow. Today will see the last of this carefree first leg of the walk as far as Lechlade, nine miles from here. There are still no clues of impending greatness. This could still be any ambling waterway somewhere in lowland England.

I am preoccupied by the colour of the sky, that profound, impenetrable blue-grey of memorable downpours. There is no escape, no prospect of a relieving shaft of sunlight with which landscape artists, daunted by the monochrome, dreary reality of many summer days, illuminate their canvas. I have a minute and a half in which to minimise the damage.

My anorak is allegedly showerproof. Now for the supreme test. I crouch under a hawthorn and lodge my head between my knees. By this inelegant contortion I present the smallest undefended surface to the rain.

It works. The anorak does its rain-repelling duty. A river flows down my back and opens out into a delta over the curve of my bottom. A secondary channel breaks into rivulets over my knees. My calf muscles are stretched painfully as I crouch. I am so delicately balanced that the touch of a fingertip would be sufficient to despatch me into four feet of clear, still water.

I muse on the hypothetical inconvenience of such mischief. How, soaked to the skin, do you beg the formality of a stranger's bathroom? How would a dripping wet person otherwise last out the day? Do I book back into a hotel, simply to dry myself, hoping the radiators are hot?

But the tree has done its best. The damage is limited to five small islands of wet on my knees and back. The staccato beat on the placid river relents until the tree is releasing more water than the sky. It stops raining.

Cricklade was originally an Alfredan burgh, cosily enclosed by bank and ditch. In a field name just below the town there is a clue to an ancient function. It is The Forty, probably referring to the forty paces in an archery range. Since the 1500s the town has been dominated by St Sampson's great central Tudor Tower. 'In lovely surroundings, abounding in all kinds of riches,' wrote an early visitor.

Charles Dickens junior wrote it off in the following terms in his close-detailed *Dictionary of the Thames* published in 1893: 'Pleasant little town, clean and well paved, but has not been the scene of any particularly remarkable events, since it shared the fate of so many other Thames towns and was plundered by the Danes in 1015.'

However, Cricklade is still a town important enough to acknowledge the river with a wide sign, 'River Thames', at High Bridge, the first of seventy bridges between here and Staines. But young men (I assume) who have a grudge against notices announcing grand things have defaced it with private inanities. Why is graffiti so tedious. Where are the witty daubers? Where is Kilroy?

The river brushes past Cricklade. Tiny craft are occasionally set upon it here to batter through the undergrowth to Lechlade, the accepted starting point to navigation. Cricklade never had the commercial justification to sit itself firmly on the river.

I walk through ways whose names speak of long abandoned uses: Horse Fair Lane, Abingdon Court Lane. Then past a pink-washed house and a farm on the edge of the town, down a narrow country lane and through a sweet wall of elderflower perfume. Milky-brown soil eroded by the downpour is drifting into the water.

The Romans made their second crossing of the river with Ermin Way at Cricklade. A few hundred yards east at Calcut Forty, is the recent crossing, relieving the town. It is an unearthly place. The river is chaperoned under the road in a strict concrete channel. The roar of vehicles is etched into a corridor of sullied ground about a hundred yards wide. Even when there is no lorry in sight, a dull, low undercurrent of sound persists.

I escape the din briefly as I pass under the road. I leave this precious silence and the noise thuds back. One part of my mind is busy repressing this awful sound, while another extracts compensations from the view ahead, a pleasant stretch of low farmed countryside rising to a distant southern rim of hills.

I look back to see the product of thoughtful landscaping. It is a miraculous vista. The awful road is no longer there. It has been erased. The view is composed of Cricklade's church tower, some tall trees, a line of hedge, the river's reed fringes, and the curve of the river. The road is totally invisible behind a high hedge which partly smothers its sound. In winter, of course, this barrier is lost: the road returns, striking out the bottom half of the spire, with lorries shuttling through the bare branches of the hedges.

Ahead there is a home for Eyore, Winnie the Pooh's friend. A ramshackled field of tussocks, thistles and buttercups. If this riverbank walk can be divided into parishes, then the next subdivision is the field. Almost every field is different. I step over a stile from a finely-tilled shrine to the Euro-subsidy, into an untamed relic of prehistory.

A family of warblers tizz across the water. The river is narrow enough to suffer a casual indignity: a short coarse concrete bridge carries a pipe across. A field has been ploughed to the river's very brim, pushed out like pastry. Whatever grew on the bankside has been smothered.

I cross Eysey footbridge. It is seventeen paces long: about twenty metres. The Thames passes under at a rush, rapidly accumulating. Drainage channels slip in unnoticed, and crank up its volume by imperceptible amounts. I eat my picnic on a fisherman's stile under the flank of Eysey Hill. No richly spread table at a Thames hostelry can match this simple pleasure.

Although the engines of agriculture can accomplish most things, this hill's incline makes it unploughable. It is an ancient marker. When the land is flat, we cannot tell where the river's course was 1,000 years ago. But a sudden hill like this must have set the northern limit of its wanderings on this otherwise level land.

Into the second of my Thermos's two and a half cups of coffee, I notice that I am sitting within a whisker of an electric fence, by Gallagher Energisers of Oakham. Today it is de-energised, but I would welcome a warning of the countryside's little perils.

There is a commotion on the other side of the high ground. It is some urgent call rising out of this or another time. Nothing is visible. It multiplies and rises to a buzzing, wailing roar. What can it be, the huge hysterical sound of an ancient people in distress?

It is not until I hear the stronger tones of men in control that I deduce that I heard a flock of sheep being driven to pasture. But I never saw either men or sheep. Without visual confirmation, sound in the countryside can outwit. This sound had struggled round the hill and assumed the malevolence of an apparition.

I walk on through an eerie place, a field newly-ploughed in June. Steam is drifting off it in ghostly swirls. There is a solitary lapwing above me, its tortured piping a mixture of lamentation and hysteria. Is it coaxing a partner or deterring me? It gambols crazily for about five minutes, worrying the skies.

Again my path, mainly grass with not too much churned mud, changes sides from south bank to north bank. Here the flow is strong enough to bear away small trees; the river passes under me with a confident gurgle of purpose. To demonstrate its growing power it swallows whole the River Ray which has straggled up from the south.

The river drifts through a drowsy countryside: it is spare and reticent with few features and names. Those names I do find on my map are quaint or mysterious – Frogpit Cottages, Plague Cottages. The explanation is in the flatness. Nobody trusted the Thames here. Early man stood back and only sent his cows on to its meadows for summer grazing. There is a more permanent and cheerfully domestic ring to the names only when the contours begin – in Cherry Tree, Sycamore Tree, and Boxhedge farms.

In Castle Eaton, three miles north-east of Cricklade, the message from my protesting legs is that the Red Lion, the first pub on the bank of the Thames, is an appropriate place to stop. I hear the incongruous clunk of steel upon steel, interspersed with technical expressions which, as I move closer, turn out to be in French. Three teachers from a Swindon College look up and throw a flimsy cordon around their identities.

Under questioning they are doubly exposed – as masters absent in school hours, released, they assure me, from invigilation during exams; and as players in the stark middle of this pub's *pétanque* piste.

'We have twenty pence on this match. It's very tense,' says Godfrey, which may or may not be his real name. A boule from Peter, quivering with

17

heavy back spin, thuds down and sends Godfrey's ball leap-frogging over the cochonet into oblivion.

'Describe us as cross country players,' says Jonathan. 'This piste is terribly English and conformist. We prefer to play like the French, all round the church, half way around the village.'

A short ricochet from the Thames, I have discovered the true all-weather sport. On the typical, fickle British summer afternoon of dancing raindrops and mournful cricketers stranded on the pavilion steps, games of boules cluck happily on under a forest of umbrellas.

The books describe boules as a highly sociable game. Landlord Hans Hauck-Rogers interpreted 'sociable' as associated with a pub and built a piste on thirty-eight tonnes of bricks and gravel, to revive the fortunes of his hostelry. The door of his public bar stands reassuringly open nearby.

His pub team is 'middle of the road', but it cannot find sufficient local competition by which to measure its improvement or decline. The nearest clubs in the British Pétanque Association are in Oxford, High Wycombe and Southampton. 'We are like darts players. Reluctant to travel further than ten miles for a match.' However, he has beaten genuine French opposition, the visiting André and his family.

I leave the Red Lion, to theatrical French oaths from the teachers, unwilling to discard my idealised notion of the most perfectly French game, played in the village square under a hot sun by inscrutable old men in berets, while swallows screech overhead.

The Red Lion may expect few riverborne patrons. The Victorian writer J. E. Vincent, in his *Story of the Thames*, concludes that above Lechlade, boating is the 'mere labour and sorrow' of penetrating the weeds past Castle Eaton and Kempsford to Cricklade.

It took an acquaintace of Vincent's in a canoe, around the turn of the century, from 10.30 until 5 p.m. to reach Cricklade from Lechlade. 'Not to be recommended except to those who can watch for an abundance of water or the clearing of leaves. And then not unless they have that superabundance of vigour in exercise often characteristic of the Oxford tutor.'

Yet slipping up river here at Kempsford, four and a half miles beyond Lechlade, is George MacFarlane. He is not only the first person I have seen boating on the river, but also one of the most remarkable. George had left Sheerness on the mouth of the tidal Thames two weeks earlier to row the river.

Many have rowed the river in the other direction, with the hand of the river firmly in their backs. No one, say the record books, has rowed upstream faster, single handed than George, although the writer William Morris certainly rowed it twice from West London to Kelmscot, ten miles downstream from here. He awaits a challenger.

George's is an inspiring story, and I am happy to tell it. He had reached Lechlade yesterday, where he took it upon himself to go through to Cricklade, his dash for the Pole, nine miles on. He booked into the inn in Lechlade so that, if necessary, he could retreat in the dark.

This morning he had laboured unfussily upstream on this dreamy reach. At Hannington Bridge, a few miles on from here, he sensed that the river was about to defeat him. It was constricting him and squeezing him off. The bridge was too narrow to allow him to lower his oars inside it. So he rowed hard at it, drifted half way in and hooked himself through to the other side.

This final section of the river is like a giant ditch in places. Pressed in by corn and nettles, he has to jink around tumbled trees. He decides to stop. Kempsford Church comes into sight, but he cannot find a landing spot. One farmer refuses him a mooring; a menacing dog warns him off a garden, so he presses on. His boat is trapping twigs and leaves; his blades are scratched.

I meet him at Kempsford where he calls it a day. He pulls the boat into the reeds and we sit on some steps a farmer had built and share a can of beer. He tells me of distant places which I shall reach by following this blue thread at our feet.

George MacFarlane is a distinguished son of the Thames. He is a freeman of the river, a Thames waterman, journeyman, lighterman and former master of a tanker which plied from the deeps off Southend to Hammersmith in West London. He is a swan upper. As a freeman of the Thames, he dressed in a scarlet cloak and rode in a carriage at the Duke of York's wedding.

His desire to row the river was born out of a boyhood impatience to round the bend in the Thames beyond Wapping Ness when he worked with his father on a skiff between Limehouse and Wapping. They moored ships, and rowed stevedores and crews to and from the boats, and served as mudpilots, 'shifting ships about'.

He went on to the river at the age of fifteen in 1942, and has been on it ever since. He came to know the river as a waterman from Tilbury to Brentford, and a swan upper between Blackfriars and Pangbourne. 'I had an urge to see the rest of it. There are only two ways: to walk it or row it.' (He rows every Sunday morning with the Poplar and Blackwall, Isle of Dogs club.) 'I always wanted to do it when I packed up at sixty, this year. My wife said "Get on and do it." '

He spent four years planning his trip. He borrowed his boat, a treble sculler or randan, from Mark Edwards, boat builder at Hampton Court. Friends made him an anti-theft device, a long wire leash, which could be strung through the boat and padlocked.

19

He left Sheerness on one of this summer's few beautiful mornings. 'The sea was like a mill pond. A coxwain in the harbour signed my logbook to prove I had left.' Using his waterman's skills he passed through London on the flow tide.

On the non-tidal river he battled against millions of gallons of land water, surging off the drenched land. Muscles, full of fight on the first day, could scarcely stretch the blades. 'I had to stop and hang on to trees to have a blow. It was practically all I could do to get round some bends. It was constant flow, like a good strong ebb tide.'

Helpful boats would offer him a tow into locks. Like a classical hero enduring his torments, he refused, as if the slightest touch from a bystander would invalidate his feat.

At Pont Meadow Oxford, his blade struck a Highland heiffer's horn, as the animal performed its own ordeal by water. 'People couldn't believe what I was doing. "Where have your come from? Sheerness?" (Astonishment). "Oh, that's a good row you are having." ' An innocently irreverent youth: 'Dad, there's that old man again.' The boat hadn't made a drop of water. He only had to bail it out after the rain.

I leave George to his fast train home and explore the village. Once Kempsford guarded an important Saxon and medieval ford, which shows how full the river could be. The church of St Mary the Virgin founded by Edward the Confessor has a horseshoe said to have been cast by the Duke of Lancaster's horse. A guidebook accords its choir 'well above average for a village' status.

At Hannington Bridge, half a mile on from Kempsford, I picnic seated on a crust of yellow lichen on a parapet. The bridge's age is past guessing, so permanent is it a part of the river which flows under it, through green ruffles which recall the rising curtain over the cinema screens of my youth.

This is water crowfoot, the long swaying strands scattered with white flowers like a water daisy. The poet Willam Barnes called it 'Fair small-feaced flower'. There is a choice of local names for it here, where the county boundary dissects the river. To the north side, in Gloucestershire, it is rait; to the south, in Wiltshire, water lily. I must enjoy it while is lasts. It has no place in the navigable river which is to come.

The river drifts on. The fields are flat, down to cereals and cattle. The map releases the occasional detail from vacant stretches of white. Brazen Church Hill to the north, but no sign of a church. Little Crouch Hill to the south. Five 'Enclosures' in antique writing signify that ancient settlers perceived a greater security on these slightly higher pastures.

In sudden contrast to the old, I find myself walking along the boundary of the new. The middle of the Thames hereabouts is the boundary of the district of Thamesdown, the sort of vibrant self-confident place which might announce its dignitaries with a computer hum rather than a fanfare.

Thamesdown sounds a suspiciously made up sort of place. Who but a committee could have thought of such a neat title? The coat of arms of the borough on a road sign reveals a split personality. First (or is it last?) we have the river Thames. This is easily identified: four waves of alternate blue and white ('a chief barry wavy, four azure and argent').

Then there is once rampantly-industrial Swindon, ten miles south of the river, whose railway engines chugged over the river to Cirencester and slashed plumes of smoke across the clear hot skies of the furthest outposts of Empire: 'a horse vert crened, breathing flames and resting the exterior forehoof on a hammer head'.

I am nearing the end of the innocent Thames. It will still drift and dream for many miles, as it slowly gathers strength, absorbing the waters of central southern England beyond here. But it's function will have changed.

This has been the Thames of Kenneth Grahame's wonderful description of Mole's discovery of the river: 'Never in his life had he seen a river before – this sleek, sinuous, full-bodied animal, chasing and chuckling, gripping things with a gurgle and leaving them with a laugh, to fling itself on fresh playmates that shook themselves free, and were caught and held again. All was a-shake and a-shiver – glints and gleams and sparkles, rustle and swirl, chatter and bubble.'

The best of the afternoon's sparingly distributed charms is Inglesham Church, rescued largely through the frantic energy and persistence of William Morris, and now in the secure care of the Redundant Churches Fund.

Inglesham Round House once marked the junction with the Thames and Severn Canal. This was one of the river's major junctions, a prime intersection on England's waterways, of which there is now no trace. The canal, opened in 1790, after a bill moved in the reign of Charles II, broke away to the north, completing a continuous waterway from one side of England to the other.

Before the railway was completed between London and Bristol, when this was a busy link, the Road House was a conspicuous mark for approaching bargemen. The salmon which once prospered in the chalk tributaries of the Thames, may have reached these waters from the Atlantic through the canal, when the river in London was an impenetrable poisonous barrier.

This momentous union of the two rivers excited the poets, but not the merchants. Trade was declining by the mid nineteenth century and the canal shut early this century. At the other end of the canal, at Stroud, close to the Severn, a group is painfully restoring the first few miles in a heroic bid to link the waterways once again.

Here, an old book promised pike, the ubiquitous monster of any murky water in my youth. It ate ducklings whole, and would take your toes as dessert. Should I test the theory? But reaching Lechlade on whole feet is more important than proving a folk memory.

2

ADMIRALS all, for England's sake,
Honour be yours and fame!
– *Admirals All*, Sir Henry Newbold.

ON A FAIR June morning, there is heavy repose in the Thames meadows at Inglesham. I meet some cows at ease. A number are blowing loudly, stoking invisible pre-solstice fires.

On the river the cruiser Braybird is flying an important blue ensign. Its master grunts an acknowledgement to me. The canoe Grebe Close follows behind. Its crew, stimulated by closer contact with the elements, are more cheerful. Both of these craft have ventured, like inquisitive people who press up to the limits of a country and peer past the border guards into forbidden territory, to explore the end of the navigable Thames. George MacFarlane was the one who made it, like a war-time hero in a cockleshell.

Navigators may disagree, but I estimate the end, or start, of shipping on the Upper Thames to be near Inglesham Church, at a line marked by an ash, its bark rubbed quite smooth by generations of itchy cows.

Here the river summons up reinforcements for the task ahead in the River Coln, which has tumbled down its tight valley out of the Cotswolds, through villages of rich golden stone.

I am leaving the river's second starting line and heading east. Lechlade to Oxford is the most perfectly self-contained of all the Thames stages. From the start of navigation to a minor summit of civilisation.

It is an empty place for dreamy wanderings. This is where romantic Oxford undergraduates came to dream. The Great Western Railway obligingly ran a railway on the north side down to Fairford, just north of here. Nothing remains of that. As a result the river is probably quieter than it was in Victorian times, which is remarkable. People tend not to visit an empty river in cars, except to fish. We must be grateful for that.

Today, practised in this lowland walking, I will press on along seventeen

Newbridge, twelve miles west of Oxford.

'Now who will stand on either hand,
And keep the bridge with me?'

– *Lays of Ancient Rome*, Lord Macaulay

miles of meandering river, through an unexpected wilderness in the, as it will turn out, rare company of boats as far as Newbridge. Of course, any genuinely new bridge would be a desecration of the Thames here. Fortunately 'new' means very old. Beyond Lechlade there is no town to break the spell.

On the half mile walk into Lechlade, the boats begin, like sleepy semis in the outer suburbs, snugly moored and pointing correctly upstream into the current. *Myra E, Clementine, Rosalyn, Low Flier.* They have little plastic cockpits. They are synthetic and inexpressibly dull. Are their absent owners grazing garden gnomes on pocket handkerchief lawns? It will be a challenge to find interesting boats. I take some comfort in C. V. and D. D. Sleeman's *Tradi*, a narrow boat of stencilled castles and roses.

A tractor is flipping over fading bundles of hay. Here, in this fastness of unexceptional meadowland, there is an exotic plant on the bank. It is a single specimen of oil seed rape, not yet dignified with a Latin name in my books. (Keble Martin, in his 1965 *Concise British Flora in Colour*, only mentions the swede rape.) It is a vulgar, washed-out yellow. The sweep of a rape field, buttercup-bright in May, is a bold, delicious prospect. Here, as nature's litter, it jars. How resourceful of it to arrive here, but oh for a flood of purple loosestrife to sweep down and engulf it.

At Lechlade, for the first time I could bathe in the Thames, but I would be wise not to do so. 'Warning. Danger to bathers. Following dredging, the river depth is increased in places.' Poor landlocked Swindonians, on their day trips from ten miles south, denied the people's simple pleasures.

Upstream, where I have come from, the River Thames simply enhances the places its flows through, elevating house prices, inspiring picture postcards. Here, for the first time, the river itself is marketable. Lechlade has carefully staged gift emporia, antique shops and tea shops with big rear rooms that suggest a rush in season. There is a library, closed on certain days, and at least three pubs.

It is a place of little conflict. Otherwise there might have been an election for its town council, recently returned unopposed. I take this is a sign of a community at ease with itself. The town notice board, as if through a time warp, offers a chariot race in the charity event week. A water bailiff is sought by Stroud and District Anglers' Association, which tries thus to persuade suitable candidates to adapt pleasure to riparian service: 'If you regularly walk along the towpath with a dog, you might be interested.'

'Did it rain today?' asks Peter Collins, landlord of the Crown. It is a legitimate question, not the landlord's stock conversation opener. It has so far rained for much of the summer. The regulars hack the weather about a while, as they might a deflating football, then turn to the subject of diet.

Lionel, at the bar, speaks up for the wide-ranging taste in food of his dog

Ricky. The splendid creature will eat most things, except cheese. To test this disinclination, Mrs Collins offers Ricky a cheeseburger. Ricky fulfils his master's words and obediently refuses. He is not invited to insult Mr Collins' admirable Hook Norton bitter with another rejection.

I leave the Crown and walk along to the church where pre-school age children are disporting on an open tumble of gravestones while they wait for their elder sisters and brothers to be disgorged from the adjacent school. This does not seem in the least disrespectful.

The poet Shelley rowed to Lechlade with friends in 1815, and dined well after an appalling diet of bread and butter on the journey. They failed to penetrate the weeds past Inglesham, and rowed back down river. Shelley's *Stanzas in a Summer Evening Churchyard* celebrate the visit.

I return to the river. A duck hangs in the flow under Halfpenny Bridge, exactly matching the speed of the water with its forward motion, thereby staying quite still.

'Lechlade does not tempt one to linger in the flesh,' notes Vincent, unfairly, in his 1908 *Story of the Thames*. 'Remarkably tranquil and its history has been of the same character.' There are arches on both sides of the bridge to accommodate flood water – 'Always a terrible trial here.'

Back on the towpath, on the south bank, I head east, past more boats: *Red Emperor, Esmeralda, Dreaming Spires, Herpager*. A mystery. *The Sagaman* has been abandoned by its crew, tethered to the bank but still noisily chugging. Would this *Marie Celeste* drift endlessly if I cut its moorings?

A pill box surveys the river glumly through narrow eyeslits. It will be the first of many. Since it became redundant as a custodian against river invasion after VE Day 1945, this pill box has disfigured the approach to Lechlade for *Esmeralda* and the rest.

Something ought to have been done about pill boxes by now. These squat, concrete fortifications from which defenders would have trained their guns, are an irrelevant clutter and an intrusion into a pleasant view. Between here and Reading I will count dozens. The preservation of one would be enough to commemorate the glorious defensive readiness of Dad's Army. A gang with hammers could knock down the rest in a week, but no doubt a gang of solicitors and the Official Secrets Act could hold them up for another fifty years.

St John's, tidily tended, is the first lock on the Thames. It has little flowerbeds, and a notice informing me that the keeper is at lunch. Still within his lunch break, he storms back and like a schoolmaster smattering the playground with admonitions, throws a sharp, routine 'Hey' at me. My feet are contravening a 'Private' notice, close to two marks on a stone which reach about half way up my calf. There is a date against each mark: November 1894 and March 1947. They signify the height of the two most dreadful floods in recent Thames history, not stages in the privatisation of the lock keeper's grass.

The lock keeper, an imposing uniformed man, has swept into his lockside house, satisfied with the power of the public rebuke. My small son would have whooped with defiance and run the other way. Chastised, I drift back to the correct side of the 'Private' to read his notices which refer to proper conduct on the river.

Father Thames is safe here from vandals like me, behind a chain. He was originally carved for the Crystal Palace, then rescued from the ruins. I do not suppose he will ever move from here.

From now until it merges with the North Sea, the River Thames is under strict supervision. Every few miles, it submits to a lock or a weir, in place of its natural fall. Thames Water's mark is upon it in elegant gun-barrel grey wood fences and gates. The Thames is allowed to follow, more or less, its traditional swerves and sweeps, but it is tame – a working river, a receptacle, a source of drinking water, a highway.

Now that there are boats, there is, as a consequence, a crumbling bank. There is recently submerged vegetation, like pieces of crumbly fruit cake. At the present rate of erosion a line of fishermen, their places marked by short wooden posts driven into the bank, will fall in by the turn of the century.

A family of coot are pulling with uneven pace for the far bank: the fledglings expend twice the effort to make half the progress of their parents. For some minutes the mother maintains an insistent alarm call, like a sharp hammer tapping on marble, to round up the prodigals.

Just over a mile further on, at Buscot Lock, the keeper, in white shirt and nautical hat, has a cactus surplus. He is solving it by free enterprise, selling his excess for 40p, 60p and £1 the pot. But there is no boat passing through his lock on this unusual dry day, so he thunders around his formal lawn with a mower.

The novices I last saw uneasily leaving Cricklade, approach Buscot lock with growing competence. Two little daughters test the cross wind with toy windmills. Cow X221 gazes with distant concentration as I climb a stile. It seems to have tried, and failed again, to puzzle the mystery of man: 'Almost had it there. No, its beaten me again.'

The National Trust property at Buscot Park touches the south bank here. The church has two windows by Burne-Jones and a monument to the Loveden family which built Buscot Park in the Adam style in 1780. It was later spoilt by the Victorians, then restored by Lord Farringdon, whose collection of fine paintings and furniture are on display. These include Burne-Jones's Legend of the Sleeping Princess, still in the original frames.

The Trust own the entire rather splendid package, the 4,000 acre park, the village and the stone bridges, across one of which I see a cat slink, distrustful of man's engineering.

For two miles I see no boats. Then a glass fibre vessel surges past with needless haste. For a minute, little mounds of water roll and throb across the river. I draw six flattened rugby balls on my notepad to show the effect. A notice at the first lock warned of serious punishment to those who speed. I must ask who has been punished and what was the fine.

The boat names are improving. *Merrie England*, a wooden craft, in Oxford and Cambridge blue, is moored on the south bank. A Boeing 727 growls into RAF Brize Norton. For some moments all inferior sound is cancelled in a noise footprint ten miles long.

The Thames has many large guardian trees. There were elms close to Kelmscott in William Morris's day. Now the trees are mostly ash with their narrow pointed leaves, the closest thing to fingers in any common tree. They stand as commanding bankside markers: others, tottering, defiantly struggle to stay upright as the waters loosen their roots.

I notice ahead a very distinguished house, about three hundred yards back from the river. It is Kelmscot (*sic*) Manor which belongs to a pure, non mechanised age. So it is a surprise to overhear the man from the Society of Antiquaries, who issues my ticket, admit that he has just accepted the gift of a Japanese digital watch. William Morris peered into the twenty-first century from the nineteenth in *News From Nowhere*, but he did not anticipate impeccable, handless timekeeping in his beloved riverside house.

Morris first rented this fine sixteenth century stone-built house, wrapped around by high walls and big enough for the large Victorian family which he never had, in 1871 and lived here until he died in 1896.

I am here for Kelmscot's brief first Wednesday of the month opening (from April to September, or by appointment). Whenever I enter or leave a room there is, leaving or entering it, a dreamy American girl or intense young man, pondering *Guenevere* or dark green bedspreads patterned with fritillaries, marigolds and daisies. It is a sanctified, inspirational place.

William Morris, socialist, medievalist, designer and poet, carried his anger, passion and creativity up and down river between his two houses, Kelmscot Manor and Kelmscott House in Hammersmith.

'Heaven on Earth,' he wrote when he discovered the manor. 'An old stone Elizabeth house, and such a garden! Close down by the river, a boathouse. All things handy.' He and the poet Dante Gabriel Rossetti moved in in July 1871 and for a time Morris was the happiest he had been in his life. He loved the 'sad lowland country, with river meadows, long silvery willows and long blue distance.'

Kelmscot has a kind, soft interior, with mellow unstained wood and furniture fabric in blue birds and bold flowers. 'Who is William Morris?'

28

asked my six year old daughter. 'He designed the material in our curtains and on our Chesterfield.'

'Every flower and every leaf? Was that his hobby?'

This design is at least 100 years old, but I find Morris's big opulent pink-red chrysanthemum heads and sprays of green leaft immortal. I have had instructions from the family to find the original. In a display in Kelmscot's attic, I find the very material, but the thrill of recognition is spoilt. It is prosaically identified as 'Sanderson's ZH614/3.' Dull news to convey to the family. They will be more interested in how Mrs Morris became King Arthur's queen.

A notice in copperplate: 'The fabrics are all old and very fragile. They suffer from handling. Please refrain from touching them.' Happily the creativity and spirit of Morris, a man to raise his voice at any offence to beauty, were more robust than the medium he expressed himself in.

An inscription in the counterpane on Morris's bed reads 'You do bring in the spring and wait upon her welcome maids of honour.' This is the bed Morris died in. In another room I find a drawing of considerable nobility, from 1896, of Morris on his death bed.

Morris' wife Jane is everywhere. In the Blue Silk Dress, 1868, over which is written in Latin 'Famed by her poet-husband, and of surpassing fame for her beauty, now let her win lasting fame by my painting.' Her mysterious beauty endured. A photograph from 1910 shows that same striking profile. In a bedroom, like some fairy treasure chest, is her jewel casket, painted by Rossetti and his wife Elizabeth Siddal.

Morris wrote of the Thames: 'Altogether a very pleasant river to travel. The banks are still beautiful with flowers, the long purples and willow herb and that strong coloured yellow flower, very close and buttery. Also a very pretty dark blue flower, I think mugwort, mixed with the purple blossom of horse mint and mouse ear and here and there a bit of belated meadow sweet.'

In the broader details, Morris's enchanting river is not much changed. The same lazy meadows, some now split by wire fences, but still in the main divided by the hedges of Morris's day. The village of Kelsmcot, perfectly cast in Cotswold gold stone, is not sullied by a single stray brick.

I return to the river bank by Morris's house. I find fewer flowers than he could have borne – in high summer only a few purple loosestrife, some flowering thistles and speedwell. But this is an important spot in the history of conversation. Morris and his friends fished here for perch, dace and chub. Refreshed with sandwiches and a bottle of claret, they talked long into the night about art and craftsmanship and Morris's vision of a new society. I picnic on coffee and sandwiches.

The fiery Morris would not have endured today's casual fisherman's debris on the riverbank before his old house. The uninhibited bellow of this early Thames conservationist could have been heard from here to the letter page of *The Times*. He wrote to a friend: 'The beautiful willows at Eaton Hastings have not been polled [pollarded] for 17 years and now the idiot parson has polled them into wretched stumps. I should like to cut off the beggar's legs and have wooden ones made for him out of the willow timber.'

Morris was enraged by the Thames Conservancy's tidy-minded cutting of riverside flowers and clearing the stream of reeds and rushes. It was to be another 100 years before the complaints of this brilliant and energetic man were widely accepted by water authorities.

When he died, the October waters were out over the low lying river meadows and all the little streams that fed from the Cotswolds ran full and deep brown. The farm labourers attended his funeral, dressed for the field, a natural touch of which he would have approved.

I walk on towards Eaton Hastings, through the writer Vincent's 'fat and rich country near Kelsmcott. Land of multitudinous willows. Abundant grass, stately elms, reeds, wild flowers, the meadow sweet, loosestrife and water lillies, by the river marge.'

Vincent recalls the method of passing down river before the pound locks were built. Boaters would remove the paddles in the flash locks and shoot the rapids as the river surged through. 'At Eaton lock in 1876 to fall for four or five feet in a light boat on top of the rushing water was distinctly exhilarating.'

Close to the site of the weir a man is bouncing over undulating turf in an ancient green motorised lawnmower. *Warspite II* stands ready to convey the house guests to quiet picnic spots. As the trees part Eaton Hastings is revealed, tiny with its own church.

I find proof that speed kills: an ash is on its side, the bank washed from beneath its roots. Already weakened, like a boxer allowed to take too much punishment, all that was required to drive it down was the first strong wind from the correct quarter.

In vain I look for the Kingfisher. Vincent and Morris found it in abundance on these waters. However the chaffinch is flourishing on this stretch. Why? I assume it thrives on the crumbs from fishermen's sandwiches.

Then a memorable event. A curlew conspicuously defies the reference book, which locates it mainly in the north of Britain. It orbits me vociferously, advertising itself for many minutes in a circle of two hundred yards' diameter. Without binoculars, I can plainly see its long curved beak opening to emit a 'kew kew, kew, kew.' Then it makes a graceful descent, breaks into a bubbly, plaintive 'ker-whee' and patters away. Within a few minutes it repeats the entire routine.

A genuine navigator is approaching Grafton Lock, two miles beyond Kelmscott. E. M. Morrison in the narrow boat *Artemis of Norton Keynes*, sixty feet long, and carrying a bicycle on its roof. Three swans and a flock of Canada geese glide respectfully aside. The navigator raises an appealing finger. Mr Wells, lock keeper, holds the gates open at Grafton, where the glass fibre *Coral I* is waiting. After a few minutes of the soft gurgling passage of water, both boats restart, three feet six inches nearer to sea level.

A mile on from Grafton is the thirteenth century Radcot Bridge, possibly the oldest on the Thames, and itself on the site of a Saxon bridge, with its ancient church-door arches. The river has long been a strategic gain line, and even the tiniest bridge was a vital catch.

This is the site of two battles. Henry of Derby, later Henry IV, defeated Robert de Vere, Earl of Oxford and Richard II's favourite. In the Civil War the Parliamentary forces were repulsed hard by here in Garrison Field by Prince Rupert in an attempted push south to Farringdon.

I drain my Thermos flask on this bridge, and ponder a connection with distant parts of the river. There is evidence that the Upper Thames was used to carry some of the stone for building St Paul's, which was taken from Burford in the Cotswold to this bridge, thence to London by boat. But there is no evidence that these twisting, shallow waters were any easier to navigate five hundred or a thousand years ago.

The afternoon has become warm with dawdling, fluffy clouds. A few yards east of Grafton Lock two men step from a red van to set clues. Later, parties of schoolchildren will converge from both banks towards the bridge under which I stopped for refreshment and, if they have followed the trail correctly, make for an adjacent tree to pick up a clue. That is the theory. The clue is 'Find the Old Man'.

If they do not read their maps closely enough, they may yet, as others have done, confront and misidentify Mr Wells at Grafton Lock as the living embodiment of the description. They will be wrong. The 'Old Man' is the neat wooden bridge itself. I promise to give nothing away. But I never see anything of the party. An unfinished story.

The river now behaves like an erratic heartbeat on the screen of a cardiac monitor, oscillating wildly through an ancient landscape. It is a wide flood plain from which settlers have stood cautiously back. But the river has held no menace for the electricity board which strung its pylons in hard, straight lines along both sides of it.

There is open meadowland, a threatened habitat, on each side. Could the river ever flood this land again as completely as in those ancient inundations? It would devastate the grazing, but do no harm to the flora, bearing down enriching deposits from the Cotswolds.

There is a curlew here again. Is it that same forlorn lost soul I saw earlier?

An ancient ash is on its last totter. I surprise a common sandpiper which makes off on swift, strong wings from a little bay.

On the north bank a man is fishing. He is wearing an American artisan's hat of deep blue, and a woollen jumper which takes no account of the heat. A vast, black cylindrical net is ready for his catch. His black and white mongrel dog gazes mournfully and with considerable scepticism into the waters which show no sign of yielding up a fish for its master. It is a fine study of the fisherman as individualist – apart, silent, patient, unconcerned at the prospect of total failure.

There is another ash tree, bent like an old man. Its heart is missing. I take the wraith's route, through this tree to the other side. Whatever nourishment it takes up passes through a fragile outer frame only a few inches thick. Yet it is vigorously, defiantly alive, with a fine canopy of leaves, like a well coiffed centenarian.

A coot family heads across stream from a bar of lilies. The young have rufous heads and yellow beaks, a touch of colouristic rebellion in their youth before they adopt routine adult black. The parents are insistent, yet the young linger. I hurry past to spare the parents the embarrassment of seeing their warnings unheeded.

A female mallard is in profound distress. It tears up and down, quacking furiously. I am perceived as a threat to be vigorously deterred. Yet she cannot begin to threaten the *Maid Penelope* which speeds carelessly past her, upstream, within a few frothing inches of her brood.

To the north, a forest of radio masts. Then an ancient barrier of ash and hawthorn droop and lurch across my path, planted in the past as shelter for cattle. Beyond them, that bright and cheering meadowland marker, the ox-eye daisy.

I am in Oxfordshire but this was Wiltshire until 1974: in that county, Geoffrey Grigson writes in his *Englishman's Flora*, people knew it as dog daisy, fair maid of France, horse daisy, and maithen. Over the river, Oxfordshire folk called it moon daisy. The herbalist John Pechey described it perfectly: its flowers, he said 'cast forth beams of brightness.'

For some time I have noticed the top deck of *Silver King* bobbing and weaving through the meadowland, marking the line of the invisible river ahead. On the water there is a lily, big oval leaves like an artist's pallet, with a single yellow flower. There are many dragonflies, a tireless aerial infantry out on sorties.

A swallow beats lazily up the river. It is a sign of change – of man's works, of a farm, church or old house. What this particular swallow heralds is Rushey Lock, a mile away. I draw closer. 'DANGER' screams a notice at the entrance to the weir alongside the lock, in white letters on strident red.

A line of poppies standing above the barley on a field-edge, underlines the warning.

As I approach a wave of activity is breaking over Rushey Lock, which looks like a film set. 'It's all happening' says lock keeper Mr Murgeson, who has the following crammed into his lock: *Silver King, King Crab, Low Flier* and *It's Magic*. 'Room for one more,' he barks. 'In uniform?' asks *Silver King*, familiarly, to Mr Murgeson, who is parade ground-neat in a shining white shirt. 'Nearest I'll ever come to it,' replies Mr Murgeson. 'When's lock inspection day?' inquires *Silver King* cynically.

There are roses, pansies and irises, but no cacti here. The wise has some advice for the beginner. *King Crab* tells *Low Flier* to keep well clear of the sill of the lock. 'You can do an awful mischief to your Z bars along there.'

Mr Murgeson plays the Hollywood director, in full control of this animated scene. Its players include ten people visible, and some below decks. As he turns the lock wheel, the sun bursts out from behind fluffy clouds, just as the best directors arrange it. Another camera angle would take in a slim young lady in red hair, trimming the borders of this impeccably preened lock. The director casually nudges the lock gate open with his behind, lighting a cigarette with free hands.

The channel blocked off by the 'Danger' signs leads to a sudden weir. A stream of yellow flowers flows off the old stone. The violence of the surge gives way to a hugh quiet pool, with a sandy fringe.

The Victorian naturalist Richard Jefferies measured the extent of the weir's foaming thus, in *The Modern Thames*: 'A thousand thousand bubbles rising to the surface would whiten the stream. A thousand thousand succeeded by another thousand thousand. No multiple could express the endless number.'

He warned of the weir's seductive dangers. He had his reverie on the riverbank disturbed by news of a dreadful drowning. 'Entirely preventable accidents happen year after year with lamentable monotony. Each weir is a little Niagara and a boat once within its influence is certain to be driven to destruction.'

Hopeful fishermen, who pay £1. 20 to work these deep brown waters between Rushey Lock and Tadpole Bridge, are enjoined 'not to walk about in the mowing grass.'

In this utterly remote stretch I stop for an afternoon drink at the Trout pub at Tadpole Bridge, a mile south of Bampton, where Morris Dancing may have originated. A mystery is solved for Cyril and Irene, crew of *Silver King*. They had seen me pursuing with notebook while they followed the river's manic swerves. 'When first they saw the men of Rome walking for the pleasure of walking, they thought they must be mad', wrote Strabo. But they are affable company. I resolve not to accept the surly face people often wear upon the water as a conclusive guide to their disposition.

At Tadpole Bridge, I cross to the north bank. A smooth meadow walk gives way to a tangle of vegetation. The river, restrained by an embankment, concentrates its nourishing power on this dank barrier.

Dragonflies erupt in clouds. I find one at rest. This riverside bandit is a piece of living geometry. Its long bottle-green body flops back at an angle of thirty-five degrees to its head. Its wings are opaque, the bright green of a blade of grass. I flush up more unidentified marvels. There is a fast-flying moth, the colour of golden syrup; and a sleek little darter like a sharpened piece of dried grass. Then, dispelling the laggardly impression of an earlier sighting, a supercharged heron sprints off the water into flight.

The landscape opens out on the left into a huge meadow, smudged scarlet with clover. Grigson confirms a boyhood recollection of mine. We used to suck the flower heads of clover. All children do this, but we forget the pleasure as adults. 'Flowers you could pluck off one by one and suck for the nectar or honey, honeysuckles,' writes Grigson. 'I will enchant the old Andronicus with words, more sweet than . . . honeystalks to sheep.' – *Titus Andronicus*, William Shakespeare.

A cordon of willows, restlessly swishing, marks the meadow's edge. Only skylarks define its ceiling. But this is a private view, reserved for walkers. The high bank I am standing on makes it quite invisible from the river.

I stand for a moment to confirm that what I am going to write down is absolutely correct. There is not a visible boat, person or dwelling in any direction. To the north the trees and hedges fade into a flat infinity. To the south, a low line of hills support a thin banner of trees. Before this stands an intermittent cordon of hawthorn and rose. In the grazing meadow is a straggle of cows in black, brown, cream and gold.

On this soft, soothing day, this is a joyous place and a challenge to those who celebrate the quality of our landscape only by its fringes, wildernesses or high points. Here, quite unexpectedly, in the middle of lowland England, midway between Buckland and Chimney, or more distantly, Oxford and Swindon, there is a discreet paradise.

In time a boat must puncture this solitude. It is the grindingly prosaic *Shady Lady* – there *had* to be a *Shady Lady*. It is flying a flag and three pennants of various pretentious hues. However, unless its crew climb the masts, they will certainly not see my meadow.

As I walk along the north bank, north-east towards Chimney Farm, I become aware of a distant pursuing noise, a raw, open engine cutting out and surging on with the unmuted snarl of a Yellow River freighter. At Shifford Cut Bridge it overcomes me, a fast arrow of a Thames Water maintenance boat.

At Shifford the Thames is by-passed. Long ago the Suez Canal strategy prevailed and engineers sliced through one of the river's more tortuous loops, excising Duxford from the commercial waterway. Now boats take the direct line, but the river still flows in the loop, where it regains its youth.

On this thick hot summer morning this backwater is torpid and drowsy. Above there is the lazy drawl of a light aircraft. The Abingdon and District Angling and Restocking Association claims Private Fishing.

The river can be crossed here by a ford. It is the lowest point on the river where, short of a full scale swim, I may walk across. There is a fascinating mystery whose answer must lie somewhere in the shelves of books already written on the Thames. This was clearly a ford of some importance (hence Duxford), but when was it last used if the river has been navigable for so many centuries?

I round the half mile diversion and head north to Shifford lock, invisible and inaccessible behind a dense screen of cow parsley, high purple-green stems and tiny, tickly white flowers. The barrier opens to reveal another of those unexpected landmarks. Shifford church, in butter-yellow stone, is adrift on the other bank in a sea of fidgeting wheat, its simple lines framed in trees.

An enormous brown dragonfly, which seems to be twice the size of any I have yet seen, hurtles past my bankside resting place, like some prototype for a new master-breed of insects.

On the other bank the Great Brook cuts into the main river, at the sort of oblique angle favoured by motorway engineers. It is a pretty, clean artificial stream, an example of those ancient works along the river which transformed the drainage of the surrounding land, once so prone to flooding.

The southern bank of the Thames has been torn and scratched by sharp mechanical teeth. I struggle through a tangle of weeds that has burst out of the disturbed ground on the edge of a ploughed-up field edge and break clear on to a grey metal bridge.

Harrowdon Hill is on my right. If you walk over high ground, distant landmarks are in sight for many hours. On such river meadow lowland as this, even at the slowest amble, the horizon is close over the flat fields. In these shortened perspectives, new features – churches, hills, copses – break suddenly into view and pass just as suddenly out of sight.

A bridge over a side channel has lost its two concrete abutments. It was marooned, like a beached ship, probably by some sudden surge of the river which washed away its supports. Little mats of green vegetation dawdle down the stream. By this means, Gloucestershire's rare fauna may be set adrift to colonise Middlesex, as the island Madagascar was colonised by lemurs out of Africa. There are no boats to be seen on this delicious drowsy stretch. This cheers me.

It is an enormous relief to step into open meadowland, untouched by chemicals, after a field of tall crops. There are red admiral butterflies in the clover. Four horses, the most perfect of animal profiles, stand out of the hot sun, patient and sedate in an ash glade.

Once riverside farmers would have graced this meadow with a fine, precise name. Instead I find a coded agricultural notice attached to a tree: 'NAC Field B'. Like an explorer, grateful for the opportunity, I unilaterally rename it Clover Mead.

This still warm air is ideal for the appreciation of sounds. A nearby bush offers a series of coarse churrs, followed by a sweet swirl of bubbling sound. Three aircraft of the Second World War shudder across the sky in tight formation.

Later a red Royal helicopter comes buzzing importantly out of Gloucestershire, over Standlake Common to my north, bound for official engagements. (Later, this simple statement would be enough to have my children packing the entire Gloucestershire-resident Royal Family, the Prince and Princess of Wales, The Princess Royal and Prince Michael of Kent into the same red bird, to some glittering Palace function.)

A hundred pins break the surface of the water edge with an audible pricking. It is a scrimmaging shoal of tiny feeding fish. There is some local magic here, working on behalf of wildlife. On one short stretch between curves in the river, I count seven mature swans. And fast under an ash there is a guelder-rose, so tightly intertwined it appears to be fused with the tree, sharing its life, sweet, pink flowers woven into the ash's lower branches.

There are the remains of a stone wharf in this quiet reach. From here, cattle must once have been transferred by river to grazing pastures. Above the river is Kingston Bagpuize – there will be no Thames name as picturesque as this. Its millenium in 1970 was celebrated with a Womens' Institute pageant. The name, by one of those splendid contortions of sound, comes from a Norman family Bachepuise.

Then there are Hinton Waldrist and Longworth, commanding views north across the Thames Valley, far into the northern edge of Oxfordshire, and south into the Marlborough Downs and the Vale of the White Horse.

These are names known far beyond this gentle ridge to generations of schoolboy trainspotters through two of the Great Western Railway's Manor class locomotives. I remember them pulling milk and fish trains past my school, like well-behaved W. A. Awdry creations.

At New Thamesside Farm the boat *Peppers* passes me with a restrained gurgle. It has smooth and expensive lines, and cradles its own small tender. Speeding on the river would demean her.

I walk on through the meadow to the six arched thirteenth century Newbridge, its uplift of sandy bricks rising to an apex. 'New' bridges are always old. In 1885 W. Senior, disputing Radcot's claim, wrote in *The Royal River*: 'The oldest, and in truth the oldest looking bridge on the Thames is called Newbridge. It has been Newbridge for at least 600 years now, yet its groined arches and projecting piers seem as strong today as ever they have been.'

The bridge, enclosed by two old pubs, the Rose Revived and the Maybush, is the end of what will be my longest walk on the river. It is crossed by the A415, bearing many heavy lorries; one of those unofficial trunk roads between important places which is not approved by the map. The bridge, built wide enough for a single medieval cart, makes them wait, snorting and flustering in meek little queues, behind traffic lights.

> WHERE are the mowers, who, as the tiny swell
> Of our boat passing heaved the river-grass,
> Stood with suspended scythe to see us pass? –
> They are all gone, and thou art gone as well!
> – *The Upper Thames*, Matthew Arnold.

I cross the bridge to the north bank, past this impatient convoy of lorries. But they do not trouble the Thames for long. Old bridges always crossed water at right angles. Because rivers flood and threaten the surrounding flat land, the roads make off directly for the high ground. So there is the occasional offensive roar, and the A415 is soon gone.

Today I will reach my first important destination. It is twelve miles from here to Godstow on the northern edge of Oxford. It will be easier now that my legs are becoming accustomed to this billiard table flatness.

In the first meadow beyond the bridge, close to Stonehenge farm, two spotted flycatchers dart out of an unkempt hedge and in complex, fluttering pirouettes snatch insects out of the air. This delicate latecomer to our summer struggles further and for longer than any visitor from the south. One is bold enough to fly fifty yards to a point close to me to unerringly select its prey from a fog of midges dancing over the bank.

With a soft cough, *Camelot II* creeps past me as I picnic in the shade of the ubiquitous ash. It is a wooden boat of distinction, with a red and black hull, brown upper quarters, with the casual untidiness of the far-travelled.

I walk the mile to Hart's, or Ridge's, footbridge which perpetuates a perilous right of way over the weir which once stood here. There are a number of other old ways across – Old Man, Tenfoot and Eaton Weir to name three where a bridge survives the defunct weir. Standing here today is a young man with a towel. He is statuesque. This unnatural pose is designed to show me he has no intention to do anything whatsoever.

37

It is perfectly clear he intends to bathe, which is entirely reasonable and not against the rules. Local people must have bathed on such unrestrainedly hot days for many generations. The river is now quite deep enough to sooth, and also to kill.

I cross the bridge and walk up to meet Poul Christensen, whose illustrious farm runs down to the River Thames on the south bank. Many people visit the farm, but for Poul the most important of these are the Fellows. Some are in nuclear science. One is a medieval historian. Another is a philosopher.

The Fellows, of St John's College Oxford, bring their own food and trail around, enjoying themselves hugely. 'They are very interested,' says Poul. 'They ask unexpected questions. Most people would ask how much fertiliser I use. The Fellows might ask why I have cows at *all*. I have to scratch my head to answer them. Why *do* I have cows?'

St John's College owns Poul Christensen's seven acre Kingston Hill farm. They also own land on the north bank. Poul considers them to be good landlords. On their last annual progress they were very impressed with his work. They agreed to change the terms of his tenancy, thereby approving retrospectively all the revolutionary things Poul has done for wildlife.

Normally tenants must keep their hedges as smart as a new schoolboy, short and neatly trimmed, and their ditches scoured. Poul's abundant hedges, bristling fortresses for birds, and protective ramparts for wild flowers, are certainly unkempt by these conventional standards. But the Fellows agreed that his hedges could grow higher and bushier. It was the first such agreement on a tenanted farm and a blueprint for conservation farmers.

'The Fellows know bugger all about farming, but they are in a position to take a long term view,' says Poul. 'They have owned the farm next door since fifteen hundred or something. They can sit back and view the ups and downs of income with detachment. They may keep this farm for another two hundred years.

'A historian and a philosopher are probably the two ideal blokes to make long term decisions. I get annoyed when they ask stupid questions but I would ask stupid questions of a philosopher. I wish they would buy a lot more farms.'

I first met Poul Christensen six years earlier when his holding, one of the Countryside Commission's ten demonstration farms, was a tiny island of deviation in a sea of cynicism. He allowed his hedges to sprout for the benefit of birds while others hacked ruthlessly away. He planted trees and dug ponds while neighbours smartened and gouged, bullying their land to over-produce.

The conversion of many farmers to conservation is one of the more satisfying recent developments in the countryside. For his part, Poul took nobody's advice. He worked out his own solution, thinking carefully and spending wisely, using the grants available to any farmer. He planted hundreds of trees, cheaply purchased. He encouraged what was already there, coaxing vigour out of hedges and ditches. Since he stopped applying fertiliser on the field edge, vetches, buttercups and forget-me-nots are flourishing in the hedge base, germinated from dormant seeds in the ground.

He persuaded the farming clubs to allot more marks in competition so the people who have been winning for years suddenly no longer win. He himself has won second place for the past two years in the Drayton and District Best Farms Competition. 'Ha, ha, ha. I haven't won yet, but I bloody well will.'

As an exercise in creative conservation he would like to re-establish sixty acres of natural flood meadow next to the river near Harts Bridge. He wants to restore such traditional watermeadow flowers as the snakes head fritillary. There are a lot of old grasses on the river's fringe already, such as quaking grass. If he withheld fertiliser, they might spread. I look forward to returning ten years from now.

Last year a birdwatcher jumped out of a spinney on the farm, and told Poul there was a pair of nesting hobbies on his land. Thereafter Poul and his family saw the pair every day, exuberant air champions, the shape of flying scythes, raising three young. 'I am highly privileged. On a May morning when I walk around the cattle down by the river, and see an early boat, and the swans nesting, then all is right with the world.'

I walk back down to the river and recross to the north bank and walk, in the map's wide white land of Northmoor, through the plushest of river meadows into a field of broad beans. But it is a worthwhile planting: the EEC is not in surplus in beans.

Then comes a succession of flat, freshly-cut hay fields, unnamed unlike the evocative Cowslip Close and Water Furze opposite. A tractor bustles past, dragging two gadgets. The first bails the hay; the second corrals the bails, like fudge, into slabs of six which are then cast adrift for later collection.

On the river's first boat house a weather cock indicates a stiff easterly breeze. I pass another hut. Moored outside is *Lazin 2*, an example of the unoriginal play on words which afflicts pleasure boats. I would like to report intelligent riverine puns, but I find no evidence of improving standards.

Lock keeper Mr C. J. Buddin stands at Northmoor Lock, bare-chested and tanned in crisp, white shorts from Thames Water's summer wardrobe. He has just dispatched *Aprilina* of London to the west. I buy his honey in a painted ceramic pot and read a sun-bleached leaflet with information on the authority's reservoirs. Will I reach Oxford by nightfall? A brisk stroll but I ought to manage it, he suggests.

Beyond the lock are little strands of purple in the bankside, a flower with the richest literary and artistic associations. This is Milais' purple looses-trife, in which he depicted his floating, dead Ophelia, modelled by Elizabeth Siddal. However, according to Grigson, this is not at all what Shakespeare meant by 'long purples', in Ophelia's 'fantastic garlands . . . of crowflowers, nettles, daisies and long purples.' He says they were actually early purple orchids.

The crew of *Miss Misty* have drawn up and are casting fishing lines without much hope, into the flow. I do not expect them to catch anything and when they pass me some time later it is confirmed. A blissfully unproductive afternoon.

A party of mallard bob in the quivering wake of *Doandah*. I can no longer cross at the Chequers pub, a mile and a half on from the lock, at Bablock Hythe. Once a 'great ferry boat' plied here. Now the pub is closed and ferry extinguished, its winding gear redundant.

Matthew Arnold, poet, brought his *Scholar Gypsy* here 'Trailing in the cool stream thy fingers wet, as the punt's rope ships round.' The ferry was convenient for patrons and walkers. The river cannot be crossed for a further six miles. Car-less medieval man found it easier to cross the river on this stretch than this twentieth century walker.

Beside the pub is Thameside Park, already well established behind a fine line of tall cypress, a community of caravans advertised by the management under such bland and inconsequential names as Tingdene Villas and Bluebird Penthouse. Residence is circumscribed by tight rules. This must make it a place of tedious but well-ordered tranquility.

A man fishes from under a voluminous green umbrella, distrusting the unexpected warmth in the air. People here have a casually determined attitude to leisure. A man with nut-brown arms and a blue sailor's cap – required headgear among the lesser navigating classes – steers *Tarka VIII* heavily past this tethered flotilla and sets it bobbing.

Eventually I explain my predicament to two young men working on a boat and they row me across in best muscular tradition for the price of a drink in the extinguished pub. Thameside Park ends, with appropriate tidiness, with a hedge. Normal Oxfordshire countryside resumes. A mallard displays itself upon a half-submerged tree root, like the avian equivalent of a mermaid.

There are cows ahead in wide, easy fields. A flock of feral Canada geese rise reluctantly to their feet and flap complainingly away, leaving a field which resembles the scene of a savage knife attack on an eiderdown.

There is enthusiastic chatter from a boat behind, for once unencumbered by chug. Two men and two children creak past in a plastic rowing boat; yellow within, white outside.

On a sharp left turn there is an elegant willow, inclined at an angle of about sixty degrees, dipping its branches into the flow. On the other bank a herd of Frisians, their heads down, swivel like black and white weather vanes to mark the direction of the keen summer wind behind them.

To my right is a hidden body of water, Farmoor Reservoir. Archaeologists found crop marks there, and excavations in the 1970s revealed Iron Age and Romano British remains. These suggested possible seasonal occupation, with summer fishing and grain growing on the flood plain. It must have been a very fertile and amenable place to live. In the winter they repaired to the hills for safety.

Farmoor reservoir covered what may have been an old line of the Thames, later totally buried and abandoned by ancient man. A drove way crossed a ford over the Thames in the middle of the settlement, where among other remains they found a scythe nicely preserved in the mud.

These wide flat gravel terraces here with fertile flood-borne soils are found from here onwards into Middlesex. The whole area has been intensely flown and photographed from the air. Archaeologists can point to almost any large gravel area along the river and show evidence of some sort of Stone Age, Bronze Age, Iron Age or Roman settlement.

Dragonfly of Marlow appears, hugging the inside curve. At the tiller is a Thames institution, 'Twig' Branch, seventy-nine, who once kept an art shop in High Wycombe. Mrs Olive Branch, also seventy-nine, is below. Their vessel is a steel-hulled narrow boat in scuffed Cambridge blue.

They are joined in the Pinkhill lock by *Tatty 'Ead IV* of Caversham, which has come roaring up from the west, releasing slivers of bank with its wake. This scene of rapid arrivals is scrutinised mournfully by a recumbent black labrador.

Mr Branch is a master navigator of no formal qualification. He and Olive have circumnavigated Middle England this summer – down the Thames to Brentford, up the Grand Union, down the Oxford Canal followed by another nostalgic foray up this reach of the Thames; a river they first navigated fifty-three years ago, two years after the Pinkhill lock keeper's cottage was built.

Twig and Olive Branch started their travels on the Thames in the wooden-hulled *Audley III*, graduating to the aluminium *Audley IV*. Twig never saw a horse towing on the river, although he has seen horse traffic on the canals. He recalls a quiet Thames, shortly after the war, before the explosion of pleasure craft and after the final decline of freight – he saw timber-carrying boats plying from the Surrey Docks to Reading. He remembers the rowing boats. 'You couldn't camp alongside the river with a punt today. The wash would sink it.'

Later, a mile downstream, I find Twig and Olive moored in a tight curve under Beacon Hill. Olive is rustling up a fried lunch. Twig, white beard, alert eye, is planning the October voyage. He is a charitable man: 'Boats haven't spoilt the river. And the erosion is very, very slow.' The biggest change is emergent vegetation: trees and bushes on the towpath.

I leave Twig, a man still captivated by the river's little charms: 'I have lain in that cabin there and watched a kingfisher fishing, inches from my boat. A boat makes a very good hide.'

Under Swinford Bridge, I find the *Lady Saphina*, a steam-driven floating boudoir of a vessel, with fine polished wood and plush seating, is tied up under. With her inward-curling stern, she is the height of seductive Edwardian charm.

On Swinford Toll Bridge, built 1777, Alan, wearing an earring and a cautionary yellow hat, bids me good afternoon. Before we next exchange words, he has extracted with both hands the sum of thirty p from fifteen cars ('two p from cars, five p from wagons'). A century ago *Royal River* described this toll-bridge as an 'annoying anachronism' but it outlived the ferry at Bablock.

Miscreants are faithfully recorded on a pad in his little wooden office: Alan's black list include a car with the new registration letter, whose high spending owner begrudged the proprietors of this bridge their ridiculously small levy. Who are the worst offenders? 'Foreigners. Bloody useless.' Some drivers return, conscience-striken, to pay their debts.

Fire engines, police cars and post vans are free. Open top buses ask for a receipt as a souvenir. Many drivers conduct their payment through the agency of small children: one man curves a hand out of a sun roof with the coins. Alan divides the road with a blur of hand movements. 'What's the matter with Sam?' asks a lady Saab driver, pointing to the surgical collar of Alan's colleague, recently emerged from a roadside hut.

This painstaking attention to the extraction of small sums brings the bridge £200 a day. It is a dangerous job: who else works, standing unprotected in the middle of a main road in an odious atmosphere of fumes and grinding gears? I bid farewell to Alan, last seen either waving to me or extracting small change from five cars.

In the calm of Eynsham Lock, just beyond Swinford, – another intriguing Thames mystery: did pigs really cross here? – there is no sign of Mr McCreadle, lock keeper. A sign respectfully informs boaters that lock keepers have to take meal breaks or attend to other duties. This lock was opened by Lord Desborough of Taplow, chairman of the Thames Conservancy, in 1928. The vandal would have to demolish the lock to remove this information, set on a marble block. The theme plant here is the rose, deep red and fragrant.

My path takes me through Wytham Great Wood, a site of special scientific interest and the subject of much study by Oxford University botanists. I discover a synthetic solution to erosion. The towpath had been gobbled up by the river here and walkers had to endure ordeal by bramble, thorn and scrub woodland.

Thames Water men battered a course through the scrub and pinned plastic binding mats on to the river bank as a foundation for protective, undersown vegetation – sedges and reeds, providing cover for wildfowl and nest sites. It sounds awfully false, but it works, a compromise between conservation and safety.

Beyond the wood, sheep are spread out unaware that one of their number is the central player in an instructive drama in which it is shown that the British public care deeply for animals; and that the river bank is a dangerous place for the unsure-footed.

A sheep has fallen into the water. A lot of people are very concerned. In earlier times our concern would have had an economic basis. We would have been frantic over the loss of an asset. Today our concern is entirely humanitarian.

'I couldn't care less what it is worth: it's saving an animal that counts,' imparts an urgent Mrs Mavis Thomas, who press gangs me into the relief organisation.

It is a major, impromtu rescue, joined by twelve people from three boats. Some, like foreign correspondents witnessing an atrocity, stand professionally aloof, and do no more than take photographs, while we toil, damply.

A rope is attached and I am detailed to pull from the bank, while small boats nuzzle comfortingly around the stricken creature. Mavis is worried about the wash from passing boats. As in any public drama, somebody has assumed control and is issuing calm orders.

'Steady, one, two, three pull!' A number of people narrowly avoid falling in. David Wibberly's flimsy canoe *Bess Ruwa*, which is a Nigerian name, could easily have been upended. We learn later that *Bess* contains all David's baggage for a four-day navigation of the Thames.

The sheep can gain no purchase on the steep bank: three men could scarcely budge it from the bottom of the three feet high slope. In *Bess Ruwa* David tows the sheep, nose pointed high, ten yards downstream to a piece of stepped bank.

We all tug, except the photographers. The animal suddenly skips on to land, like a piece of soap popping out of a wet hand. At first the sheep appears to be lame, but this is only the stiffness of long immersion. The sheep shakes herself vigorously and trots carelessly back into the herd.

Within minutes she is absorbed by the woolly throng and we cannot pick her out.

'Britain is the only country where so many people would spend so much time saving an animal,' remarks Mrs Thomas, inviting us aboard *Twm Barlwn*. We all feel rather pleased with ourselves. She hands me coffee in a Caerphilly Castle mug, and apologises for the lack of Welsh cakes. She and Ken live near Twm Barlwn, at Goetre in Gwent. They explain that the twm, a piece of high ground, is a semi-sacred place of pilgrimage on Good Friday.

Fellow rescuers David and John Wibberley from Minchinhampton in Gloucestershire, share the Thomas's hospitality. John is an agriculture lecturer. He tells us the animal we have saved is a mule ewe, mottled grey, white face, worth about £65.

They outline their enterprise, now slightly delayed, which is to row the River Thames as far as Teddington. It is pleasing to see a father on an adventure in the company of his university-age son. David tells us about his little tub *Bess Ruwa*. 'It's so small, people think its a tender to a yacht, but it's not, it's our boat.' It is a very insubstantial craft. 'You stop rowing to scratch a fly off your nose and you spin round like a top.'

I walk on a few hundred yards to where the river Evenlode stretches languidly in from the west. Another half mile and the Oxford Canal joins at Yarnton Mead. This is as important a junction in our waterways as the union of M1 and M6 is to our roads. The canal links the River Thames to almost every navigable waterway in the Midlands and the north of England. But there is no ceremony; no long line of boats waiting to come and go in a fog of fumes, just *Silver Day* slipping down out of the rolling Midlands fields.

This is the most northerly point of the River Thames. It wriggles and dances uncertainly, turns north, checks, thinks again, loops back, then lurches south. To the north there is a ribbon of slow-moving traffic on the A40, by which the clever men of South Wales came to Oxford.

It is early evening as I pass under the A34, Oxford bypass, under a car carrier crammed with new Fords, Harry Shaw's coach and two caravans. There is an obelisk, dated 1886, commemorating men of enduring obscurity in some way connected to the river: R. Bucknell, mayor and F. Twinings, sheriff.

3

THE clever men at Oxford,
Know all that there is to be knowed.
But they none of them know one half as much
As intelligent Mr Toad.
    – *Wind in the Willows*, Kenneth Grahame.

MY FIRST SIGHT of Oxford, a masterpiece among European cities, comes at the uncomfortable frontier of the city's ring road. As I pass under the roaring traffic at Thames Bridge, which carries the A34 trunk road west and north, I become aware of what seems to be a forest of churches, in an exceptionally devout village. I realise this is my first glimpse of one of the long distance walker's greatest privileges, Oxford's dreaming spires.

This place, suffering the sort of traffic that used to pass through the city, is as awful as it is in order that Oxford, with its thirty-nine colleges and a reputation as one of the world's leading academic institutions can retain some of its medieval peace.

There are other ways to approach Oxford. Jude, in Hardy's *Jude the Obscure*, saw the city first from the high ground to the south-west, where most of the artists still gather. But this is the aspect the river offers, and it is magnificent, even if horizontal. The view of the city, still three miles away, reminded me of my first visit to Ely with its majestic cathedral, clearly visible from many miles across the flat plains of East Anglia. Reaching Oxford is, in a temporal sense, just as gripping an experience.

In the context of what has come before, it is a tremendous shock. From mile after mile of drowsy river meadow, with tidily unobtrusive settlements, to a place which is, at the same time, one of the finest architectural concentrations in Britain, a thriving car city employing over ten thousand people, and a burgeoning centre for technological development, all set down in the quiet centre of England.

Oxford, seen across Christs' Meadow.

'The most effective kind of education is that a child should play amongst lovely things.'

— Plato

The city and its reputation overwhelms everything about it. Only the Thames, which has an existence before and beyond Oxford, can compete with its eminence. But I will have to wait. Oxford is like a sumptuous painting set in a frame with a very wide and dingy border.

The city is very clearly contained within ring roads. Here, at Lower Wolvercote, the A34 crosses the river, close to the famous Trout Inn, an ivy-covered stone building to which better-off undergraduates repair. At the southern perimeter, about two miles south of the city centre, the A423 crosses the Thames just south of Iffley Lock, underlining the city.

Oxford marks the start of a neatly self-contained thirty mile section of the Thames which ends at Goring Gap, in the geological sense the scene of the river's greatest breakthrough, seventy million years ago.

My intention is to pause in Oxford, then reach Abingdon, eight miles south, by late evening. Would a day in Oxford be sufficient? Hardly. More like a week, warned the keeper at Godstow Lock, a few yards on from Thames Bridge.

Close to Godstow Lock are the remains of Godstow Abbey, the 'House of Nunnes' where Fair Rosamond, supposed mistress of Henry II and subsequently poisoned by a jealous Queen Eleanor, was buried. On the east bank is the most ancient surviving part of Oxford.

There is a story of a Japanese visitor arriving in the city and asking to see the city's oldest thing. He was tugged right out of the city to behold this nondescript green space of Port Meadow, a damp wedge of green two miles long, which narrows to a point and impales the city centre.

Its appearance has changed little since people first lived on the meadow in the summer, certainly as long ago as the Bronze and Iron Ages. It contains burial mounds dating from 1500 BC. The meadow may have been given to Oxford by King Alfred when he founded the city. In 1940 the exhausted men of the Oxon and Bucks Light Infantry rested here after the evacuation from Dunkerque.

Four times in three hundred years the City fathers have tried to snatch the land and build on it: on each occasion they have been repulsed by the time-hallowed status of the artisan's rights to it. Local people retain grazing rights to this day. I walk on down for two miles through Medley and Osney, the spiritless western flank of the city.

The Thames and the city of Oxford share each others' celebrity. I find only one thing wrong. The city's founders built Oxford a few hundred yards too far to the east. If they could have conspired to make the river the centrefold of their city they could have created one of the truly great marriages of nature and architecture.

As it is, Oxford is still the only large community, apart from Reading, on the Thames outside London, and the Thames was once a vital resource. It supplied fish; it powered mills for fulling cloth and grinding corn; and it provided cheap transport. River trade to London, 111 miles away, and beyond to the Continent was flourishing by the twelfth century.

I reach the second oldest part of Oxford at Folly Bridge, the only proper entrance to this spectacular city. Oxford is significantly different from almost any place in Britain, because it is still doing what it has done for hundreds of years in much the same way.

On a rain speckled day young men in tweeds and young ladies in seemly long black dresses with heavy buckles swoosh past on bikes. The ladies and the bikes are the only give-away that the university has arrived in modern times. Otherwise I could be looking at any of the countless generations of students who may proceed, on unsurpassable credentials (matched only by Cambridge), to the highest positions in national life.

The timeless flow of academic achievement seems untouched by the outside world and looking at the perfect state of the old buildings, I am inclined to think, particularly untouched by wars. The city's fabric certainly seems to have been spared.

But then I remembered Lord Stockton, the former Harold Macmillan, pondering the lost fellow undergraduates of the 1914-18 War, so poignantly recounted in Vera Brittain's *Testament of Youth*. We will never know how our lives might have been enriched by those squandered talents.

The river greatly eased the problem of building so many colleges. Much of the construction material was carried here by river. The oldest is Merton (1264). There are about twelve thousand students at the university now, about 4,300 of them women. The liberation of the woman student is the most dramatic turn in the university's recent development. The tradition of single sex colleges has been swept away, and there are now only two colleges exclusively for women.

There was a time when roughly half the Cabinet would have been the product of Oxford. The rise of red-brick graduates is only a recent cloud on Oxford's horizon. An utterly random trawl through the graduate list of the twentieth century reveals Hilda Margaret Roberts; who went on to become the longest serving Prime Minister of the century; T.E.Lawrence (Lawrence of Arabia); Dorothy L.Sayers; W.H.Auden; Richard Burton.

I turn off Folly bridge into St Aldates, the cradle of Oxford. The site of the ford just south east of the bridge was probably the reason this great city was set here at all. The river was the thin blue line between Mercia and Wessex.

The city grew up around the gravel promontory where the Thames and Cherwell met, on the south side of present day Oxford. The first written evidence of Oxford is a reference to King Edward the Elder turning it into a stronghold to guard the entry to Wessex. In 1071 King William's man Robert D'Oilly built Oxford Castle down here and the long Causeway.

Even without its university Oxford would be illustrious. It was one of the most important towns in Saxon England and one of the largest towns in England in the early Middle Ages, when its history was recorded in greater detail than any other place.

It has the oldest civic seal for any town in England and one of the richest concentrations of classical buildings in Britain. Some commentators go further: 'The most beautiful city in England with a larger and richer display of academic architecture than any other.'

Then there is the geographical significance of Oxford, in the middle of Middle England, roughly equidistant from the Solent, the Thames Estuary and the Severn.

We know a vast amount about medieval Oxford. The masters of the university, which had no formal beginning – there were scholars before 1200 and it had gained a European reputation by 1300 – came somewhere below the fletchers, dyers, tanners, and builders in status. In *The Miller's Tale*, Chaucer wrote of the carpenter at Osney who owned a house with four rooms, one of them let to a certain Nicholas of the university.

The first students studied only theology, rhetoric and logic but their problems were timeless. After seeing some students cavort in tipsy abandon down Broad Street, young men in mortar boards and girls in prim black gowns, I came across the following historical exchange. 'The money you so liberally gave me last time for my study is disbursed,' wrote a despairing medieval student to his father. 'I am in debt to the tune of five shillings and more.'

'You will now cease from ribald behaviour,' came back the stern reply, 'knowing than on no account will I give you any aid while you behave thus madly and outrageously.'

I walk up past Christ Church with its opulent bell tower, Old Tom, completed by Sir Christopher Wren. It is the largest of the colleges, founded by Cardinal Wolsey. There is overwhelming certainty to life in St Aldate's: at five past nine every evening the six tonne Great Tom Bell still tolls 101 times to signal the closing of the gates to the original 101 scholars.

Then I turn into the High Street, past the colleges – St Edmund Hall, Queens, All Souls, Oriel and Brasenose – crammed together like weighty tomes on a shelf, wondering how I should begin to unravel Oxford's superlatives.

One American tourist, at least, has discovered his personal goal. 'Here it is, Ag,' he drawls triumphantly, outside the Radcliffe Camera, built by James Gibbs in 1739 to house Dr Radcliffe's physic library. The huge classical dome of the Camera 'counts for quite half in any distant view of Oxford buildings' wrote a contemporary observer.

Walking along Broad Street, which must be one of the most bookish places in Britain, with the Bodleian Library just around the corner in Cattle Street, among the six libraries entitled to a copy of every book published in Britain, and one of the few from which no book can be borrowed. This rule applies even to monarchs. When Charles I was at Oxford during the Civil War, the librarian feigned illness every time the King asked to take away some reading matter.

Then there are the many outlets of Blackwell's Books. I browse for an hour through the astonishing Norrington Room, which has the largest single display of books for sale in the world. Outside, I chance upon the site of one of the many turning points in English history which can be located in Oxford. The traffic is dividing around a sober suited man of theatrical bearing, standing on a metal cross embedded in the road.

Over the traffic he is addressing a camera poised above him on the roof of a Range Rover. He is talking I assume, but in what language I cannot deduce above the din, of Latimer and Ridley. They were burnt at the stake on this spot in October 1555 for refusing to renounce Protestantism, while Cranmer, who was to be similarly executed within the year, gazed supportively down from the city wall.

In the Civil War the King withdrew to Oxford, possibly the only place with sufficient dignity to put up a displaced monarch. The Royalists minted some splendid coins, including the golden Triple Unite, and Half Unite, gilded slabs which must have jingled deliciously, but not in the soldiers' pockets.

A massive canvas by Jan Wyck in the City Museum shows the siege from high ground to the south, smoke drifting off the fires of the patient besieging Parliamentarians camped to the west of the city, not a single boat on the river which divided and ran down the west like runner beans cut in strands. To continue the culinary theme, it was said that the Royalists would never have given up had not the ladies of the court felt the need for fresh butter on their early peas.

After the Civil War the university came to dominate city life. William Cobbett, in *Rural Rides*, sneers at Oxford's academic status: 'Upon beholding the masses of buildings at Oxford, devoted to what they call "learning", I could not help reflecting on the drones that they contain and the wasps they send forth.' Henry James is more complimentary: 'Oxford lends sweetness to labour, and dignity to leisure.'

But the city has a few independent claims to fame. James Sadler became the first Englishman aviator when 'with firmness and intrepidity he ascended into the atmosphere' in a hot air balloon to a height of 3,600 feet.

He drifted out of the city on a light north westerly and came to earth, alive, near Islip, a few miles east.

In 1874 Sarah Cooper developed Frank Cooper's Oxford marmalade, 'an essential part of the English Gentleman's way of life at home and abroad.' In the 1890s another William Morris began repairing bicycles in his Oxford home. Two wheels led to four and by 1913 he was making Morris Oxfords. His original Cowley works is now part of Rover Cars.

Dr Roger Bannister ran the first four minute mile here. Penicillin was first administered to a patient in Oxford. The yellow ragwort, orginally from the slopes of Vesuvius, began its invasion of the railway cuttings of Britain from escaped seeds of specimens planted in the Botanic Gardens up against Magdalen Bridge on the eastern entrance to the city.

Today Oxford graduates have helped make the city one of Britain's most flourishing manufacturers of scientific and medical products. Oxford Instruments, a high technology company which started in a garden shed in North Oxford is now worth more than £200 million on the Stock Exchange.

My progress around Oxford was after all threatening to consume a week. Just time to seek out *Heads and Hands of the Apostles*, by Raphael, at the Ashmolean, the first public museum in Britain, and still heroically refusing to charge people to see its wonders.

But no time for Holman Hunt's *Light of the World*, first version, at Keble College Chapel; or for the claw and beak, all that remain of the dodo, that tragic bird, symbol of extinction, at the University Museum. Oxford's once whole specimen predated by a hundred years the sophisticated taxidermy techniques that would have saved it.

By mid afternoon I decided to make for the river. But which river? The Thames running through Oxford has many runnels, 'more in number than your eyelashes' wrote Keats. It curls and splits then rejoins with itself, then splits and fuses again after its union with the Cherwell close to the south-west side of inner Oxford.

The map is full of confusing twists and twirls of blue. Sideshoots of the Thames become Bulstake Stream, Botley Stream, Seacourt Stream and Hogacre Ditch. Some, like Weir's Mill Stream, tell of their ancient function. And, all the while, a separate arm of the Oxford canal steals down the city's flank, on the west side of Port Meadow.

I picked up where I had left off, at Folly Bridge, at the bottom of St Aldate's, which is where by tradition the Thames draws members of the university and the people of Oxford for recreation.

The river, like a successful socialite invited to the best parties, has impressive literary associations throughout its length. This stretch has one of the best.

July 4th 1862 was cool and wet. Four people set off in a gig to row up to

51

Godstow for a picnic. One of the four began to give the first telling of a story which opened thus: 'Alice was beginning to get very tired of sitting by her sister on the bank and of having nothing to do.'

The Reverend Charles Dodgson, alias Lewis Carroll, was a maths tutor at Christ Church, a few hundred yards up from Folly Bridge. On that boat trip he told *Alice in Wonderland* to the three daughters of Dr Liddell, the dean of Christ Church. 'Ever drifting down the stream; Lingering in the golden gleam; Life, what is it but a dream,' wrote Carroll later, commemorating the occasion, in *A Boat, Beneath a Sunny Sky*, twisting the meteorological truth.

By the late nineteenth century the Thames had become Oxford's particular outing for high days and holidays. It remains a place of colourful ease and exercise. In May there is Eights Week; in June a procession of boats on the river; in July the City regatta; in February, Torpids, the college rowing races. There is little punting on the Thames: that elegant diversion is reserved for the more tranquil Cherwell.

I pass Salters, passenger launch proprietors, a famous company, which ran daily services from Oxford to Kingston. The through journey took two days, the boats stopping at Henley for the night. Today, from Oxford, they will take you no further than Abingdon. If you think Salter's schedule was fast, Hilaire Belloc once walked from Oxford to London in eleven hours.

There are many boat yards along this stretch. A shining shaft is upended on a stand for a craftsman's final touches. Dingier craft are stacked on shelves.

Then I am snapped out of my riverside reverie by a brazen radio voice from an alternative culture. 'Say hullo to Gary, Kerry, Keith and all in Upper . . .' invites a Radio 1 person, inspiring the toils of a blue hatted artisan, at work on Pembroke College's new student residence.

In a city, a river acquires an active and sinister function: people fall into it, lose things in it, dump the proceeds of crime in it. The river invites people to end their days in it, and to dispose of those whose days are unnaturally ended. There is a police launch on hand for such eventualities.

A few yards downriver, the police presence was not sufficiently prominent to deter Master Fletcher from scrawling, with suspiciously precise use of the apostrophe, 'Fletcher was 'ere. OK.' The pleasure boat *Reading* chuckles past, leaving little wake. I see a college spire, not as in a dream but in a nightmare, partly obscured by a drearily functional 1960s flat block.

On the opposite bank is more original Thames flood plain, Christ Church meadow. It has bobbles and ridges, has never been built upon and is untouched by the machines of agriculture. It is held in trust by Christ Church College as green countryside in the heart of the city. The successful fight against proposals to build a road through it in 1965 was described as the 'bloodiest battle' that ever took place over an environmental issue.

I meet Jan Hallwood, a Magdalen College scout, who arrives on a three wheeled bicycle at Isis Cottage, built in 1910. At her front door, fringed with red roses, Mrs Hallwood tells me that six years ago she and her husband read the sort of advert that sends some sensitive readers shivering with anticipation to the telephone. The three lines in the *Sunday Times* said: 'Cottage with 1.5 acres on the river. One mile city centre.'

During term the bank is an animated scene of brisk young persons rowing sharp swift boats and people shouting encouragement from banks. Isis Cottage is a sort of turning point, from six a.m. onwards.

A few years ago pack ice floated down the river. It froze again last winter and the family passed twelve days without fresh water. 'We dug holes in the river and boiled the water. The lock keeper was wonderful.'

Just over a mile south of Folly Bridge, at Iffley Lock, there is an ornate stone-built bridge, and a Stonehenge device, a roller slip, built by the Victorians for hauling small boats on rollers over a dry hump, to bypass the lock. It probably cost the builders little more for that graceful touch than it costs today's engineers to besmirch the river with ugly concrete slabs.

Iffley has been spelt eighty different ways in the past thousand years. It has a fine Norman Church with a massive tower. A few yards to the south – in built-up areas the riverbank is full of these sudden shifts from the sublime to the awful – I come upon *Oxford Regent*, pulled up under the Oxford ring road, a dreadfully loud place.

On the fringe of a large swampy plantation of alder, Thames Water's strict rules of speed and litter are being widely ignored. Urban fringe society is at leisure. A youth of about fifteen jumps into the river before a warily admiring posse of young girls. 'I'm doing nothing. I'm just standing here dripping wet,' is his unspoken message to me.

I have now left graceful Oxford. It was the only place where I found 'Isis' an appropriate alternative to 'Thames'. Study the Ordnance Survey map and you will find 'Isis' alongside 'Thames' all along its blue line from Gloucestershire.

Now consult a local person. No local uses the name: Isis is a classicist's affectation and the sort of name you might expect to find in Oxford where Mr Toad's 'clever men' congregate most densely. It seems ideal for riverbank cottages and tea rooms with frilly curtains and poetry in the lofty style.

I meet, raised on a plinth, a piece of high quality stone, bearing no explanation whatsoever. Some important legend has been torn off. It has nothing to say either on the subject of grand departures or on merely slipping away, but a lot about riverbank thuggery.

53

The countryside returns, to the east of the suburban village of Kennington. The river has lost its shine and has turned opaque under a squall. But it is benevolent, warm, summer rain. The sky has spent its malice in a wicked June. It is certain to finish in two minutes. At Rose Isle I pass a cordoned-off clump of new trees which will give a solid shoulder to this long meander in ten years' time.

Set fast in the mud are sad, expired examples of the Victorian boat builder's art. They include a boat of Venetian aspect with high blue prow, the *Lady Wendy*, heavily holed. She is quite beyond recall.

In an hour's steady walking from Folly Bridge I reach Sandford-on-Thames, three miles south of Oxford, a place where gentrification has taken its first, modest grip on the river. It is a place of illusions. There are smart riverside wood-clad and brick houses, with balconies and picture windows perched in tight medieval formation over a high metal wall, intended to keep the river out.

A kingfisher, the first I have seen on the river, heads across 100 yards of open meadow from the river. By now, half way through an average day, it must have caught at least forty minnows. It banks obligingly to flash its blue back, swivels again to reveal its orangey-chestnut underside, then arrives at its nest with a chirrup.

The river becomes sluggish, deep and brooding. Didcot power station comes into view, simmering on the horizon. It dominates this flat landscape, a plain biscuit after Oxford's rich gâteau. I hear an explosion of profanities from the other side of the river. I look for a gang of navvies digging up the bank, but it is only two boys fishing.

'The Thames is "swearing free" ' wrote Richard Jefferies, the sensitive Victorian naturalist and writer in *The Modern Thames*. By 'free' he meant quite the opposite of 'devoid of'. 'You may begin at the mouth off the Nore and curse your way up to Cricklade. A hundred miles for swearing is a fine preserve: it is one of the marvels of our civilisation.'

A dribble of curdled smoke struggles up from the burning stubble of a large cornfield. The land begins to rise on the eastern bank. The colours in the fields range from a dull fawn to a deep-reddish brown.

Silver Enterprise, moored by the boat house at Lower Radley, opposite Nuneham Courtenay, contains the nephew of a five times Wimbledon champion. Philip Dod volunteers this connection in the course of a general chat about his vessel's capacity to sail across the Atlantic. 'It's designed for heavy seas,' says Philip. 'It's really too deep for this river. We can touch bottom. We have to be careful where we pull in.'

Would Philip, who was in air-sea rescue in the war, dare to cross the Atlantic in her. (Nonchalantly): 'Oh yea.' Pause, then from below, 'I wouldn't.' This is Mrs Marion Dod. Philip says she would be seasick.

We turn to Philip's remarkable aunt, Lotte Dod. 'Wimbledon champion in 1887, then mixed doubles with my father, then ladies doubles with her sister. Then she gave up tennis and became all-England lady golf champion. Hockey, no, archery, was next. Silver medal in the Olympics, then eighth in figure skating in Europe. Then she played hockey for England, became one of the few ladies to go down the Cresta Run and climb the Matterhorn. All she had from Wimbledon was a silver toast-rack. Playing today, she'd have been a millionairess.'

Mr Dod is the embodiment of the interesting depths which casual riverbank conversation can plumb. He has a creased, weathered face. He lost an eye at the age of eight playing football. We watch a yellow brimstone dance past his prow, while he concludes his unprompted recital of family sporting prowess with an account of how his father played chess with the younger Dod's schoolmaster, who was West of England champion, and beat him three times before dinner.

I leave the overwhelming Dods and walk on. Across the river is Nuneham Courtenay, five miles south of Oxford, site of unprecedented royal bliss. We can only guess at the perfect content the young honeymooning Queen Victoria experienced in that light-brown stone building, Nuneham House. 'One of the most delightful residences on the Thames,' wrote Charles Dickens, junior. 'A famous place for picnics and water parties'. But not today. It looks very private.

Was the royal privacy maintained then, as today, by the very pleasing line of mixed trees on the other bank? A grotesque pink and white wood boathouse with high sloping roof comes with the estate. The village, which formerly stood near the house, was removed some distance north-east in 1760 by Earl Harcourt who wanted the site for his landscape garden, another of Capability Brown's achievements.

The matching pairs of cottages, which face each other across the main road, show the tidy mind of the destroyer of old Nuneham. The squire, in addition to rehousing his underlings, had an odd idea of improving them by the institution of orders of merit and prizes of virtue. 'The attempt did not answer the sanguine expectations of its promoter,' observed Dickens.

I walk on for about two and half miles, under little riverside spinneys and skirt an uncut meadow, in quiet farmland under a low hill. I enter Abingdon by a reedy backwater, which the map insists is the Abbey Stream. A small white butterfly passes in energetic flutter. I reach Abingdon Lock. Four swans are working the waters, their invisible heads detained underwater.

In Abingdon (twinned with Argentan, Locca and Schongau) a small floating hotel, *Le Sans Egal* of London, is tied up, with its blue plastic ornamental chairs stacked inwards, its patrons ashore. But I make for the former Birmingham Canal Navigation tug, *Bevan*, built in 1914, which I had seen that morning in Oxford.

Bevan is the nautical equivalent of an old, patched bulldog that has seen many fights. Nick Perfect, estate manager at a school, paid £50 for her. 'She really was a bit of a wreck,' says Nick. 'But she's got wooden knees and she's magic.' *Bevan* used to pull horse-drawn boats through tunnels.

The tang of Morland Brewery's hops wafts to the very door of St Helen's church in the middle of Abingdon, which is as broad as it is long. (Technically, its nave and chancel are of equal breadth.) Welcome, says a sign in seven languages. There is an invitation to become a 'holy duster'. Saints Matthew, Mark, Luke and John behold this invocation to cleanliness from stained glass.

> I CALCULATE that with these legs [the poet] Wordsworth . . . must have traversed a distance of 175,000 to 180,000 miles – a mode of exertion which, to him, stood in the stead of alcohol and all other stimulants; and to which, indeed, he was indebted for a life of unclouded happiness, and we for much of what is most excellent in his writings.
> – *Literary and Lake Reminiscences*, Thomas de Quincey.

If it wasn't for Oxford, Abingdon would be terribly important, the first biggish place on the river. It has had its moments. Abingdon Abbey was refounded in 924 by King Eadred at the junction of the anciently-named river Ock, a British word for salmon (and a clue to where the Thames salmon spawned).

By this time the upper Thames was already an important commercial redistribution centre, receiving cargoes of high quality goods from the continent, which threatened an early trade deficit.

The abbey, mindful of the remunerative trade passing its portals, became an early Thames manager, digging a new channel for the river in the early eleventh century when the main river was silting up. But the monks could never hope to tame the Thames. In 1316, calamity. The abbot and monks were all swept away in the swollen river in an ill-advised attempt to ford it.

Today the centre contains a monument to civic failure to stop people writing their names on things. I can't really blame the authorities for letting it happen but I did find the library of daubs on the open ground floor promenade of the original and ancient County Hall in the centre of Abingdon rather depressing.

Today I will take a modest stroll along eight miles of the Oxfordshire Thames to Day's Lock at Dorchester, which is a baptismal point if not a watery cradle of British Christianity, pausing at the melting pot for twenty-first century power. I will find that, after the river has been compromised by Oxford's many roads, it regains its youthful innocence.

I leave Abingdon on the east bank, opposite the mouth of the old Wilts and Berks Canal, which joined the Kennet and Avon Canal in 1810, and took a lot of trade from the Upper Thames. Close to my path three new trees are neatly snapped off level with the top of their supports. I find no example of careless vandalism as painful as the beheaded sapling, unless it is a swan with a fisherman's float in its gullet.

At the edge of Abingdon is an early example of Thames corner cutting. To the east of the river are several channels which turned this sheep pasture into an island. My path is the east bank of the river on Andersey Island, which is about half a mile wide.

Across the Thames are some modest 1960s houses, their gardens running down to the water. 'Very select riverside houses' are being built next to the Abingdon Marina. From here to Docklands the side of the Thames is, as the estate agents say, a much sought after place to build a house.

Then the corporate features come to an end. I pass contented pigs up to their hams in grass and reach Culham. There is a neat scatter of manor houses, a church and a renovated barn. A kestrel is hanging in the humid morning on slighty upturned wings ten feet off the ground.

Kennet 2, a Thames Water boat pulling a trailer full of twigs and leaves is leading, at a crawl, an impatient flotilla of five boats. This is Culham Cut, which slices off a river meander past Sutton Courtenay. The fifth boat assaults me with high volume Radio 1. I escape to the original river – recorded thus in one book: 'More enjoyable by far' – which runs in a loop to the south.

The kestrel drops to a level of increased readiness. It is being mobbed by a party of swallows. The kestrel responds irritably with a fidget of its wings. I picnic on this long, quiet side reach.

In this little village's church, All Saints, are buried Asquith and Eric Blair. I find a mock Tudor house with a Romeo and Juliet balcony which juts out over *Lady Decima* and *Flaming Fantasy*. The water-borne suitor might approach his task thus: 'O, speak again, bright angel! for thou art as glorious to this night, being o'er my head, as is a winged messager of heaven . . .' It would just about work on the right sort of scented evening in this reach, untroubled by through navigation for over 100 years.

The 1885 *Royal River* had it even then as 'A beautiful little back water, brilliantly pied with water lillies.' But some details have disappeared irrevocably: that writer found the corncrake in an adjoining meadow. The younger Dickens wrote: 'During the month of May, the meadows by the riverside resound with the note of the landrail, or corncrake, which is heard far into the night. The nest is not infrequently cut out by the mowers in the grass fields.' Today the bird's habitat is as remote as these books' literary style, swept off the face of southern England by agricultral changes.

It has become a sultry day of hot wind back on the main river just beyond Culham Lock. The *Sans Egal* lumbers past, its ornamental chairs still unused. From the bank I can see a white concrete futuristic building half a mile to the north. Its soft, reassuring lines suggest a vacuum-cleaner museum.

But cosmic forces are harnessed here. Men in white coats have just outshone the sun. This is JET, the Joint European Torus, a research programme at the UK Atomic Energy Authority's Culham Laboratory. I am tantalised by nothing less than the birthplace of a potential source of safe power for the twenty-first century.

A simple phone call draws me in. I identify myself to the security officer at the gate with a credit card and I am directed to John Maple, Culham's information officer, a man still eager after receiving five thousand visitors this year to discourse on fuels. We talk about the benign purpose of this soft-edged building. 'It's the process that happens in the sun. We would like it to happen here on earth.'

This is nuclear fusion research. Unlike fission, which involves splitting the atom and terrifies many people, fusion is the process of heating up gas to very high temperatures, and it is very safe. 'But we have to be even cleverer than the creator,' says John. 'We must heat our fuels to 100 million degrees or more. Although it sounds incredible, it is possible, because we only need heat a very small quantity.'

Why are we deploying so many men in white coats to harness fusion? 'Common sense and strategic reasons, not because it is some great white hope.' As we speak, the White Coats are inside the evacuated magnetic chamber, which is shaped like a giant doughnut. A few days earlier they passed an enormous current through it and heated less than one tenth of a gramme of plasma to 140 million degrees centigrade, many times hotter than the centre of the sun.

Once they have heated the fuel to great temperatures, they must hold it in a magnetic field, trap the neutrons in a blanket, then slow them down to produce at sensible temperatures – a few 100 degrees centigrade – the heat source for electricty, generated in the conventional way.

The JET project began in 1983 on this research station of the UK Atomic Energy Authority, when the European nations agreed they needed to build a bigger doughnut to achieve their purpose. Inter-governmental back scratching brought JET, the world's leading fusion experiment, to the side of the Thames. At first the European Commission was unable to decide on a site. But the UK won West Germany's support after the SAS helped rescue German nationals from a hijacked plane in Africa, and JET came to Culham.

It will be the year 2030 before the CEGB receives fusion electricity. John invites me to return and complain to him if its inception is delayed beyond that date.

John Maple leads metaphorically back to the Thames as I hunt for the credit card that I might need to buy my way out of this place of white-hot promise, and simulated fork lightning – they also test the ability of aircraft to withstand electrical storms.

I walk back to the river bank at Culham Lock. Combine harvesters whirl and chomp. The distant smudge of the Chilterns drifts into view. The Thames, which has rolled unchecked from its source, must now prepare to break through the line of hills which divides southern England.

A line of pylons darts to the finishing line at Didcot power station, its cooling towers enveloped in smoke, like a brooding, active volcano. A family of goldfinches glean the oil-seed rape. A coal train grumbles uphill from Didcot and over Appleford Railway Bridge behind an ancient diesel. Goldcrests, with a sweet gurgling, cavort in the fringe of a maize field. The full range of subsidised crops is on view.

I am proving an obvious truth. The further away from a settlement, the better is the quality of my path. Two or three miles out of a town, beyond the range of the weekend stroller, I have the luxury of real grass under my feet. Within a built up area, I plough through a surface the consistency of brown Windsor soup.

The vessel *Cognac* is being passed by *Nevenco*. Why such haste? *Cascade* arrives, spraying transistorised musical accompaniment. 'Get your nose in there, it's not bad.' Two middle-aged men, dressed only in shorts, leap for the bank. Soon I hear over my right shoulder the sound of hammer on stake. I meet very few walkers, and rather more boats. However, they only speak if spoken to.

Gay Countess tails *Stort of Warwick* like a swift navy cutter running down a smuggler. Two young marauders on the *Countess*, brash and ribald, bellow to three girls on the bank. 'Don't worry. It's only the name of the boat.'

There is a lollipop line of pollarded ash, and a herd of cows at slumber on the south bank. The herd on the north side, as if in a different time zone, are back at work. There is a pleasant red bridge ahead with a church in the background. On the right is a caravan site filled to Hong Kong density.

Clifton Hampden, five miles along the bank from Abingdon, is a village of steeply sloping thatched roofs. The church of St Michael and All Angels, an example of Sir Gilbert Scott's early work as a restorer, has a peal of five bells. The tenor bell was cast in 1845, the others in 1844, by founders C.

and G. Mears at Whitechapel, London. Departing worshippers disgorge past a noseless bishop gargoyle and peer straight over a cliff into the river, like unwitting lemmings.

Gilbert Scott also designed Clifton Hampden bridge, built of local bricks in 1864, but he could not have imagined it would also become one of Britain's most extraordinary bird boxes. In the 1950s it held the largest colony of house martins in the UK, with four hundred nests and was declared a site of special scientific interest.

I recross the bridge and pass two neat black heiffers with freshly burnished hoofs, at the start of the pleasant vacancy of a wide open water meadow. It stretches for miles. It is a hot, full-bloomed summer afternoon.

The Thames is the colour of dark green marble. A man is up to his thighs, in eyeshield and black shirt, stalking perch among the water lillies. The shape of this bank has not changed for centuries, except that every year the river, like a salami slicer, claims another fine sliver.

I see a head on the water. It recalls that famous grainy study of leadership by example, when Mao Tse-tung swam down the River Yangtse in the mid 1960s. This man is moving steadily and slowly against the flow. *Midnight Blue* approaches, with a green T-shirted lady on the prow, legs wrapped in sleeping-bag against imagined cold. Will the swimmer make it to the jetty? The boat passes him safely, and it becomes clear he could swim all afternoon if he wished. He spares me a glance, quite casually, from mid river, like some new life-form consisting only of a self-sufficient, disembodied head.

For some time I have swung round Didcot power station in the south, like a passing space object temporarily trapped in orbit. Now Didcot away on my right is losing its force and the power of the mysterious Sinodun Hills begin to prevail. They draw me southwards.

On the opposite bank at Burcot, manicured lawns switchback down to the river. At each change in incline, there is a little support camp consisting of a scattering of garden furniture where the traveller may stop for refreshment. At the river's edge, there is the more permanent repose of a garden house.

Ahead is the timeless outline of the church at Little Wittenham, and the hill fort on the Sinoduns. An eerie tranquility steals over the scene. There is not a boat or a man-made feature, except for the distant, grinding harvester. There is a relic of an old cereal field here, the cornflower, or bluebottle, the only alternative colour to a green sweep of a quarter of a mile long.

I cross a stile. A heron barks across a meadow flecked with buttercups. A carpet of thistles releases a blizzard of seed heads. The species has not yet succeeded in colonising the other side of the river. A huge four-winged dragonfly hawks among them like a First World War ace, and audibly snaps on some invisible insect life.

Over a stile and the first clear glimpse of the Chilterns, capped in trees. In this passage through unfolding England, this is the biggest single landmark. I reach Day's Lock, eight miles from Abingdon and a quarter of a mile south of Dorchester. There are Pooh sticks for sale at two p each.

The remains around Dorchester are some of the best examples of a late prehistoric landscape in Britain. Man first reached the Thames Valley about four hundred thousand years ago. Finds from around here show that in Palaeolithic times he would have hunted mammoth, woolly rhinoceros, cave bear, lion and arctic fox.

The Sinodun Hills are an outcrop of the chalk deposits which form the Chilterns. They would have been an important landmark to travellers passing on a north to south route and to boats on the lock-free river, which was navigable from the estuary to up beyond Oxford until the Middle Ages.

The hillfort at Wittenham Clumps, on Castle Hill in the Sinoduns, would have been a dominant vantage point. From this ten acre hillfort, consisting of a single ditch and rampart, the keen-eyed would peer far into the nothern Thames valley and south across the Vale of White Horse to the hillforts on the line of the Ridgeway on the Berkshire Downs.

St Birinus came to Wessex as the Pope's special envoy and baptised Cynegils, King of Wessex, in the Thames almost exactly under my feet where I stand on Day's Lock Bridge, waiting for my Pooh sticks to pass under. Later he founded a bishopric which stretched to the edge of Northumbria.

There is great antiquity spread around my path for the short walk into Dorchester. The footpath takes me through Dyke Hills, which made a 114 acre enclosure defended by a massive double bank to the north and east, the site of a settlement at the time of Christ. They found an altar to Jupiter and Augustus here.

> The fortresses at Dorchester and at Sinodun are among the most speaking monuments of the earliest history of our island. But it has lately occurred to the owner of the ground that a few shillings more of yearly profit might be gained by turning pasture land into arable; and to such a sordid motive these precious antiquities are being sacrificed. At least a third of the dyke has already been lowered and will gradually be utterly destroyed beneath the yearly passage of ruin's merciless plough share.

Only the picturesque language of this impassioned outburst sets it before the familiar litany of twentieth century destruction of habitat. This is from an article in *Saturday Review* of July 2nd 1870. It was an early example of the power of conservation journalism. The landowner was persuaded to stay his hand and the massive outline of the grim earthworks is still much as it was then.

The greatest threat to this area came after the Second World War with extraction of the gravel reserves, borne down by the Thames at times of great spate. Rescue excavations were carried out ahead of the diggers between 1946 and 1951 and what was found established Dorchester as one of the classic neolithic sites in Great Britain.

Dorchester, once an important stop for coaches on the London to Oxford road, and now bypassed, is still a favoured place with its timbered houses, thatched cottages and quiet inns.

Edith Gratia Steadman OBE, 1888 to 1978, is its most famous adopted daughter. In the chapel of St Birinus, there is an eloquent testimonial to her. It stands within what was the most peaceful place I found anywhere on the Thames, in the abbey church of St Peter and St Paul. Why is Miss Steadman, appointments officer at Harvard University so honoured? The reason is that she cared so much for Dorchester. She twisted the arms of wealthy Americans on Dorchester's behalf and her largesse paid for the restoration of the museum. The Queen Mother visited Dorchester and took tea with her. Miss Steadman's benign features are preserved on a gargoyle outside the abbey.

I read a note from the Victoria and Albert museum, informing the abbey authorities that their excellent chasuble is even older than they believed – late fifteenth or early sixteenth century Italian, pre-Reformation. So I am looking at a glass-covered artefact worn in the celebration of mass by an English bishop who owed his allegiance to the Pope in Rome.

> GORING played East Preston on a field the hedges of which had long been tenanted by rabbits. One rabbit emerged for his customary evening nibble, and Mr Somerset, who was batting, hit a cricket ball at him with such force that it killed him on the spot.
> – *Over*, Hugh de Selincourt.

Retrieving the river the next day, I lose myself on a high point somewhere near the roof of southern England. My quickest route lay over the fields, past such homely landmarks as Oak Tree Farm and Ladygrove Farm. Then head-high crops divert me from the footpath and I stray into that indecisive white land the map leaves vacant for imaginings.

For a few moments, under a sunless sky, I am alone with prehistoric man in a wide ancient place of safe heights above the threatening river valley. Then the familiar details of southern England lock into place: the

Marlborough Downs, merging into the Chilterns, one long roll of blue-grey hills with their prehistoric paths linking the West Country to East Anglia, and the Roman road striking up from the south to Dorchester.

Within a few minutes I am back in the map's safe custody in Little Wittenham. A wren bursts out of the porch of the church, which is overwhelmed by two massive horse chestnuts.

From Day's Lock, I begin the stage of the walk which has the most emphatic of all finishing lines at the river's only significant barrier, the Chilterns at Goring. The river breached this wall, the chalk of the Corallian Ridge, unimaginable aeons ago, seventy million years, to form Goring Gap. In more manageable numbers there are eleven miles of bank swapping between Oxfordshire and Berkshire.

I pass a fisherman wearing a grimace of concentration, casting his line into the squall-agitated waters. It's a mean day of racing showers, but I'm weather hardened by now. The path is undergoing its regular personality change, from narrow fenced-in corridor on the edge of a town, to broad open water meadow.

There have been improvements here from a hundred years ago. *Royal River* noted 'The towing path grows almost wild for so highly civilised a country as that through which the Thames flows, and the pedestrian wades to the knees through rank brambly grass.'

The river Thame curls down to join the Thames three hundred yards due south of Dorchester in a final flourish of a bend, like an extravagant royal signature. The Thames gains new vigour from the alliance. A duck loiters in the Thame's dying inches. It is a bad year for butterflies, a good one for dragonflies. The crew of *Gay Monarch 2* have improvised a cricket pitch of uncertain bounce on the far bank.

A mile and a half on, as I approach Shillingford, the back gardens of some riverside houses present the first touch of domestic untidiness I have seen from the Thames outside Oxford. From the Dorchester bypass comes the swish and dull grind of traffic. I walk past tacky little aprons of mud next to the river, feeding places for cows. A small boy in red jumper is willing the waves from *Summer Ranger* to lap over the top of his red wellingtons.

At Shillingford there is an Elizabethan building with black and white exposed timbers, encased in cream and red brick, side on to the river, to which it offers the yawning mouth of a boat house. Shillingford's three-arched bridge built in 1926 probably superseded the Keen Edge ferry. Keen Edge is corrupted Thames-speak for cane hedge, which by careful linguistic routing brings me eventually to understand as the long extinct osier beds on the bank.

A swing gate and a stile of very long standing has been extinguished, and the ferry at Mill Stream no longer runs. Inadvertently I walk along somebody's private drive to reach the village, and into a confrontation. I am met by a locked gate leading to the road and the owner who has coincidentally arrived by car. I explain the mistake but he is not sympathetic.

The problems of access to the bank are not new. Jerome K. Jerome, who is buried at Ewelme, a few miles north, was moved to homicidal passion in *Three Men in a Boat*.

> The selfishness of the riparian proprietor grows with every year. If these men had their way they would close the Thames altogether.
> The sight of their notice boards rouses every evil instinct in my nature. I want to tear each one down and hammer it over the head of the man who put it up until it killed him, and then would bury him and put the board up over his grave as a tombstone.

Chastened by this carefree brutality, I walk out of Shillingford through a tall stand of lime trees, with gnarled and indented bark. My way along the banks from Thames-side villages is marked with increasingly decorated walks. Past the trees, a black umbrella with feet, and a multicoloured one without feet, stand in my path. They shelter a woman and child, who observe a stoical fishing father, unprotected from a sharp shower.

By the village of Benson, a mile and a half on, the boat names are climbing up market: *Elysium Echo*, *Excalibur* (with radar). A plaque tells how far I have come and how far I have still to go: Cricklade Bridge 63 miles; London Bridge 92 miles. The distances come with a catchy homily: 'East, west; homes's best,' presented by F. N. and D. McNamara.

'You are trespassing on my lock,' The lock keeper can be an intimidating official in uniform when he tries, as strict as an Eastern European border guard, without the gun. Out of growing exasperation at the footpath's bank-switching, I have crossed the river by the weir bridge from the north to the south bank at Benson, which is not allowed (although perfectly safe for an adult with the experience of more than sixty-three bank/river miles behind me), and now I am on the private side of his lock. My second show-down in fifteen minutes.

He contradicts my map and tells me I am on the wrong route. The footpath is crumbled away on the river's left bank. I will have to walk on the road. I argue that the current Ordnance Survey map which still shows the footpath is the best authority and, with the sudden indignation of the challenged, invite him to prosecute me. Not waiting for a reply, I hurry over his lock to the fence. Afterwards I reproach myself for my outburst, but it is a temporary upset. Awkward encounters on the riverbank are dismissed with your footfall.

On reflection, the lock keeper was right. An ancient curved seat of doubtful benefit to the spine clings to a precipice, softened by white bryony and nettles, where the footpath has surrendered to the river. There are teasels, and purple loosestrife, with their heads of five petals, like straggly starfish. Some tight-lipped fishermen of the roll-your-own-cigarettes disposition, hunch into the damp wind like jockeys.

Two great crested grebes speed away from Dire Straits. It is reassuring to see the grebe here. Once this handsome bird, with its sharp Concorde-depressed beak and rebellious chestnut fringe, was persecuted by Victorians whose ladies adorned their hats with grebe feathers. Their numbers fell to about forty over the whole of Britain. Their recovery and expansion is one of the ornithological success stories of the century, although it is due more to an increasing habitat in the form of abundant flooded gravel pits than a more inviting river. On my walk they have been as commonplace as ducks.

Wallingford gives me a sullen welcome, in the form of a scattering of non-biodegradable bottles alongside my path. Some boys have built a little fire by way of lively diversion on this pale morning. Perhaps it is a retrospective commentary in smoke to Tusser, author of *'Five Hundred Points of Good Husbandry'*. He had miserable memories of his education here:

> What robes, how bare! What college fare!
> What bred how stale! . . .
> Then Wallingford, how wert thou abhor'd,
> Of sillie boise.

Another notice promises farm eggs, honey, milk, butter. A day-old calf stands in a state of utter trust, as a lady milks its mother in the open field. There is a benign agricultural spirit nearby. At Howbery, on the other side of the river, Jethro Tull developed a drill for peas, beans and wheat in 1701. He also perfected pulverisation which allowed him to grow wheat for thirteen successive years without manure, unwittingly inventing the grain mountain.

I enter Wallingford, in earlier days one of the most important crossing points above London. Its first wooden bridge was built in AD 600. In 1006 it was sacked by Svein Forkbeard. Thereafter, however, its fortunes rose steeply.

William made his first crossing of the Thames here six days after the Battle of Hastings. The warmth of his welcome persuaded him to grant the town an hour's extension of *couvre feu* (curfew), designed to quench dissent and intrigue, from the eight o'clock which prevailed elsewhere.

Wallingford at Domesday had a mint, a Saturday market and twenty-two resident Frenchmen – a sign of extensive trade. Its castle became one of the most important in England, and Wallingford itself one of the most significant towns.

The original Wallingford bridge, built in 1250 of Marcham quarry stone, was nine hundred feet long, only fifteen feet shorter than the old London Bridge. This huge span on the relatively young river says much about the danger of flooding. There is speculation that the same builder worked on both bridges.

In 1142 Matilda fled Oxford across the frozen Thames here in the camouflage of a white coat. It became her stronghold in the civil war with Stephen. The town suffered cruelly in the next Civil War, at the hands of Fairfax, the Cromwellian general, who took it in 1646 after a long siege.

I walk on out of Wallingford. A continent of blue sky is called into being out of a cloud bank to the east, just before noon, thus fulfilling the morning's weather forecast seconds short of the deadline. Sunshine illuminates the town river in its many animated functions: mothers and children playing; old men walking; small boys fishing; walkers relaxing their dogs.

On the other banks there is a stately crenellated place, Mongewell House, where once the bishops of Durham resorted for relief 'from the fatigues of administration'. My footpath passes over a reclaimed lawn, and descends into a thicket. A jet fighter steeples into RAF Benson, once the seat of the Kings of Mercia. I am heading due south, scuffing up a snowdrift of hay on a newly-cut meadow.

Fair Mile mental hospital is on the right, a traditonal gaunt and red-brick pile. A life-buoy holder holds no buoy and a lot of litter. I have met among anglers wise men of the deepest perception of nature and countryside matters. But they also have among their number people of the most loutish insensitivity to their surroundings.

Suddenly a noble apparition: gliding through the middle distance and springing over the river in a wave of bricks is Brunel's great way west, the main railway line from London to Bristol and Wales.

I cross Papist Way, which points straight at the river, suggesting to me a link to a secret ferry reserved for the persecuted, who didn't care to risk Wallingford. My problem is purely secular. I have walked into some beaten-down fisherman's cul-de-sac just short of the railway bridge. How do I cross to the east bank, which, it has now become clear, was the right route for me?

There is nothing for it but the two-mile trudge back to Wallingford. An hour later I reach the meadow beyond Moulsford railway bridge, and I feed a coot with celebratory crumbs from my picnic.

The coot lingers as might an abstemious lady at a cocktail party, saying

'Well, I don't normally drink, but I'll just have the one,' pausing to check she is not being observed. A high-speed train, with an engine at both ends, roars diabolically up from the west across the bridge. The coot, with its stonemason's hammer-tap, sees off a competitor.

I reach South Stoke, half a mile on from the railway bridge, walking on the mingling of two notable paths. For the past two miles the Thames Path has been overlying a far more ancient way, the Ridgeway, which follows the prehistoric drover's route over the high downland on the south side of the river.

On this side of the Thames it heads north to Ivinghoe in Buckinghamshire, close to where I write these words. The Ridgeway is one of our oldest roads, the main channel of communications between east and west, part of Icknield or Ickleton Street. It was one of three long-distance routes of prehistoric man, the trackway of the tribes, joining the country of the Iceni in the east with the Dumnonii in Devon.

It was twenty-two yards wide at the time of Enclosure. Flint axes and cleavers traded from Grimes Graves in Norfolk litter its length. The megalith builders who made Stonehenge used it, splashing through a wide forded river near this spot.

The union of Ridgeway and Thames Way takes me past those cheering symbols of the English village, The Malt House, Vine Cottage and Plum Tree Cottage. St Andrew's church, South Stoke has a flint-built fifteenth century tower – early English decorated and perpendicular.

It is a 'lively focal point for worship in our village beside the river Thames,' writes the vicar, Dr Philip Nixon. He has placed a small advert in the parish newsletter. 'The remains of the stone cross which fell down from the roof of the church some years ago: if anyone wants the pieces for a rockery, please ask.' I suspect there are some of Brunel's navvies reposing in the churchyard after their heroic labours.

In the Perch and Pike, Joe is telling Arthur of his diminishing credentials for the game of cricket. 'I'm too old. When I'm fielding and the ball comes towards me, I just ignore it. I can't see the bloody thing.' They turn to the concerns of old men. Arthur reveals that his late wife encouraged him to set money aside for a pension. 'She insisted. I wouldn't have bothered. Now I'm glad I did.'

Walking away, I wonder too late if those two men, subsiding into memories, could help me find the ploughman, if he was still alive, who in 1960 found Berkshire's finest treasure, the Moulsford Torque, a one pound gold necklace unearthed high up on Moulsford Down.

The corn is cracking in the sunshine as I leave South Stoke, still on the Ridgeway. I walk into Goring past various riverside improvements and enterprises. There are smart road signs, such as Penny Piece, in gold letters on a green background.

In Goring, I call on Mr Salisbury, estate agent, who sits at his green desk with gold angle-poise lamp, conveying the certainty that the Thames sells houses. Mr Salisbury is telling me the price range I must inhabit if I wish to live by the Thames in Goring.

Frontage commands a twenty per cent premium, he imparts. Goring owes everything to the Thames. It would be a 'nondescript' village if it had no Thames flowing through it. 'Add "on-Thames", and even without frontage you have a premium there.' The village of Purley, near Reading, has been upgraded by this suffix, to the satisfaction of local estate agents. You don't need a royal warrant.

Clients have short-distance ambitions in this area. People move from Streatley to Goring (two hundred yards) and from Goring to Goring. I leave Mr Salisbury with the reassuring information that should I ever succeed in buying into Goring, I would be rewarded by solicitous shopkeepers addressing me by name. It is the charm of the place. I walk down the hill the few yards to the river.

Goring and Streatley have made one big mistake recently. They allowed a concrete bridge to be built across the river. You cannot disguise the unloveliness of concrete, in which wood is only an embedded, strengthening feature. You cannot paint it. You can only watch it turn a hideous browny-grey.

'Have you taken a photo across there?' asks a boater to a lady in a turquoise swim suit on the craft's roof. 'Amazing, the number of tree colours.' The Victorian artist, Leslie, acknowledging the scenic allure of this part of the river wrote: 'The village of Streatley swarms with geniuses and their aesthetically dressed wives.' Another writer called it 'the Mecca of landscape painters.'

These are Goring Fire Station day-ticket waters. Fishermen have time to count the seductive little glimpses into this majestic wall of trees cordoning the very end of the Marlborough Downs. The trees are already touched with gold on this summer day. Much of the high land on the south bank, The Holies, Lough Down and Lardon Chase is owned by the National Trust which is trying to repair their damaged chalk downland.

Brunel tracked north of this valley, forcing through in his own way through the chalk barrier, a little west of the village. There is a road through here, but set high to avoid the floods it makes little impact: the trees stifle the sound of traffic.

A man with thick red arms, blue T-shirt and swept-back peaked cap is extracting a hook from the gaping mouth of a fish which he grips in a dirty rag. 'Another one,' he airily informs his companion, as if he has just shelled a pea.

In soft sunlight my path breaks out into a stupendous view of the smoothed western edge of the Chilterns. Slopes of newly ploughed fields are dusted with chalk. A heron saunters upriver. A snarling Inter City 125 hustles over Basildon Bridge. I am through Goring Gap.

The Mill at Mapledurham.

'What, man! More water glideth by the mill,
Than wots the miller of.'

– *Titus Andronicus* (Act Two, Scene I),
William Shakespeare

4

PISCATOR. Come, now it hath done raining, let's stretch our legs
a little in a gentle walk to the river, and try what interest our Angles
will pay us for lending them so long to be used by the trouts; lent
them indeed, like userers, for our profit and their destruction.
                                        – *The Compleat Angler*, Izaak Walton.

FROM HERE TO Henley people begin to take the Thames seriously.
They discovered it in the nineteenth century, when the early trains seemed
jet-propelled compared to stage coaches. They could be in Belgravia for
morning coffee and Pangbourne for late lunch.

At Henley they made heavy demands on their wardrobes and imitated
the Venetians. Only Reading, the second major conurbation on the river,
could turn up its nose at it. Jerome K. Jerome was very nasty about this. Its
present prosperity owes it nothing whatsoever.

In its early middle-age the river continues to look stunning. This is a
twenty-mile section which will take me three days. Today my walk is along
this increasingly busy Thames. I will have insights into its distant past,
examine one of the best living examples of ancient river-powered commerce, and have my path checked by its noisy present.

A short step downstream from Basildon Bridge I meet Mike Hall. He
drives me to the south side of the river, where a typical Thames mystery was
resolved. Aerial photographs had showed a muddle of crop marks in the
middle of the field. Archaeologists are never sure what crop marks mean
until they dig them up. Initial excavations in 1985 had revealed Bronze Age
burial mounds.

A pipeline was due to come through. 'We needed to dig this site before
everything was mashed up,' says Mike, the Thames Water Authority's
archaeologist. They expected to find at least one Bronze Age burial mound,
and they did. But they found much more: 'a full house of history, from the
Stone Age to the Roman.'

We are standing in the most visual feature, a small framework of stones. At first Mike and his colleagues thought it was a shrine or temple. It incorporated Roman building material – flat bricks, probably re-used, with flatter stones, red bricks and flints.

They identified it as a corn drying oven. This was an arable area in Roman times. Corn harvested off this site would be brought here to be dried before it was stored. It was a fairly large facility, drying a lot of corn for a substantial settlement. (Local farmers still grow corn on this rich soil; only the link with the local market is broken.)

A Roman storage pit contained some broken pottery and scattered building material. Between here and the hedge there are five or six more storage pits.

These and most of the local burial mounds were on an upper terrace. But one was found half off and half on the river's flood plain. 'Perhaps it was someone they weren't so concerned about. Perhaps it didn't matter if great-grandmother's toes were washed. Or perhaps the plain was affected by some kind of climatic regression.'

The site will be covered with polythene, and infilled with a material quite distinct from archaeological deposits, such as brick rubble, so that archaeologists yet unborn could not confuse it with Roman remains. Then enough soil will be piled on to it to prevent it being nibbled away by ploughing. 'We are in effect covering it for ever. It's too nice to smash it up gratuitously for the sake of a few pounds' worth of hardcore.'

We have progressed through four periods of archaeological time. A splendid example of industrial archaeology, Basildon Railway Bridge is an original Brunel structure, with its extra two tracks grafted on when the commercial potential of privately financed transport became clear. We walk under this open-air cathedral and Mike applauds smartly. 'What a lovely sounding arch. Listen to that clap of thunder effect.'

The most recent addition to river archaeology here is the pillbox, part of the Second World War southern defences, based on a line formed by the Kennet and Avon canal, the Downs, Hungerford and Newbury. Today it is a fisherman's toilet, and unlovely. But it makes this little corner fecund with history.

'It is a nice place, with the bridge, ducks and alder and willow. But we are looking at the totality of man's manipulation of the Thames. First they put in weirs that had nothing to do with navigation. Then the river was made navigable and finally the almost entirely pleasure machine it now is.

'People ask me now where the river used to be? When? At Domesday or Magna Carta or the Roman Invasion? I don't think we can tell. Somewhere within this flood plain.

'It can swill around quite happily and cut its course where it wants to, between one set of chalk downs and another or one set of gravel banks and another, but that is not the exact course. What people see on the map as "Thames" is only today's perception of the river. The aspect of it is different and I'm sure we wouldn't have recognised the old river.'

There are many things the historian still doesn't know about the Thames. They would have had wharfs, bridges, fords and capstans at the flash locks. There is little trace of any of these today.

They don't know how big the Thames valley's population was. 'It's a mystery. We are not finding the burials to substantiate the amount of settlement we know was here.' So did they practise that cleanest form of disposal, immolation? Mike doubts the dead were launched in flaming boats down the river. They would probably have burnt people's crops and killed somebody else.

'Everything we can see, including the route of the railway, built because this valley offers the least resistance to a nice straight line, is here because of this few yards of dense silent grey water.'

We look into the surge and guess at the key moments in man's perception of the Thames. When did they see the Thames as highway? 'From the earliest times, and we don't know how early, when somebody found that if they dropped a tree branch in, it floated.'

People made rafts or dug-out canoes, then full-blown boats to take things up it. 'These craft were certainly here, but if you found one today by dredging out a backwater you couldn't tell if it was a log boat or a bit of debris. One bit of waterlogged wood is much like any other. A lot of archaeological evidence has been lost.

'All the organic stuff, textiles, leather, the clothes people wore, the shoes, the beds they slept in, the houses they lived in. All gone. We have to take this on trust.' Did the river have any preservative quality? 'It might in those places of nice hippopotamus-like mud, but there isn't too much of that.'

But now, from the number of crop marks, the number of finds of artefacts dredged out of the river, we know that people have been here since probably the earliest Stone Age, certainly the middle Stone Age. The earliest human remains found in the UK at Swanscombe in Kent are quite close to the banks of the Thames.

If the river ever ran dry, archaeologists would have a fruitful time on its bed. How did things get into the river? 'People would throw them in to appease the river gods, to make the goats fruitful or their warrior sons successful.' So we have the Thames as wishing well.

From the back of his car Mike produces a Bronze Age spear head found in the river in Sunbury, and hands it to me. It dates from around 750 BC. Mike looks at this eloquent survivor as if assessing a lost umbrella.

'Someone might have been holding it for battle when it fell in, or the boat

73

capsized under him, or it might have slipped off a horse crossing the ford. There are all the reasons you can think of for it being in the bottom of the river. They can't all be true, but one of them must.'

Mike drives me back to the north bank and I take up the path, walking the hundred yards on from the bridge to Gatehampton ferry house, half a mile east of Goring, and under the shoulder of the Chilterns.

Flo and Lil turn away from their bankside station on my beckoning cough to explain the true significance of fishing. They *don't* fish for the frying pan. Indeed, they care not if they catch nothing.

Their fishing sons and brothers are their inspiration. For ten years they have been renting this ferry cottage. The fishing is not very good this year. The perch have taken over. 'Almost equal to the pike in boldness and voracity, and bites at some periods at almost every kind of bait', informs Dickens.

'Do you mind if we just go and look for something?' inquires Flo. They emerge with a curdled photograph of a man from 1892 in a full beard and fine hat, working the long extinct ferry on the other side of the river. Once he lived here 'in the solitary cottage under a line of full-headed pollards.'

Our conversation is suspended as a Concorde climbing west bursts the sky, its vibrations causing some rearrangement to the geology of Southern England. It will be in New York before I'm in Purley, five miles on from here. I pass a picnic party of young people, who freeze into the deportment of shop window dummies. The only sound or movement is the gentle tizz of champagne bubbles.

William Senior, writing in *Royal River*, describes an extinct river industry here, the osier farm. 'Out of the river, formal growths of tall green sheaves seem to flourish within a ring fence. Men, women and children are busily engaged. The tall slender sheaves are bundles of withies that have been reaped from the islands and osier beds, and punted to this depot. Here they are planted *en masse* in the water and the cut branches preserve their vitality until they are required for use.

'The girls and boys are very handy at the operation of peeling. They take up a withie from the bundle last landed, draw it rapidly through a couple of pieces of iron fixed to a stand, and in a twinkling the bright green osier has become a snow-white wand. This humble colony of workers, about whom little is generally known, is one of many engaged in an out of the way industry, hidden from the eyes of the world, in some nook of the Thames.'

But the osiers' retiring craft was already threatened by rampant Victorian industrialisation. At the Inventions Exhibition of 1885 at South Kensington, 'an apparatus for willow-peeling was shown amongst the labour-saving machines.'

I walk east on an exquisite summer day. Before long my path is forced upwards in Hartstock Wood into the flank of the Chilterns. A speckled wood butterfly, creamy brown spots, flits between islands of sunlit turf. I drop into a beautiful dry valley, bent like an elbow. Beech trees cloak the top. A mile and a half later I walk down into Whitchurch and Goring Heath, twinned with La Bouille, Seine Maritime. From all points of the Thames hands of friendship are stretching metaphorically across Europe.

As a mere pedestrian, I cross Whitchurch Bridge for nothing. But sitting at a steering wheel I would be challenged for my two pence by the young Sarah, red haired, short blue dress, representing the Whitchurch Bridge Company.

Where do I find the bridge company? 'In New Zealand, Australia, South Africa – all over the world,' says John Jones, bridge manager, who is at work in his garden. Individual shares have been handed down since 1792. The owners stick them in drawers.

I will find nothing on the subject in the Berkshire libraries, he tells me. The present chairman, a Dr Micklem, a descendant of the original proprietor, lives in Leighton Buzzard, Beds. 'But I know more about the bridge than he does,' declares Mr Jones. 'I couldn't tell you how much we take. I don't have a counter. I'm not prepared to sit and count all these tickets.

'The company is responsible for keeping the bridge in good shape. We have just finished painting it. If it falls down tomorrow, by law we must put another one up sharply, and provide a crossing for pedestrians immediately.'

Mr Jones has been a publican and ground manager at the Oval for Surrey Cricket Club. 'I'm quite happy here. I've dropped out really.'

He is worried about erosion. 'Boats scream through and wash the bank away. It has halved the size of our garden. They are given notices telling them to travel slowly, but they come flying out of that lock with the notice in their hand.'

He is worried about lorries. 'When the bridge is thrown open at night we find thirty-two tonners trying to go over. The limit is ten tonnes, so it's out of order. They come down in twos and threes. We rush out and turn them back sharpish.'

I cross the bridge, in search of river bank creatures. In Pangbourne I find, easily enough, various foxes, coots, squirrels and badgers, on display outside the garden centre. But they have no moles, or water rats. A mole is a subversive influence in the modern lawn, and not a creature to be celebrated in a plastic likeness.

There is a Duck's Ditty restaurant, next to a shop boasting 'the very best in video'. Eventually I find three versions of *Wind in the Willows* in W. H. Smith, between *What Katy Did* and *What Katy Did at School*.

Kenneth Grahame, a Scot, sometime secretary of the Bank of England, ended his days here in Church Cottage, twenty-four years after publication of *Wind in the Willows*, which strikes me as one of the most successful evocations of an impossible rural perfection.

The river Pang slices luxuriantly through this town of ancient passage. I wonder when did Ye Old George Hotel acquire its silly prefix? I return to the river past the Peking Garden, the Copper Inn, the Cross Keys and the church of St James the Less, where Grahame's funeral service was held in July 1932.

'And perhaps the most touching things of all were the flowers, sent by children from all over the country, with cards attached in a childish scrawl, saying how much they loved him,' wrote his agent's secretary. 'The grave was lined with thousands of sweet peas and the scent was unforgettable.'

Back under the railway bridge. Grahame had little opinion of the early railways: 'The iron terror that scurfs the face of our island and has killed out the pleasant life of the road.'

A shop selling ladies' négligés stands opposite the Working Men's Club and Institute, whose colour is a confusing Conservative blue. I turn east into Pangbourne Meadow. This is National Trust land, but its seven acres have not tested the descriptive powers of the Trust handbook's editor, who writes sparingly: 'This pleasant area has some interesting flora.'

There is a high, majestic stand of trees at the start of some of the best of the Thames landscape. 'Many lovers of the River Thames declare that, take it all in all, there is no sweeter spot from source to sea than this,' notes *Royal River*. The river sweeps under that great shoulder of southern England, the Chilterns, which end with a high wooded scarp on the left, and continues in a wide three mile curve around to Tilehurst – an exhilarating hour's walk.

Striding out of Pangbourne on the south bank through Sulney Mead, I meet a huge, empty expanse of water, flanked by graceful lines of tufted, pollarded yew on both banks. The Thames, where Grahame walked in his declining days, has reached maturity. The map shows this as a reserved corridor of white land. This water meadow has been spared development by the sheer inherent destructiveness of the river. I imagine the mighty lake across here in the flood of 1947.

There is an exuberant swirl of swallows. A damselfly displays an incongruous blue against the gold of the wheat. An echoing, lazy lap of water survives long after the passing of the boat that generated it. A jet drawls through the hazy cloud. Ducks shuttle urgently.

In time this sweetly soothing picture is disrupted, as a pond is disturbed by a tossed pebble. The lock releases a flotilla: *Girl Friday, Benson, Fiesta 3, Costa Packet* and *Vade Mecum*. A diesel locomotive growls past on the main line.

At Mapledurham a cow descends to drink from the river. The lock keeper is selling summer flowers. I have to leave the bank for a few hundred yards here and divert through the newly enobled Purley-on-Thames. A man with a backpack instinctively shoots up from his repose in a bus shelter as I approach, like a sentry caught sleeping at his post.

I begin to feel the lack of Thames ferries acutely. Once again I need a car to convey me to the other bank, where, just upstream from the lock, I meet a miller.

Traditional millers were much troubled by rats. Not Mrs Mildred Cookson. Traditional miller that she is, heaving sacks in the old way, pursuing the ancient mores, she will not encounter a rat.

There is high technology trickery here at Mapledurham mill: no cat, but a squeak, which I took to be a toiling wheel. In fact it is an electronic high pitch frequency that torments rats and drives them away. 'I have never had any rats, except once. It looked ill. It fell into that pit and disappeared.'

We stand over a pile of hessian sacks slumped together. Each contains about a hundredweight of *Acquila* corn, harvested from the steep local Chiltern slopes. Next year it will be *Moulin* or *Mission*. Some insensitive bureaucrat has decreed that the grain be measured in kilos. But lengths in the mill are defined in feet and inches.

Mrs Cookson tests before she mills, to see which of the local grains come up best for flour making. First she bakes bread from it for her family. Next the bakers she supplies make a test batch. When they are satisfied in the matter of the Hagburg falling number, which tests the gluten content, they put about seventy tonnes of the chosen flour away and Mrs Cookson switches into truly medieval mode, except for the rat scarer.

She takes six hours to mill a tonne of flour. 'Better flour, definitely. I grind it slowly between mill stones as opposed to – I'd better not mention names – certain brands, with their electric millstones belting round at seven hundred revs a minute. Ours go at two hundred and fifty. We retain all the natural oils which give the flour its unique flavour. It comes up smashing for bread and cakes. Orders are up.'

It is the only working mill left on the Thames, and one of the few in Britain with a wooden shaft and water wheel. Domesday Book records its value as twenty shillings. It stopped milling flour in 1900, and produced only grist until the mid 1940s. Then it shut for thirty years. The internal machinery slumbered as in a fairy tale until the restorers conjured new life out of it in 1977, at a cost of £30,000.

Once, practically every village on the river had a mill. There was a community of mills on this stretch of the river, at Goring, Wallingford, Pangbourne, Streatley, Cleve, Caversham, Henley, Burfield and Calcott.

77

Wind and water milling was effectively killed by the import of foreign wheat, which began around 1900.

The key to a mill's quality is its stone. Mapledurham's is freshwater quartz (French burr) from near Paris. It is built up in sections. The cracks are filled with plaster of Paris. Iron bands hold it fast. It is then dressed in the traditional pattern.

Mrs Cookson guides me through the mill's fine old timbers. 'Elm in the waterwheel, oak on the shaft, oak teeth in the first wheel, apple on the next. The central section is five hundred years old. This is a lovely mill.'

The miller's is a routine of checking, lifting and running upstairs. 'I spend an hour checking the piling and greasing. Then I put the grain into hoppers. It can take twenty minutes to lift the bags to the top with the sack hoist. Then I mill for six hours. All the time I'm listening for a changing pattern of noises, which tells me if something is not quite right. I can usually work it out from top to bottom. For instance a wedge has fallen out, or a paddle has come loose.'

In former times, a man and his boy and three helpers would have worked this mill's four pairs of stones and two wheels, powering oak crunching machines and associated water-driven gadgets. Today Mrs Cookson runs the mill, quite alone.

She presents me with a bag of flour with this testimonial, as ghostly millers smile approvingly over her shoulder. 'It's very nice to eat bread, where apart from growing the grain, you have done all the other processes yourself.'

Queen Elizabeth I used to be entertained at Mapledurham Court for summer weekends. The church was one of the best beneficies in the Church of England, a good starting point on the Church's career ladder.

Driven back to the south bank, I walk on for a mile past Tilehurst, where I meet the unkempt fringes of Reading. This reach of maturing river has its own name, the Kentwood Deeps. Between Poplar Island and Appletree Eyot, hard under the railway line a kingfisher is released from my bank to the other as if on a tight thread drawn sharply in. There are whizzing trains, and a factory.

'Free Stonehenge 1985' counsels an old daub. This intense plea from the hippy consciousness is a clue to the nature of the remarkable assembly I am shortly to meet. A High Speed Train glints away in the western sun. There is the acrid whiff of locomotive brakebox.

I hear what sounds like the amplified summons to a phone in a factory. But it is not a factory. The town has been overtaken by an event that drives local people out in the sort of refugee convoys that clog the roads of a country when invasion is imminent. It is the Reading Rock Festival.

The first signs are young men seeking bucolic refuge in a field of cows, next to the village of tents. They wear sleeveless leather jackets and display bare arms. Some are hacking at a tree, with the uncertainty of returnees to nature.

I am to walk through this bizarre, rather menacing community on the public footpath. Will they rush at me with knives or smother me with welcomes and drag me, like a long lost friend, into their celebrations?

The trained ear can unscramble the sound of twenty 'ghetto blasters', all playing different music. Bottles without messages are bobbing in the river. I see a grinning policeman holding his boot in mock threat over the face of a recumbent fan, displaying the enforced humour obligatory on these occasions.

'We have't seen any bands yet, we are just sort of in the water,' says a voice from the river. This is Peter Hunter, a Niagara Falls head of Pre-Raphaelite red hair tumbling down his neck. He and his party are standing in the Thames like semi-submerged oracles on this warm summer day. He offers me a bottle of Ruddles County beer, which is providing communal refreshment.

He explains how the joyous decibels will overwhelm Reading in the next few days and nights. The sound rises from the festival field, travels north across the river, bounces off the houses on the other bank and surges back to reinforce and reinvigorate the sounds that succeed it.

A man with 'FM' on his shirt fly kicks beer cans into the river. *SitPax*, a Thames Valley Police launch, arrives, with what admonitory intent I never discovered. Flooding out of Reading to the festival fields is a wide river of fans. A black youth is selling Monsters of Rock T-shirts. 'Want to buy one, mate,' he inquires.

> I NEVER saw a man who looked with such a wistful eye
> Upon that little tent of blue which prisoners call the sky.
> – *Reading Gaol*, Oscar Wilde.

From Reading the bankside path will take me the seven miles past Sonning, another of those timeless villages of long declined importance, to Shiplake, one of the Thames's earliest dormitory towns, which has an unlikely literary connection with Wigan – Eric Blair, George Orwell, lived there.

I find Reading a self-sufficient place, a busy prosperous town in a region dominated by the development of the microchip. Its speciality is 'biscuits, beer and bulbs' according to the tourist brochure. It is the most unpretentious place I have yet met on the Thames. Most of its citizens couldn't care less about frontage.

After the din of yesterday, I am interested to discover Reading's historic place in the development of quieter, unaccompanied music. A monk at the Abbey is credited with composing in the thirteenth century the endless canon 'Summer is icumen in' one of the earliest examples of secular music.

Reading has Romano-British origins. Roman broaches and horseshoes have been found all over town. Its first inhabitants settled on the gravel terraces where Suttons Seeds are now based.

The town was once a focus of enormous reverence. The abbey was the greatest in the kingdom, with the very best mementoes – a piece of the Lord's shoe, a tooth belonging to St Luke, and, less likely, a sliver from Moses' rod. In 1135 Henry I's body was conveyed here, wrapped in a bull's hide, and entombed before the high altar.

Chaucer in *Parliament of the Fowls* describes the feasting after the wedding at Reading Abbey of John of Gaunt and Blanche, daughter of the Plantagenet Duke of Lancaster.

Parliament, driven out of London by plague, frequently sat here. The town found early prosperity in the cloth trade. It had royal backing. Queen Elizabeth I sent a mulberry tree to encourage its silk industry. Thereafter Reading switched from cloth to beer. In 1700 it had twenty-one breweries and 104 pubs.

Today's Reading draws a variety of enterprises to its waterfront. On the Thamesside promenade, which runs for a mile before Caversham Bridge – Reading may not be very interested in adorning its river with fine houses or gardens, but it has given the river a solid footpath – I find an office called Microsoft. With its smoked brown windows, bijou radiators, and a computer at every desk, it encapsulates the spirit of Reading.

Maroon and white buses bustle over Caversham Bridge which is hanging with baskets of flowers. A ford here was replaced by a wooden bridge in 1239. In a chapel by the bridge they kept one of the many spears alleged to have pierced Christ's side, 'the principal object of idolatry within this realm.'

I meet Norman Nicolson in Thames Water's big squat building next to the bridge. We drink tea brewed from water drawn from a Thames tributary, an aquifer on the River Kennet upstream from Reading, renowned for its trout. 'Tastes a bit of chlorine,' reports the expert palate, 'but I think we can safely drink this.'

What of water direct from the river itself? He is close enough to his territory to swing down a bucket from his high office in Nugent House, hard by the river and scoop up a sample. He would have no hesitation in drinking it, suitably treated. 'We can't say there is no hazard in Thames water, because mathematically that is not true, but it has been through a very sophisticated treatment and disinfection process and it is very rare that we find any live bacteria in it likely to do any harm.'

Twelve million people live inside the Thames Water catchment area, a quarter of the population of England and Wales. It contains 'all those bits of ground where rain that falls finds its way to the River Thames valley rather than the Severn or Trent,' a vast watery empire, stretching from the North Sea to Gloucestershire.

Can he tell me when you could last have safely drunk from the river. 'Before the Industrial Revolution. Freshly discharged sewage effluent would make people ill.

'People ring up and ask "Is it safe to swim in the Thames?" Our reply is that where there is freshly discharged sewage effluent it is not safe. I couldn't say there is more or less risk than swimming in the sea.

'There are still so-called bathing places. Runnymede is still much favoured. There are risks, but they have been taken over the years. Most little boys swallow the water. I don't expect it to be any worse today. You can build up immunity, I suppose. It would be foolish to bathe downstream from outfalls, which are generally on the downhill side of all major towns. Reading puts her sewage into the Kennet.'

I convey a common public misgiving, that the river is a doubtful murky colour. 'It is hardly a natural river,' Mr Nicholson reminds me. 'It is an impounded river with forty weirs. Outboard motors stir up the mud. I too would rather look at the gin-clear Colne at Bibury. But I think what we have is quite good.'

I leave the river's nerve centre and walk on, past new houses on Heron Island, with their red tiles, milky-brown bricks and minarets. They include, of course, private moorings. A developer would no more build a new house on the Thames without private moorings that he would leave a suburban semi without a garage.

The packaging of this island is finished even before the completion of the last 'three/four bedroom luxury home'. A fresh carpet of turf has been laid down to the river. Next to the island, behind the fading craft *Little Bustard*, two ancient ladies sit reading, like characters from a 1930s tea advertisement. Once the riverside offered timeless seclusion: now it is the promotion in the estate agent's window. Oscar Wilde suffered grievously close to here, imprisoned in Reading jail for his homosexuality.

I walk on into Reading's biscuit quarter. Here the writ of Associated Biscuits runs even to the river. The company owns 'sole fishing rights' on this section. 'Any person found fishing such private waters will be proceeded against' bullies a fading notice. On another, proclaiming 'No day tickets', Cliff, Daren and Joe recorded they 'was 'ere'.

Little waves chase and chatter under the bank, the product of the colliding wakes of two boats. *Kingston Romance* heads up the Kennet, which leads into the Kennet and Avon Canal and eventually the Bristol Channel. For adventurous boats, it is the quickest way to America.

In late March 871 the advancing Danes reached Reading from Peterborough and Thetford at this point, using it as a base in their operations against Wessex. It isn't known if they travelled overland and met their supporting boats or came entirely by river. But they had brought their wives and families so they were clearly planning a long stay.

They landed here 'to the right of the royal vill' on King's Mead between Kennet and Thames, on a site chosen for the Abbey.

Close to this point the Kennet squeezes into the Thames under the railway line, past some gas holders, a workaday composition that reminds me of Birmingham. I count nine swans. Boats are buzzing here and there in search of lunch spots. The appearance of a police boat has the same sort of dramatic effect in slowing them down as a police car might on the motorway.

I cross the river to enter the news broadcaster's Tower of Babel, where men and women listen, for their living, to every bulletin of any significance from anywhere in the world.

In the former Caversham Manor there is a sense of national purpose carried out with quiet diligence, running as a thread up and down this former mansion's elegant staircases, in and out of its abundant old rooms.

Caversham ought to be, but isn't, a name to stand alongside Bush House, Lime Grove and Alexandra Palace in the BBC galaxy. It is a huge pile, set magisterially on a ridge above the Thames.

Signals are received here, translated, edited, transferred to tape or teleprinter and dispatched within minutes to the world's newspapers and radio stations. The list of Caversham scoops include news from the Falklands War and events in Iran, taken from Teheran Radio for want of correspondents in that country.

The best view of the stars comes from the pure heights of Brazil, but the same reasoning does not apply to the siting of a radio monitoring station. Even if the service had a clean map to chose from they would come more or less here, rather than the Cairngorms due to a surprising lack of radio interference.

I walk on to the edge of Reading. The last building is an unnamed former pub. I think once, then twice before stopping: there are fierce dogs, Prince and Sheba. But I am encouraged when I see John Clark feeding twenty-eight swans.

Anne and John Clark invite me in. They are eating their lunch at stout, sparred tables. There are tubs and hanging baskets full of bright flowers. This was originally the Broken Brow, then the Dreadnought. It is now the unversity sailing club. People often gaze longingly over the fence.

'I have to say "Sorry",' says John. 'It is no longer a pub. It would have been a nice little business, not exactly busy, but busy enough. People come here to enjoy a bit of peace and quiet, then they have to go all the way home for a cup of tea.' However, there are ways for enterprising ice-cream vans to reach the bank.

John and Anne guarantee the welfare of many wild birds. Their daily feeding, alone, satisfies about thirty swans. 'We have had a genuine black swan, jet black with deep red beak and white underwing, consorting with the others. There's a heronry in those trees. Look, there's a heron now, in that tree there. And there's a white goose. He travels with all the Canadian geese.'

One day John's dog Prince challenged a passing walker. The man was surprisingly unconcerned. 'He said he didn't mind. He owed his life to a dog that lived in this pub. He told me he was walking home from Sonning during a flood when he fell in. He couldn't swim. A labrador from here jumped in and pulled him out.'

John recalls seeing an Indian washing in the river, just as he might in the Ganges. 'He had his sheets and was flapping them out on the water. I couldn't believe it.' He tells me that the authorities occasionally sanction another, ceremonial, use of the river. Recently some Reading Sikhs hired a boat to scatter ashes on the water, under a weir. 'Years ago they used to try immolation. That had to be stopped.'

The Clarks are more concerned about casual abuse than ritual use: they are moved to fury by the plastic bags full of rubbish and bits of furniture they occasionally see floating by.

It is easy to slough off the city. I walk out of the Clark's gate and Reading is over. On the two-mile stage to Sonning I am passed by *Zavola*, a substantial wooden boat, with a gap in the middle. A man with white hair is navigating while a younger lady with blue shorts paints the front. A tortoiseshell butterfly wanders across their bow.

Tiny drops are wrung out of a mottled blue-grey sky. Just before Sonning, a plaque outside the Bluecotes School memorial gate, honours Denys Amos 'greatly loved master of this school, who was drowned Jan. 26th, 1953.'

A mound in this big wooded hill to my right, Holme Park, marks the site of the old Bishop's Palace where Henry IV locked up Isabella of France, queen of the deposed Richard II.

This was once an important church address. There were 'bishops of Sunning', between 909 and 1107. The church was used as pro-cathedral. Ordinations were held here and, once at least, the consecration of a bishop. Later Wessex bishops, who took Sonning as an additional title, had a palace here.

Sonning is as 'pretty a little place as can be desired' in Dickens' book. Today it is frightfully well preserved and a trifle synthetic. There is a gale of rose perfume off Sonning Lock, a photogenic place. From here I am sucked into the huge silence of St Andrew's Church. A shaft of sunlight picks out the names of men killed in war. The memory of the lost youth of this century is a renewed shock on this intense summer afternoon.

I stand on Sonning Bridge, a restful sort of place in soft red brick in the sunshine. Upstream where it is narrowed by islands, the river looks like a lake. Two mallard are snapping at each others' tails in a frantic circuit of froth. A red shirted man with knotted handkerchief on his head sits impassively outside the White Hart, parodying the Englishman at ease in the sun.

Walking east, I am once again in flat meadowland, stretching away on both sides of the river. Fields of deep gold fold into the western flank of the Chilterns on my left. There is a huge blue mobile pump to refresh the field with river water. A man in a white hat, steering a small boat, executes a U-turn to make a landfall.

I walk on for about a mile on the west bank, along the quiet side of Hallsmead Ait. There is an inlet containing a blue and white boathouse, some snapping house martins, and a drawn-up boat. A group of mothers and children occupy what might be the best bathing spot on the Thames. Sunlight and distance has reduced the potency of Reading's sewage. Next to them an old ash dips its fingers tenderly into the flow.

Shiplake, 'pleasantly planted on the riverside' (Dickens, junior) was served, together with Henley, by a sleepy little GWR branch line which still wanders up from Twyford. It has two contrasting literary associations. Eric Blair (George Orwell) lived in Station Road as a boy; Tennyson married Emily Sellwood in the church of St Peter and St Paul. The house names give clues to property prices swollen by the passing flow: House by the River, Bright Water, Dabchick.

Later in my walk, I came across the only person I met who admitted to sleeping in the open air, on or alongside the Thames at night. The tap of wooden hammer on peg used to be a familiar sound on summer evenings as hearty young men pitched their tents on the Thames' islands and banks. The green space around Shiplake Lock was 'a favoured camping-out spot for boating men who do not fear the risk of rheumatism,' according to *Royal River*.

The afternoon turns sour. Later there is rain on the still, deep green waters at Shiplake. Just above Shiplake, the river Loddon slips into the Thames. This is the poet Pope's Lodona 'The Loddon slow, with verdant alders crowned.' A mystery surrounds the flower named after the river. In a survey on the site of the Maidenhead flood protection scheme local naturalists discovered this internationally rare species, the Loddon lily, the first time it had been seen in thirty years, in a backwater boats cannot penetrate.

The Loddon lily story is worth telling. More enchantingly known as the summer snowflake – hanging bells of white flowers, green tinged – this flower seems too good to be true. And so it is, claims Geoffrey Grigson.

The Flora of Berkshire noted it growing, here, on an island opposite where the Loddon joins the Thames. Grigson is unconvinced. He cannot believe that the snowflake, 'so excitingly conspicuous' and grown in gardens since the sixteenth century, could turn up on the Thames two hundred years later, apparently growing wild. He favours the prosaic, glaringly practical conclusion of a Sherlock Holmes, that the seeds floated down the river from gardens where it was cultivated. He can even believe that the snowflake was planted by the Loddon to give retrospective validity to Pope's poem.

> IT is reported that in the 1891 annual Head of the Thames Royal Regatta a Cambridge coxswain, Francis T. Ebright, steered his crew into a submerged boulder, sinking the shell, only ten yards from the finishing line. In 1892 he did not appear in the annual regatta.
>
> – Legend on a T-shirt at the Henley Regatta, 1988.

This is a leisurely day. I am to meet a true conservationist friend of the river and then reach Henley, three miles from here, in time for its outrageous annual jamboree.

In the morning I meet Alastair Driver on this quiet reach. It was he who told me about the rediscovery of the Loddon lily. He also gives me his infallible advice on how to spot a kingfisher, this bejewelled bird which seems to try to hide its brilliance by the speed of its flight.

Once I recognise its call, a sharp zit, zit, zit, I may expect to see a lot more. It stands out like an emperor in a football crowd. 'Once you hear them, you usually see them. They are not all that scarce, although they are suffering from the effects of land drainage.'

Alastair Driver is paid to see and care for kingfishers and other river creatures in the course of his working day. This athletic young man has a favoured job among naturalists. He is conservation officer for the Thames Water Company.

His task is to politely persuade his colleagues in the engineering department to treat the river's natural lines sensitively, for the benefit of wildlife. He has, for example, persuaded them to build into their works earth cliffs two metres high, nest sites for kingfisher and sand martin, another species evicted by the smoothing and shoring up of river banks.

The river catchment is a vital wildlife habitat. It supports a huge range of creatures, from gravel Cotswold trout stream, to Essex saline estuary. Attention to conservation is now cast in the river companies' official duties, after many years of indifference.

Alastair detects a 'tremendous improvement in attitudes'. He has seen work done according to the dull, old orthodoxy on some tributaries, in trapezoidal channels dug in straight lines with both banks scraped to an inhospitable forty-five degree angle. But many river engineers already cooperate, often without much persuasion.

The river bank is under constant manipulation, to relieve flooding, improve drainage and repair damage. The engineer has a choice of materials, artificial and natural, at his disposal, from concrete and steel piling, to walls of vegetation.

In areas of high erosion around locks and weirs the robust solution prevails, in concrete and steep piling. Elsewhere Alastair recommends a more creative conservation. One approved method is willow spiling, where the skills of the medieval hurdler are applied to the river bank. Willow stakes are driven into the base of the bank, and branches are woven in between, like the laying of a hedge. The stakes grow, producing a natural screen and a living barrier.

A boat churns past us and thumps an erosion warning against our feet, in the form of angry, reverberating waves. Alastair is concerned about the number of boats on the Thames, and their speed. 'You can actually *see* the bank crumble as the wash hits it,' he says.

Crumbling banks diminish the river's wildlife, and create a sparser food web. There are fewer sites where certain species can survive, and this increases competition for other sites. The effects are felt as high up the food chain as swans. Alastair wants to create alternative habitats and enrich the food web, by building up bankside vegetation, particularly in quiet backwaters.

Alastair believes the only way he can genuinely further nature conservation is by creating new habitat, 'not related to any potentially damaging activity we are doing.' Between Godstow and King's Lock, above Oxford, engineers improvised a reed bed and small island by using the river's own materials, rather like grafting hair on a bald man's head.

They built a large floating boom to protect the area from boatwash, 100 metres long, across the outer bank of the crescent-shaped meander. Behind the boom they planted reeds and lilies dislodged from elsewhere on the river. Plants were rooted in wire mesh baskets, flattened and depressed into the silt. The site was green within the year.

Now we discuss the supreme test of a river's health. There are no otters on the the Thames. But Alastair has heard of recent sightings in the Upper

Cherwell valley, possibly of otters moving from the river Ouse catchment to Wales. He wants to protect, 'or at least keep land drainage hands off' some sections of remote watercourses feeding the Thames where otters are known to pass through, with a view to releasing a breeding pair, if none stop of their own accord.

When was the last otter seen on the Thames? Alastair doesn't know. Otters have escaped from collections. They cannot easily be told apart from natural otters. This muddies the issue. The return of otters to the Thames may be the ecologist's unattainable goal: too much boat disturbance for this shy, sensitive creature to tolerate. But he believes the river's natural fabric and wildlife have passed the worst of their decline. They will improve, as long as pollution can be contained.

Thames Water is rescuing and even creating islands. At Wargrave, a little way above here, the parish council campaigned for a small island to be reinstated. In a few weeks the engineers replicated a task which might have occupied geological forces for ten thousand years.

The island had been eroded to a quarter of its size of a few years ago. Some underwater alder tree roots preserved a residual foundation, but there was nothing visible above water level. They sunk a cordon of piles around the original bank line. Willow spiling stakes were knitted into this frame to protrude above water level, and the frame was filled with soil. The island is now stable enough to withstand the buffeting of boats leaving an adjoining marina.

There are dozens of islands on the Thames. They are an important habitat, less accessible than an equivalent corner on land. While the exclusion of dogs and foxes cannot be guaranteed, islands provide a valuable breeding habitat for the more sensitive species, such as moorhens and mute swans.

In the Maidenhead area alone, Alastair believes there may be at least ten which deserve protection. He is anxious to maintain waddling-access to islands. 'It is no use piling them so they have a two foot drop on the edges and ducklings cannot get on or off.'

If the edges have to be piled, he proposes dropping the level at the tail of the island to give access to birds. They did this on the island at Temple Weir Pool, after Alastair recommended that the piling be lowered. Lo and behold, a pair of coot nested on the island's tail the following spring.

Thames Water has created several small islands from nothing, in the open river. An excavator mounted on a barge lays a square of wire mesh baskets in the river. Silt from the river bed is piled on to this foundation and it is gradually built up into an island, two or three metres square at the surface, enought to support the nest of a mute swan.

I walk on towards Henley on the west bank. Alongside the grass path I find a little metal mushroom, dated 1903, with the legend: 'Towing path, 14 feet to river.' I measure the actual distance. The mushroom is now no more than four feet from the line of the bank. Its inscription has been interpreted as a challenge to reduce the distance yet again: it is precisely twenty-two inches from a little man-made inlet.

Two women saunter past, hands behind backs, in brown plastic macks, the uniform of the drizzly day. There is a formal garden on the other side, with a forelock of branches. A scrummage of walkers out of Henley is snatching at second-hand books, many of them of the Barbara Cartland tendency. They shun the only genuine literature, an original Penguin *Lady Chatterley's Lover*.

A long wooden walk leads over a rushing weir to the Henley promenade. A man in tattoos and a blue shirt observes to his wife that it is starting to rain. 'This is the tree for us,' he says, indicating a welcoming yew. They discuss the bird life. Tattoo man correctly identifies grebes. 'They are all ducks to me,' admits his wife. 'Isn't it awful.' Two more women pass under umbrellas which announce Busch Gardens, Williamsburg, Va.

The grebes begin a terrific piping. 'They always come to the same nest. Isn't it lovely,' explains one of the Williamsburg, Va., couple. 'The next time you ring me and tell me it's beautiful sunshine, I'm not going to believe you,' says her companion.

Bjorn Lundberg from Stockholm studies the river: he expected it to be much wider. 'Parking lot for boats', he says, gesturing at the thronging craft. I tell him you can't walk along the bank for the entire length – there are houses in the way. 'Ah, their privacy,' he responds with understanding, as if we are talking of some hallowed concept understood by any nation.

'The water. It gives something special. You can do so many things with water. You can fish, you can swim, you can take the boat. The water gives pleasure to people, if it's the roaring sea or a smooth surface where you can see the sun glittering, like a living picture.'

I walk into Henley, a venerable place. 'The ancientest town in the county' in the opinion of an old guide. There was a Roman crossing here. Later it became an important trade centre. Cargos were unloaded here and taken by road to Goring Gap to bypass a tricky stretch of river.

In the Civil War the town split between King and parliament. It's historic records were 'pillaged by rough soldiers.' Prince Rupert used the Bell Inn as a base during the Civil War. An elm in front of the inn is said to have been used to hang spies.

Henley was known for its maltsters – the sharp tang of hops from the Henley Brewery catches my nostrils. Then there was its hiring fair, Britain's greatest glassmaker, and a pioneer of the navigable waterways. Humphrey Gainsborough, brother of the painter Thomas and Congregational minister for the town, did not let his spiritual duties blunt his inventive genius. His first achievement was to drive a road over White Hill, near the town.

In 1770, faced with an increasingly sluggish, wayward and trade-hampering river, the Thames Commissioners met to discuss the merits of a canal between Sonning and Isleworth. Humphrey was on the committee, in his capacity as minister. His counsel was to improve the Thames rather than duplicate it: he set about inventing the modern lock system, designing the locks at Henley, Boulters, Marlow, Temple, Shiplake and Sonning.

I walk into the centre of Henley along Friday Street, which hints at an old function. The stream off the river ran here, containing the fish for the townpeople's meatless Friday.

Some of the town's houses have the patterned brickwork and balconies of a south coast resort. The town sells mugs which read 'I love Henley'. But this affection is commonplace: the word 'love' is rendered by a red heart.

Henley Bridge has a singular status on the river, the bridge most highly praised by a prime minister. 'Not a sight in the island more worthy of being visited' reported Horace Walpole. It is indeed a fine structure, but there's family interest.

William Hayward built it in 1786, with embellishments by the sculptor Anne Damer, Horace's cousin, who executed the masks of Isis and Father Thames. After her debt-ridden husband shot himself, her horizons expanded. She was introduced to the Emperor Napoleon in Paris. He presented her with a diamond snuff box carrying his insignia.

Nelson sat for her and she gave a copy of the bust to the King of Tarjore 'to win the Hindoos from the worship of ugly idols'. Then to solidify her own reputation, she presented a bust of herself to the Uffizi in Florence.

On this stretch of the river, downstream from Henley Bridge, I meet a startling obstacle. The First World War seems to have been delayed. It is the Henley Regatta, fused like a barnacle to the social calendar, an idealised celebration of distant times.

A time traveller from the 1880s would not require much eye rubbing to recognise *Royal River*'s 'banks blossoming with artificial colours'. The sartorially impatient have dashed ahead into the 1920s, but the dominant theme in costume is still Edwardian.

Anything remotely contemporary is an outrage. 'Henley bans the mini skirt' notes a headline from the local newspaper, over a story about a provocative threat to the status quo, engineered by the national tabloid Press, who decked a young lady in the offensive garb and stationed her outside the Steward's Enclosure.

The Henley Regatta is the nearest thing we have to a Venetian pageant –

men in boaters and blazers; women in ribbonned and beflowered hats and the highest fashion in long dresses, every floating thing commandeered.

There are men with violin cases, little clipped moustaches and dark glasses. Does the Mob's influence extend even to Henley? But no. These are real violinists come to serenade guests drinking Taittinger and Rene Florency Premier Cru. A bottle costs a day's wages for the lady serving them in the Pimms Champagne and Seafood marquee. *Choir Girl* bobs past, with a special umbrella to keep its champagne cool.

I am on the Berks station, standing downwind of steak being grilled for sandwiches. This is a poignant aroma for me, to which I succumb. I first tasted steak sandwiches on my wedding night. Close by, Tony Connor of Eton, ('Hats for the Gentry') is conducting his business by credit card (£6 for the Henley boater).

For want of the correct pink or green badge, I am excluded from the Stewards's Enclosure. The badges drip from lapels and bosoms like monocles, or a superior form of price ticket. A selection from Gilbert and Sullivan seeps out of the stronghold of the Steward's Enclosure.

Smart men in light blue suits and dark glasses defend the exclusivity of lesser pavilions, which stretch along the towpath, offering, for £125 a head, 'corporate hospitality'. The complementary boaters are colour-coded: Lloyds Bank is green, Racal Chubb a dainty lemon curd, Ontario Tourism a wholesome maroon. An ensemble strike up *Eine Kleine Nachtsmusik*.

The river procession begins. *Windsor Castle* creeps past. In mid afternoon, some of its clientele are already dancing to a traditional jazz group. *Caversham Lady* offers the discordant competition of a steel band.

'Things have changed over the years down this end' complains a devotee. And so they have: 'Welcome to Remenham Meadows. Have a great day' drools a notice. Helicopters clatter in. At Temple Island Enclosure where the buildings suggest busy agriculture for most of the year, the crop is now people in boaters and wide-brimmed hats.

Two sturdy tractors tug trailers full of sardine-tight, slightly soused guests. It is a comical sight and the victims share the fun. A natural free-enterprise consequence of the decision at a public meeting in 1839 where towns people realised they could exploit the best stretch of water in Britain. They started the regatta in the same year.

At the start of the course the head of a prostrate cox peers out from a prow at the beckoning spire of St Mary's church, a mile and a quarter upstream. The boats are physically held by young men lying stretched out on pontoons while a starter, patrician figure in blazer and red peaked cap standing in the bows of *Amaryllis*, a long sleek motor boat, informs the crews with timeless authority: 'When you are both straight and ready, I shall start you like this' (demonstrates lowering of red flag). 'Go.'

The two boats jerk away against the flowing river with staccato judders, and *Amaryllis*, bearing various honoured guests including a lady of antique and genteel bearing who gazes into a middle distance of memories, roars after them towards St. Mary's. I suspect the cultivated air of antiquity at the regatta does not extend to the measuring of the course, which seems to have been aligned by laser beam.

Three officials rise precisely to their feet at *Amaryllis*'s stern, one is in a cap, two in boaters, like accusers at an ancient Greek trial. This ritual is repeated every four or five minutes, in boats called *Magician*, *Enchantress* or *Bosporos*. Some of the competing craft carry abstract or self-deprecatory names. *The Immovable Farce*, self-fulfillingly, is well behind.

The next race is begun before the one in front of it has finished. Henley does not admit the possibility of shipwreck interfering with the smooth course of competition.

The juxtaposition of extreme, pampered indolence with straining, manly endeavour is startling. It is as if two images are being accidentally super-imposed on a screen. (A third, if you count the bewildered hire cruisers stealing past.) I suspect that if the competitors decamped to a deserted stretch of the river a few miles away, few of the carousers would notice.

'Is it a castley castle you'll be staying at?' murmurs a mother to a blazered son in a discussion of summer holidays plans. Empty champagne bottles loll against plastic chairs. A tall man in a deep wine-coloured boater plucks at a double bass at the Old Blades marquee. Confused moorhens fluster around the booms that mark the edge of the course and seal off their territory.

The police launch *Tillingbourne* apprehends *Poppin 18*, illegally parked near a drinks tent. Ribald suggestions from the semi-recumbent clientele: 'Tow him away'; 'Put a clamp on him'. The single scullers Messers Harris and Ashmore toil heroically past. The *Bosporos* pursues relentlessly, its umpires stern and frowning on failure. A cyclist with 'Row Naked' on his T-shirt tries inconsiderately to cleave a way along the towpath, through the promenaders.

I have attended one of the world's most imposing fancy dress parties as a casual uninvited spectator, wandering along the river bank free of charge. I would not have come close to Ascot. My grandchildren may be assured that nothing will have changed when their turn comes, except for the vintage of the champagne.

5

WEDGES of gold, great anchors, heaps of pearl,
Inestimable stones, unvalued jewels.
– *Richard III*, Act I Scene IV, William Shakespeare.

THERE IS A distinguished stretch of the river ahead of me. The next twenty-two miles includes the river's last lingering in rural England, before it falls away south into Surrey. There is the most frequented Victorian fun spot; the inspiration for one of the most famous pastoral idylls; the best and the second best houses on the river, the finest railway bridge, the nastiest road bridge and the world's most famous public school.

Today I set out for Cookham, ten miles on, leaving Henley's multi-coloured party and throbbing helicopters, still delivering guests. Beyond Remenham, and Temple Island, with its Grecian temple for a prow, the river bears right in a glorious arc to Marlow. The mighty curve of the river is defined by the sharp steep edge of the Chilterns which do not seem to draw any closer in half an hour's walking north of Henley. It is perhaps the most memorable, and certainly the last grand, natural view available on the river.

The Henley Centre, Fawley Court, is on my left, built by Sir Christopher Wren. Men in shirtsleeves have broken off from their high endeavour and are strolling on the lawns of this management college. On my right a field of fresh earth, newly drilled for next season – tomorrow's breakfast laid the night before.

The sites of Roman villas dot the high ground around here. Appreciation of a beautiful place to live, unlike our changing taste in art or music, is constant.

At Hambleden Lock, two and a half miles on from Henley, my navigating inner eye has seen the building on the other bank many times before: it is Hambleden Mill, pictured on the front of my Ordnance Survey map. This mill is 350 years old and the latest in a series.

Holy Trinity Church, Cookham.

'I am afraid he has not been in the inside of a church for
many years, but he never passes a church without pulling off
his hat.'

– *Life of Johnson*, Boswell

I inspect the bye-laws at the lock, displayed like pages of a book on blue boards. 'Keep fingers off ropes'. 'Persons are not permitted to bathe in the locks or lock cuts.' You are not allowed to wash lorries in the Thames, which seems entirely reasonable.

The Victorian writer Richard Jefferies might have relished Thames Water's strict regulation of the waterway. He poured out a mid-nineteenth century lament for an abused river in *The Modern Thames* (1885). He found anarchy on the river. People did as they chose. 'There does not seem to be any law at all, or at least there is no authority to enforce it, if it exists.'

People shot birds from boats, and from the towing path: 'Moorhens are shot, the kingfisher have been nearly exterminated, or driven away, and if there is nothing else to shoot at then the swallows are slaughtered. The result is that the osier beds in the eyots and by the backwaters are almost devoid of life. I suppose we shall not see the ospreys again. The wild red deer can never again come down to drink at the Thames in the dusk of the evening as they once did.'

Close by was the site of the Aston ferry. This is its sad story. The ferry must have seemed so natural, no one thought it would ever go away. But when the last ferryman died there were no young men to take it on. First, his punt was allowed to wash away in a flood. Then his marvellous tiled and weatherboarded punt shed was allowed to fall down.

Somebody could have made a reasonable part-time living running the ferry. But public money has been spent on a new bridge at Temple, down river. There used to be a ferry man there too. If the money from the bridge was invested, it could have made a ferryman rich in the summer, charging ten pence a passenger.

In an advanced technological society we can't find the men to sit down and run a ferry. If you go to Southern Ireland, you will find ferries still run by charming, intelligent men who just happen to be ferrymen. Where are our philospher ferrymen? All dead.

It is late morning. I am sitting in the Flower Pot Hotel at Aston, two hundred yards back from the river. Built into the brickwork is an out-of-date message: 'Good accommodation for fishing and boating parties.'

The man on the stool explains to me that there are no longer any boating parties, but the procedure was as follows. The chauffeur would mind the boat and inhale the cool river vapours while the smart passengers slept in the Flower Pot.

The acting landlady has applied to New Zealand House for bar staff. She finds the Antipodes a source of good workers. 'They work terribly hard and only want six square meals a day. But we can only offer one cast iron bath between six.'

I have walked into a passionate discussion about changes and talk of changes at the pub, after Fred, whose reign as landlord has recently ended. The lady with the glass of wine is concerned that the fish have gone from the walls, leaving large unfaded patches. She points to the void vacated by one particularly imposing chub.

Once the brewery had masses of displayed fish, she relates. It paid £5 each for them, caught on the river. Stanley Mead, the man who took them, around 1902, was prolific. 'Then they decided we didn't want fish, so they took them out. They sat in the cellar and went for auction at fantastic prices, £250 or £350 each.'

She saw a cased chub in a second-hand shop the other day. 'That was the Isle of Wight. Things are a bit cheaper there. I thought, those fish are like the ones Fred had.'

I leave the Flower Pot, trying to imagine Fred's more perfect regime, and on the way back to the river I see a green woodpecker clattering into a riverside spinney. Two sandpipers make off from an inlet where cows drink below Culham Court, scooting and jinking across stream. One brushes the water with a wing: suicidal in a jet fighter. A large congregation of Canada geese argues and dithers over seating arrangements.

On the other side of the river is the village of Medmenham. St Mary's Abbey, on the bank, was the base for Sir Francis Dashwood's Hell Fire Club. Dashwood did a turn as Chancellor of the Exchequer. He did not impress. His budget speech ended in, according to an observer, 'the loudest laughter ever enclosed between Hansard brackets.'

John Grigg, primary school deputy headmaster in London, intercepts me on the bank. He has been waiting for some time for somebody with a camera to photograph two chub he has caught, to support his claim after his evidence has been returned to the river.

'Both really good fish.' He has been there since ten. 'I had a bit of lunch, cheese sandwiches. Chub like cheese and I threw some in. My line went straight round. [He demonstrates this with an arched arm.] Chub are notorious for grabbing bait. Nothing tentative.'

'Leather-mouthed is he, and for a while strong withal when first hooked,' wrote the younger Dickens. 'From the fact of his desperate rush when first feeling the barb, very strong tackle is requisite to secure him.'

John takes the fish from his net and they slither and slap before my camera. They are the biggest fish he has caught. 'Three and four pounds.' For him it is a private triumph appended to a pleasant day.

On the edge of Hurley, builders are transforming a barn into a house. A lady in the riverside cottages overlooks the quiet side of the island. 'How long have you lived here?' I inquire. 'Forty years,' she replies with a smile which stamps satisfaction on her life.

I am in the repose of the backwater. A couple are sitting in a swinging canopy seat. The lady is snuggling her nose into her husband's neck, while he responds with a radiant smile. Both are over seventy-five years old.

Alantha hums out of Hurley Lock. An energetic grandmother is kicking and throwing a ball, under an enveloping horse chestnut. A party of old ladies attend to the details of tea. It is an ancient ritual, puncturing the timeless slumber of the riverbank.

Once this place was the start of a royal progress of great importance to the elected citizens of the new royal borough of Windsor and Maidenhead. On October 18th 1974, in torrential rain, the Queen set off for a ceremonial progress intended to launch the borough, on a journey of split second timing to Magna Carta Island, alighting at villages, receiving presentations in her launch.

I turn a few yards off the river. Peter Freebody receives me in his tiny upstairs office at his Hurley boatyard. He is a big, rambling man under a volcanic tangle of curly hair rising to a whispy apex. His beard matches his old, brown leather waistcoat, which he wears over a wine-red jumper.

I say: 'If people want traditional wooden boats of distinction built these days, you are one of the few yards to which they can come.' He replies: 'We are the *only* one.' So I asked him why did the others make the mistake of leaving only one yard on the river?

Peter Freebody's family roots have been immersed in six centuries of Thames water. I will not meet a man more firmly fixed on this river. He can take the broad historical view in which the recent sudden decline of the Thames boat builders is a brief passage.

'It has to do with the financial position of boat businesses at the end of the last war. If they were prosperous, the sons were educated well, and did not go into the workshop to learn the trade. Then customers said they didn't want high class work.

'They went into glass fibre boat construction and became marine garages, and in the financial difficulties of 1974 they didn't have any skills to fall back on. In the end the property became another block of flats.

'I believe that when we show customers what is available the big problem is to hold them back. Given my head I'll spend a man's money and he'll get a lovely job. But sometimes they can't afford it. As a craftsman, I'll repair your dinghy for forty pounds or rebuild a steam launch for a hundred thousand pounds.'

Peter's matriarchal grandmother, Dot Freebody, was in business at Caversham Bridge, continuing a long family involvement there of Free-bodys as ferrymen and bargemen. The earliest mention of Freebodys at Caversham was in 1257.

His grandfather went to the auction of the Medmenham estate, covering much of the Thames valley from Marlow to Henley, and bought the land where the yard now stands, for £250. To their surprise they found a family connection on this very land, a John Freebody, Hurley bargeman, who died in 1642. The wharf here where he tied his barges up is the millpool where they run the boatyard.

In the 1840s the Great Western Railway opened up the riverside towns. In 1840 a train ran at fifty miles per hour from Twyford to Paddington, faster than the average rush hour speed on the M4. People flocked from London, to live or on day trips to Windsor, Henley, Reading and Maidenhead.

The old Thames families, such as Bushnell, Hobbs, Wootton, Parrott, and Cooper, former gravel diggers or bargemen, were drawn into the fabulous boom in private leisure boating from the late Victorian period onwards, first hiring out dinghies, then using journeymen builders travelling up river. Later they became builders themselves.

Peter gives me a candid insight into his business history. 'I've behaved in a very unconventional manner. My first bank manager told me "Peter, don't you realise this is the age of paper cups and saucers. You are wrong." So I moved to another bank.'

Peter leads me into the magnificent relic of a workshop. Radio 1 is in disharmony to the tapping of a steam hammer. A tea kettle the size of a locomotive smoke stack hisses to the boil.

Richard Way, craftsman, thirty-nine years old, explains a splendidly arcane approach to building boats. 'Very little management, lots of craftsmen. Because we don't repeat our work, it is impossible to develop a flow system. We don't get used to doing any particular job, unlike a manufacturer producing the same boat.'

The yard's overheads make its hourly rates very high, so they generally build and rebuild only high-priced traditional wooden craft, steam launches or traditional open river launches like this Gibbs, or that Brindle.

'It's like grandfather's broom,' said Richard. 'Two new handles and two new heads but still grandfather's broom.' He points to a boat, brand new except for the keel, but still an old boat.

Richard Way comes from generations of craftsmen. He lived in this village, went to university, came here for six weeks in his vacation and stayed. An intelligent, articulate man, he could have done all manner of things. He also runs an antiquarian bookshop in Henley.

'To become a good craftsman you have to overcome boredom. Many youngsters don't overcome it, and very few adult boatbuilders want to stay boatbuilders. I am the only person to have stayed here any length of time. Three out of five apprentices are not very good. There is a gap between the old boys and the young. See that man with the broom in his hand. He must be the best joiner on the river.

'It takes a long time to do a good job on a fine boat. How long? For that sixty foot boat, twelve years. That's not the time to build it, but the time consumed for the owner to find the money.'

Until now the yard has had much more work than it can ever handle. Staff have left to spread Mr Freebody's revivalist gospel in their own businesses up and down river. 'Otherwise, nobody is prepared to put up with wooden boats as we are.'

Peter Freebody interjects: 'We don't build replicas, but we may not be able to improve on a design. Say a customer wants a steam launch. If you fed all the known facts into a computer, you are likely to end up with a similar looking hull to what was about at the turn of the century.'

He cites the slipper stern launches, a sumptuous little craft whose stern tapers to the thickness of a wafer. The water burbles beautifully as it runs. It has the 1930s feel of a streamlined locomotive. At night passengers rolled out the mattresses and slept aboard.

'Every riverside family had a go at building slipper stern launches but John Andrews evolved the most perfect shape. Since then everyone else has been afraid of being accused of cribbing, so they produced their own shapes. My family did, Hobbs of Henley did, Meeks of Marlow did, Townsends of Bourne End did. But none of us, because we couldn't copy, could get them as good as Andrews.

'Now Andrews has faded away I have done the most natural thing, having three of Andrews' ex-staff here. We are now continuing the line and we credit them, in the Andrews Greyhound, built by Freebody.'

He points the yard's creations out, like old masters. 'This is a Gibbs. See its cockpit. They would sit in it for an afternoon or for lunch. It would have a big folding overhead canopy, like a 1930s Lagonda.'

They are restoring the *Nefatire*, an 1880 steam launch, forty-five feet long. Richard Way found her in a field in Yorkshire on his holidays. He traced her movements: from the Thames to the Trent, via Edingburgh. She belonged to a man of substance, probably lower down the river where there were more big houses. He would have maintained a boatman as later generations would a chauffeur.

We pry under a plastic cover. *Alaska*, luxurious with a big gilded bird on her prow, slumbers gracefully in her cocoon. Richard points out the yard's identifying loving touches. 'We try to soften every corner. We put broad boards on deck, which is risky because they could buckle. But it's very beautiful, a symptom of Mr Freebody's opulent approach to boatbuilding.

'Everything was put back as original. It has a big white funnel, a fine wooden wheel, and a proper steam engine and a lovely saloon. It must have been very fine even for the turn of the century. The old boatbuilders couldn't build an ugly boat.'

I walk on the mile into Marlow and meet two men staring intently downwards. 'The Victorians were afraid of water, so they sat well back. I suppose it was unclean, all that disease.' Tony, wearing ear pads, gives me this historical assessment reluctantly, half suspecting I represent the interests of The Crown, safeguarding the monarch's claim on buried treasure.

He had been waving a metal detector speculatively from side to side, like a blind man's white stick, on the eastern edge of Marlow: he falls to his knees, gouges out a dollop of turf, then, finding no treasure, replaces it like a careful golfer.

His companion Bill, equally unsure of me, has found some Victorian pennies, spilt from the pockets of long-dead picnickers. His best finds were a George II coin and a Victorian half crown at Maidenhead. He shows me some pennies which bear the fuzzy outline of the Queen Victoria's head. I am instantly gripped by memories of frosty mornings, negotiating business in a sweet shop on the way to school.

Bill warms to his subject. 'In some fields by the river, you can find really old coins, hammered silver and stuff.' He gestures towards impenetrable mid-river. We would have some fun underwater. We would find all sorts of interesting things out there. He leaves me with surprising news from below ground. 'It looks very nice here, but a few inches down it's a tip, rubbish grassed over.'

The poet Shelley lived in Marlow, in West Street. Mary Shelley recorded: 'The poem "The Revolt of Islam" was written in his boat, as it floated under the beech groves of Bisham, or during wanderings in the neighbouring country.' Mary prepared her own *Frankenstein* for publication here.

Marlow is a sensible place, where none of the newer buildings have been allowed to detract from the old. A Hungarian might see a hand he recognised in Marlow Bridge. It was built in 1831 by Tierney Clark, the man responsible for the bridge linking Buda and Pest.

In the church is a monument to Sir Miles Hobart, the worthy baronet who locked the doors of Parliament, I assume from the inside, until important taxation resolutions were passed. Dick Turpin, highwayman, and Lord Cecil, stalwart of the realm, stopped here for different reasons – the latter on his short cuts from Hertfordshire to the gout cure at Bath.

I leave Marlow, pausing like a dutiful tourist at the Compleat Angler, the famous pub which commemorates the illustrious fisherman Izaac Walton. I cross a bridge over which the A404 dual carriageway hurries past the town on to the south bank.

' "What lies over there?" asked the Mole, waving a paw towards a background of woodland that darkly framed the water-meadows on one side of the river.

' "That? O, that's just the Wild Wood," said the Rat shortly. "We don't go there very much, we river bankers." '

I am in Quarry Wood, Cookham Dene, which runs up the hill on the south bank east of Marlow and is the inspiration for Grahame's Wild Wood.

On October 22nd 1908 *The Times Literary Supplement* published one of the century's least influential book reviews: 'Kenneth Grahame has disappointed us. There is no getting away from that melancholy fact. The chief character is a mole, whitewashing his house. No doubt moles like their abodes to be clean, but whitewashing? Then a water rat, of all animals the one that would never use a boat to navigate a stream. As a contribution to natural history, the work is negligible.

'The puzzle is, for whom is *Wind in the Willows* intended? Grown up readers will find it monotonous and elusive. Children will hope in vain for more fun.'

I once read the book as I walked to work, over parched grass in the 1976 summer, such a drought as would have dried out even Rat's streams. I treasure each escaping page of this disintegrating paperback, (105th edition, reprinted fifteen times).

Grahame spent much of his early childhood at Cookham, where he acquired his passion for the Thames. Peter Green writes in *Beyond the Wild Wood* (Webb and Bower, 1982): 'The stretch between Marlow and Pangbourne, and in particular around Cookham Dean . . . had the most powerful and emotive associations for him. He had known it during his most impressionable period as a child; he had returned to it in middle age, drawn by compulsive and no longer to be neglected memories.'

My path struggles through the wood, then up on to the heights above the Thames. Butterflies are bouncing on harebells in turf as crisp as lettuce. The river is half a mile away, over Cock Marsh. This was once a cliff over an abundant river.

There are bushes strung along the high ground like little islands of opportunity, each enclosed within a shore of footprints. I have stumbled across a blackberry mine. My notebook is still heavily stained with the incriminating purple. I gorge. A middle-aged couple are affronted that a stranger shares the secret, and will be more so when they are joined by another pair to whom I will shortly disclose the mine's whereabouts.

This is one of the river's steepest slopes. It ends abruptly and I am drawn rapidly down on to Cock Marsh, damp lowland in which a Bronze Age hero or bejewelled notable was buried in a tumulus. A wave of cows breaks over the hump.

On the opposite bank the railway noses into Bourne End, disgorges, and backs out to Marlow. It is half a terminus. This is one of those trundling secondary lines, served by a busy little diesel with no qualification to work anywhere else. *Kingston Warrior 2* drawls by with three prostrate bodies on its roof.

I have passed in succession three young women, each in the company of a dog. Even a 'Good afternoon' is not sanctioned on this footpath. They must display entirely neutral expressions to any unknown man they meet, and promote a defiant air of self-security. If that doesn't work, the dog is the final defender. It would be a bold woman who would, unaccompanied, do what I am doing. Mistrust and fear on Cookham Marsh and Moor, as elsewhere.

This is the riverbank as recreation. Cookham is walking out: this vivid civic animation recalls the Italian town, where ambulatory display is taken seriously. The White Hart advances its custom ahead of the opposition, through a sign on a riverside tree. *Zenique, Titania* and *Pentad* are tied fast, all well composed luxury – polished wood, padded seats, and table lamps.

Festivity III is more proletarian. She is crewed by New Zealander Barry Coutts, electrician from Feltham, and his wife Anne. They left Hampton Court for a seven day expedition, to see if they could endure fourteen days on a subsequent occasion. Sarah, Caroline, John and Con make up the company. Shade is ship's dog.

John, who has been round the world, strolls on to deck, playing the admiral. He was on the *Ark Royal*, so he knows port from starboard. 'You are writing about twits on the river. Where were you when we were docking?'

'We are not like some,' says Anne, defending family honour. 'That girl the other day. You couldn't say she was steering. She was giving it full bore on the governor – if only she had reduced revs. The rest were too drunk.'

Whither are they voyaging? 'We put the binoculars up,' says John. 'We say "Let's moor here." Peace and quiet. Nice landing place. Nice people coming past.'

Today Cookham is a pretty little riverside village. In Holy Trinity Church there is a picture gallery of incumbents. In the village centre a notice displays the town's colour-coded flood warnings. Gold means general alert; washed-out red indicates heavy rain and probable flooding; urgent, deeper red signifies definite risk. 'The expected scale, level and timing of the flood in this particular area will then be given.' I spend the night on higher ground.

* * *

101

> OF all the great things the English have invented and made part of
> the credit of the national character, the only one they have
> mastered completely in all its details is the well appointed, well
> administered, well-filled country house.
>
> – Henry James.

Cookham is a place of ancient significance. The Saxon Witenagemot met
on its banks. Roman weapons have been found in its stream. The village
had attached to it the seven medieval hundreds of Cookham and Bray. On
the island of Sashes, a third of a mile east of the town, there was a defensive
burghal fort.

Once the Great West Road ran through here to Silchester. The centre of
gravity shifted from Cookham centuries ago when the crossing was
switched to Maidenhead. It took a passionate artist who trundled his
materials around the village in an old pram to make if famous again.

Today, on the short four-mile stretch to Maidenhead, I will search for
traces of Spencer, visit an amiable servant of the queen and decorative
ornithology, and walk in the shadow of England's finest hotel.

The smaller the place, the greater the weight of any genuinely significant
artist upon it. In his youth Sir Stanley Spencer would dash home every
evening to Cookham from the Slade Art College in London, on that little
railway line I saw earlier. Throughout his life the village was a puzzled
backdrop to his drama. Today his influence here has retreated to the
permanent exhibition in the King's Hall.

I enter and walk about, trying to dodge Spencer's emotional punches.
But the room is so small it is impossible to escape them. In his 1920 *Last
Supper*, I find a searing sense of exposed guilt and accusation. The choking
Judas; the interlocking feet of the disciples; their inquisitorial eyes. The
company are seated in the stark brick interior of a prison. The bread is
cracked like a stone.

'As he is anxious to complete his painting of the churchyard, Mr Stanley
Spencer would be grateful if visitors would avoid distracting his attention
from the work.' This tactful invitation to leave the artist alone is placed on
the battered old pram.

I was aware of something so huge I hadn't even noticed it as a painting. It
is *Listening from Punts: Christ Preaches at Cookham*. It swamps this small
room in a purely physical sense by taking up the best part of a wall. It blows
through my mind like a gust from an intense, passionate bellows. Its effect
is not diminished by being only half-finished.

'I love the undrawn bits,' opines the lady at the cash desk. 'This is a very
small selection of his work. Much is in private hands, other galleries and the
Imperial War Museum. It is fascinating to think what it might have been.'

She is talking about the unfinished work, whose power pursues me out of the door.

Spencer did some bold things to this village. He depicted Christ standing at the doorway of Cookham Church in his *Resurrection*, now in the Tate, as if he were the butcher in his doorway. I walk over the moor in Cookham, which Spencer painted without fuss or passion.

Close to Cookham Bridge I find the master of the Queen's swans. Mr John Turk's smiling face is enframed in a white beard. On the 1st July 1963 he succeeded his father, who had taken up the same appointment on the 1st July 1922, as Keeper of Her Majesty's swans and cygnets on the River Thames. It was a royal appointment on a paternal suggestion: the young John had been helping his father since he was fourteen.

We talk in Mr Turk's new office at his Cookham house. His former office burnt down two years earlier. The Thames is running high outside his window. It has risen fourteen inches in a day.

The job, part-time now but full-time two keepers ago, seems less a matter of vocation than of preordination. His father, who took over from Richard Abnet, had served as swan marker for the Dyers' Company since 1906. His uncle, Richard Turk, was swan marker for the Vintners' Company, from around the turn of the century, and his son followed him.

Mr Turk served in the Merchant Navy from 1931 until 1947, took a job for eight years, then joined his father during his illness. 'I have no sons, only grandsons,' says Mr Turk, acknowledging that the Turks' royal service on the river will soon be over. 'One is training to be an electrical engineer, the other is only four, ha ha ha.

'The swan is a beautiful bird. I grew up with it. As a boy I would be with my father at swan upping, and when he caught swans before the regattas at Henley, Marlow, Staines and Kingston. I used to watch and feed them.'

Mr Turk's custody of the Queen's swans has coincided with the advancing and receding problem of lead weights. For some years angling bodies, and, to their shame, government ministers, denied the evidence or delayed the counter measures.

Swans had always been troubled by fishing lines. But cotton would break and metal would rust away. Lead was more serious. Swans picking up grit to masticate their food would ingest lead weights. Then the lead poisoned their blood and they died painfully and inelegantly.

In the mid 1970s the population began to decline noticeably, at a time of greater activity by fishing clubs. Research by the Edward Grey Institute at Oxford University clinched the debate and a ban was introduced in 1987, enforced in bylaws up and down the river.

About half the swan deaths could be attributed to lead poisoning. Mr Tuurk once took a weight of half an inch out of a swan. Another caught at

Cookham had twenty pieces of lead shot in its stomach. Now many anglers are using non toxic weights. In his declining years in this noble appointment, Mr Turk reports an improvement.

Until the seventeenth century, when the turkey was introduced, swans were kept as a source of fresh winter meat. At first the monarch laid claim to all mute swans. No one was allowed to own a swan without royal permission. The Vintners' and Dyers' companies, whose charters date from 1470, have for many years, for services rendered, been the only other legal owners of swans.

Ownership is signified by an incision made in the soft gristly lip of the beak. The Vintners make one nick on each side of the beak (corrupted into the pub name 'Swan with Two Necks'); the Dyers make a single mark. Royal birds are unmarked.

Swans had to be marked if ownership was to be retained. The marking ceremony, swan upping, takes place in July, now only between Sunbury and Pangbourne. The swan keeper and two swan markers attend under their banners, rowed in fine ceremonial boats.

On the first day they row from Sunbury to Windsor, where they salute the Queen and drink her health; on subsequent days they sail to Marlow, Sonning and Pangbourne, then work their way back. The mute swan nests in the same place every year, but there is less work than there used to be. There is a single pair nesting at Cookham on the stretch to Bourne End, where there used to be four.

A century ago *Royal River* noted this: 'No one can journey a mile or two along the Thames without noticing the swans, as they float on some quiet pool or come ruffling up towards some passing skiff in defence of their young. The abundance of swans on the Thames is due to the fact that they are carefully tended.' The power of royal patronage over the swan must have been great indeed to spare it from the appalling random massacre of bird life on the river in Victorian times.

Young swans don't scoot around all over the river like undisciplined duckings and goslings. They are tightly bound by family loyalty. The sighting of swans is announced with the call of 'All up'. Then markers try to corral the birds against the nearest bank. Boats move up in a line. The first and last point towards the shore; then they close the gaps to cut off escape. Otherwise the cob would lead his family out. If there is an open bank they put men ashore as the boats decrease the circle.

The swan fights. The markers catch it by the neck, and pull it into the shore, put it between their legs and smother the wings with their knees. Once the parents have stopped flapping about, the cygnets become docile, and sit calmly in the boat.

The birds are trussed, wings and legs, with rope. Beaks are examined, then cygnets are marked, with a dab of tar to close the wound. A single owner of both adults claims all: if parents belong to different owners, the cygnets are divided equally.

When there is an odd number the owner of the male takes the odd cygnet. Royal birds account for about half of the swans in this area. The remaining birds divide equally between the two companies. Marking over, the pen is released, followed by the cygnets, then the cob.

I recall the childhood advice which I never tested, that a swan could break an arm or a leg. Capt Turk, who together with his colleagues, has received painful blows from the thick knuckles in a swan's wings, tells me the bird might not break an adult's bones, but it could badly hurt a child. He sees danger when swans come ashore to be fed. 'They could take a mouthful of fingers in their beak. Sudden movements disturb them.'

The swan population on the Thames is now static. There were more than eighty cygnets between Sunbury and Pangbourne in sixty miles, with eighteen breeding pairs in 1987. 'Not an awful lot, but we hope to see a steady improvement, with fifty per cent survival, rising soon to perhaps twenty-five breeding pairs.'

Birds used to be pinioned to keep them close to the river. They were able to fly only a few hundred faltering yards. This practice was recently discontinued. Now Thames swans fly around freely. The price of their freedom is collision with overhead cables, telephone wires, bridges, trains and road vehicles. This extends Mr Turk's duties: he cares for swans throughout the year, driving out to the injured and distressed.

Other factors count against the Thames swan. There are now few quiet areas and backwaters. Gravel pits are a secure alternative habitat. There are predators: pike and rat will take a tiny cygnet or an egg out of the nest. Mr Turk has heard of a rat rolling a swan's egg with its nose and paw. Large dogs will attack a swan.

But the man whose family has tended the swan for the whole of this century believes they are now secure. He leaves me with a word about river traffic. 'The river is becoming very busy indeed. Over an hour to pass Boulters Lock. But it is the Queen's highway.'

I leave Cookham and head south on the west bank. Cliveden can be seen from only two places on the river: one is the island directly below the house, which belongs to it. This is a temporary view, strictly for the house's benefit. It is not intended for the mere bank-side gazer. As I proceed under the lee of the hill, the house sniffily disappears.

The other view is at a point five minutes by boat down river, where a cloak of trees draws back to disclose the house in its full wedding-cake extravagance. Cliveden on its cliff is our nearest equivalent to a Rhine castle. But by the time you reach here the opportunity to inquire about a room, at £150 for a night, has passed.

In his two studies of Cliveden hanging in the house, Edward John Niemann pressed this fabulous pile through a time warp. Using artist's licence, he depicted in the 1872 study a house earlier than the 1862 Cliveden. Both were painted from under a big weir here.

Cliveden is forty-five minutes from Heathrow airport by road, or five minutes by helicopter to the pad by the main gate. It takes slightly longer by the *Susy Anne*, a 1911 Edwardian river launch, which won first prize for its restoration at the Henley Regatta in 1986. There is room for ten passengers, and the trappings of Cliveden's rarefied excess: a boatman, a footman, drinks and hampers.

Cliveden, owned by the National Trust, (proprietor: the Hon John Sinclair, Savoy-trained former manager of the Lancaster, Paris; butler Stuart Johnson) is by far the grandest of the small number of country houses, turned hotels. Bedrooms where Sir Winston Churchill, Lawrence of Arabia, Rudyard Kipling and George Bernard Shaw may have slept are available to the less distinguished masses.

Impoverished owners of decaying stately piles are watching Cliveden's bookings with interest as a possible model for resuscitating their otherwise hopelessly expensive properties.

In terms of pedigree, commissioned by the Duke of Buckingham, owned by a prince and various dukes and one fabulously rich American, it is set apart from any other hotel in the world. It was also one of the first stately homes with central heating.

I plunge into deep marshmallow-soft cushions, in front of a hissing apple-wood fire, fed by two deep wicker baskets, in a French Renaissance fireplace.

For an hour I share the rare privilege of Cliveden guest power. 'You dictate to us, as guests used to,' promises Nicola Roberts. 'Press a button to get what you want.'

The John Singer Sergent study of an exceptional Edwardian beauty, Nancy Astor, dominates a corner. On the wall opposite are the Duke of Buckingham and the Countess of Shrewsbury, the first owners.

Fakery touches the restoration, but sparingly. False wood fires, fuelled by gas, burn endlessly in Lady Astor's sitting room, and the boudoir. In the Barry bedroom, the convincingly heavy bathstands are modern reproductions, made in West Germany.

The National Trust wanted to do the best for the house which was in poor repair. It granted a forty-five year lease to the hotel group Blakeney, which spent £3 million on refurbishing and modernising it. The conversion brought is as near as possible to the original: a historical hotch potch. 'Homely and comfortable rather than precious,' says Nicola.

Guests glide self-indulgently around. They are five per cent more likely to be American than British. And if they are British, they are likely to be important executives whose company accountants recognise that breakfast in Madame Pompadour's dining room is a powerful stimulus to good work, and therefore a justifiable business expense. There is a maximum of forty-nine guests to sixty-five staff. The hotel is rarely full.

Nicola explains how they might turn certain people away. 'We are prestigious. We want to attract a certain clientele, so we might tactfully say to certain people that we are not the correct venue, that it is too grand and that they might prefer a marquee on the lawn. We are saying "This is what Cliveden is, this is what it's worth and this is what it costs." '

The house offers stupendous views of the river from the parterre, due south to Maidenhead and Bracknell. Lord Astor acquired the statues in the grounds and terrace from the Villa Borghese in Rome. 'We have the originals, they have the replicas.'

The original house was built in 1666 by William Winde for a scale of entertaining intended to rival Windsor Castle. Much of it was burned down in 1795: in 1850 the Duke of Sutherland commissioned Sir Charles Barry, co-architect of the Houses of Parliament, to design the present mansion.

In 1893, Queen Victoria lamented the sale of 'dear beautiful Cliveden' to a mere American, William Waldorf Astor. Although heir to a vast American fortune, Astor was entirely European by inclination. He cared for Cliveden, and in turn gave it as a wedding present in 1906 to his son Waldorf and his bride Nancy.

Lady Astor is credited with extraordinary personal magnetism. She became the first woman MP, contesting and winning the Plymouth seat which her husband had to vacate on his accession to the peerage.

With breaks for war, the rich, famous and brilliant cleared their diaries to be guests of the Astors here. Cliveden was given to the Trust by the second Viscount Astor in 1942 but remained the family home until the death of his son in 1966. It was here, in the house's last private days, that the ill-fated liaison was struck between government minister John Profumo and call-girl Christine Keeler. Stamford University, California, had its overseas campus briefly here. Students hung washing out of windows and strummed guitars on the lawns.

It is now in much better condition than when the Astors owned it. The public can still visit three rooms on Thursday and Sunday afternoons, and the grounds are open daily between March and December.

The company wanted to recreate the style and atmosphere of a private house party. There are personal maids, parlour maids, butlers, valets and footmen. Breakfast is served in the traditional Edwardian way with guests arranged around one big table.

We are in the main dining room, in pink and purple. (Today's menu: Bavarois of smoked trout encased in smoked salmon and set in a dill and mustard dressing, followed by delice of rich chocolate mousse, served on a coffee bean sauce; wine – Muscat de Beaumes de Vinise, Domain Cayeaux Nativelle). The room was plucked from the Château Daniere. 'Rather fabulous. The centre dining table is original.' It offers a choice of Spodes: white with gold trim in a 1860 design for breakfast; for coffee, a 1890 design, and for afternoon tea, 1898.

As I leave Cliveden's outrageous hospitality, I pass a guest jogging dolefully, and at no extra charge, into Hanging Woods, the dense cloak of beech, oak and hornbeam, chestnut and sycamore which excited *Royal River* into ecstatic description. 'All the trees in England seem to have congregated on this bank . . . very probably a relic of the primeval forest which once covered so large a part of England.'

From the river, the picture is less bounteous. 'Stop the rot,' implores a National Trust sign. There is a public appeal to repair the damage of Dutch elm disease, drought and gales with planting. It is an ambitious and generous rescue attempt, whose fruits will be tasted by the visitors of the twenty-second century.

The short walk from Cliveden to Maidenhead brings me back to the main channel of urban Thames Valley prosperity, which is aligned on the main railway and the M4 motorway rather than on the river. The northward loop which the Thames has made since Reading, was its last visit to rural England. From now on the river's scenic delights will be carefully rationed.

Dickens wrote in his *Dictionary of the Thames*: 'Between Maidenhead and Marlow is perhaps the best known and most popular part of the river. And whether for the angler, the oarsman, the artist or the simple tourist, for picnicking, and it has been even whispered "spooning" to say nothing of camping out, there are few places in England to beat the Cliveden Reach at Maidenhead.'

I reach Boulter's Lock. Boulting is a milling term. This was the site of Ray Mill, one of twenty-eight mills between Oxford and Staines. Most of them are recorded in the Domesday Book. The original lock was built in 1746, the first above London Bridge. It was worn out by 1826.

One of the most animated paintings of Thames boating, by Gregory, hangs at Port Sunlight Gallery. It depicts Boulter's Lock in the days of skiffs and punts. Craft are leaping forward out of the lock, released with a starburst of colour and youthful vigour, and the self-confidence said to come from washing in the soaps of the gallery's founder, Lady Lever.

It is not the same today. Today Boulter's is the fashionable place to be stuck in a queue of humdrum glass fibre hire boats, and artless weekend cruisers. Between three and four hundred vessels pass through in a day, and delays can exceed one hour.

There are twenty thousand registered craft on the Thames. Twelve thousand launches: the rest are hire craft, house boats, steamers. Anything that floats must be registered; then there is no authority to prevent them all pushing off from the shore at one time and pressing their right to pass through the river's forty locks. I shudder at the prospect.

> YE distant spires, ye antique towers,
> That crown the watery glade,
> – *Ode on a distant prospect of Eton College*, Thomas Gray.

The Thames valley here is both an illustrious and a slightly uneasy place to be. It floods. Perhaps people take the river too much for granted in their huge ambition to live in and set up business in the flourishing corridor. As I will see later, perhaps they ought to be more careful about which flood plain they choose to inhabit.

From here it is six miles to Windsor, about which artists did not tell fibs – it was too well known – and Eton. The two places, joined across the river, contrive to be equally famous on international lists of inhabited castles and prime minister-producing public schools. Eton has turned out nineteen, although its productivity has slowed down a little recently.

I walk a mile or so inland to the northern tip of Maidenhead to inspect an apparently ordinary piece of farmland on the river's floodplain. But Cannon Court farm is a remarkable storehouse of history, one of the richest paleolithic sites in the UK. More hand axes have been found at this Stone Age axe factory than anywhere else, including the largest flint hand axe, about twelve thousand years old.

Maidenhead acquired its status late by Thames standards when the road to the west was diverted through here from Cookham. The town did a fine trade in overnight accommodation among travellers on the Bath Road who preferred to cross highwayman-ridden Maidenhead Thicket, west of the town, by day.

The present bridge dates from 1777, a good period for bridge building – the crossings at Lechlade, Radcot, Godstow, Dorchester, Wallingford, Henley and Richmond all date from about this time. It was built by John Townsend of Oxford with the architect Robert Taylor, who conceived many fine houses before the Adam brothers cornered the market.

Maidenhead is the scene of good times which must have rivalled

Henley's. Champagne and punting parties in Edwardian days; Gaiety Girls in the 1920s, their contribution to civic conviviality recognised in Gaiety Row, a stretch of riverside. Raleigh stayed in more sobre mood at the Greyhound during his trial for conspiracy. Whether he celebrated after his acquital is not known.

The town Maidenhead had its share of philanthropists: the Victorian George Herring who made his money on horse racing and in the City left £1 million to charities. The bridge builder Robert Taylor remembered Oxford University with £180,000 for the teaching of languages.

I find some minor astronomical rivalry. Slough's William Herschel may have discovered Uranus, but Maidenhead's William Lassells, who died here in 1880, discovered a satellite to Uranus and showed Herschel's claim to have found a further four to be an optical illusion.

On the bridge which carries the A4, the old Great West Road from London to Bath, over the River Thames in Maidenhead there is a plaque with these words: 'This tablet records the grateful thanks of the people of Maidenhead for the kindness and generosity of those in all parts of the world who gave help during and after the disastrous floods in March 1947.'

One hundred families were evacuated. Beds were set up in the town hall. The Commonwealth sent aid to replace furniture and domestic effects. The RAF moved in to dry out homes with special machines.

I can measure the awful power of the flood. Under the bridge, where the path resumes on the left bank, the plaque bearing the March 1947 water mark is four feet above my head. There are coy riverside names, Apple Tree Cottage, Waterside, Thames Cottage – all flooded to the tops of their sideboards in 1947.

The path sets out south from Maidenhead under another Brunel bridge, which carries his main line to the west. It is the biggest single brick arch in the world, a graceful, golden surge.

When the site of Brunel's river crossing at Maidenhead had been decided, the Thames Commissioners stipulated that it must not obstruct the towpath and the channel. Brunel solved his problem, made more difficult by not being able to cross at any great height, by designing two of the largest and flattest arches that had ever been built in brickwork. Each had a span of 128 feet with a height of only twenty-four feet three inches to the crown.

Like prophets in an Edward Lear limerick, his detractors predicted that it would fall down. And at first it seemed they were right. The eastern arch soon showed signs of distortion. But this was the contractor's fault. He kept up the wooden supports, which convinced some that the bridge was not yet safe. A violent storm, one October night in 1839 blew them all down.

A railway official was called out in the night to look at the bridge, which

110

was reported to be in a dangerous condition after a stormy night over a swollen November river. The early train must not cross it. The official passed a lantern over as much of the surface as he could and, of course, found nothing out of place. Brunel's triumph stands to this day.

The artist Turner set his 1844 study *Rail, Steam and Speed – The Great Western Railway*, on the bridge. 'Once thought unintelligible by many spectators, it is now one of the most popular and well known of all paintings', writes David Thomas in *J. M. W. Turner* (The Medici Society, 1979). The artist's broad gauge engine is shown running ahead of a wet swirl of gold and blue.

This is an appropriate image for this day of gathering storm. The grey ribs of an Atlantic depression are edging in from the west. Peter and Elizabeth Day in *Pilchard* are listening to Radio 4 when I interrupt them, with misgivings.

Pilchard is an enchanting little boat, low and snub-nosed, with a homely little box superstructure in stately navy blue, the fruit of passionate renovation. It was originally an open Andrews launch, with a slightly longer back.

'The previous owner put a rather unfortunate glass fibre top on it,' Peter explains. 'We ripped that off and rebuilt it in marine ply because with her shallow draft she would be top heavy. She handles well, but blows about in a high wind.'

Peter worked in the visual effects department for BBC TV. He took early retirement eighteen months ago. 'It's very exciting being retired.' As we speak, a gin palace of a boat goes roaring past. By that analogy *Pilchard* is a well matured little Islay malt whisky of a craft. I am not a boatman. I was seasick in my only yacht voyage, in an east coast estuary. However, I detect in some boats the most beautiful design of any man-made moving thing.

On the west bank, there is a waterfall of greenery on the side of a house. Bray comes into view: its edge is ruined by tasteless pre-war houses, its heart scarred by the aching undercurrent of noise from the third of the great crossings in this short reach of the River Thames, the M4 motorway bridge. There is, however, a fine inn, the Waterside, there, if only I could cross to it.

Nobody remembers that the first cricket in Berkshire was played here in 1773, at Oldfield, a former archery ground. Everybody remembers the vivacious vicar of St Michael's, possibly Simon Aleyn, who attended the 1543 martydom by burning of Pearson, Testwood and Filmer at Windsor and found the flames 'too hot for his tender temper'.

He resolved to swim with the prevailing religious orthodoxy as set by the monarch and was variously protestant and catholic, changing four times, under Henry VIII, Edward VI, Queen Mary and Queen Elizabeth. He achieved his purpose of remaining vicar until he died.

Today the west wind is pumping the angry blare of lorries up the towpath from Bray. I reach the New Thames Bridge (Ministry of Transport, built by Freeman Fox and Partners, completed March 1961) and climb some steps which lead engineers to the motorway's side.

I peer into a hostile kingdom where they have abolished sensitivity. There is a continuous haunting wail of engines and a blur of logos and names: *Wuzerreisen*; *A.Quinn, Sales*; *Allia, the Last Word in Bathrooms*. I can be reassured at least on the bridge's strength. Its elite corps of welders were chosen after examinations of x-rays of their past metalwork.

The bridge is made of drab spars in a wearily functional architecture. As I pass underneath I am alarmed by a loud rubberised flapping directly overhead. The wheels of lorries are visible, pounding overlapping tongues of rubber on expansion joints.

I pass Monkey Island, two miles below Maidenhead, segregated from the River Thames by two hedges, and the motorway din is immediately staunched. Two beetles, crisply black with oily, feathery legs, trickle across the path. I divert to Dorney Church, past an outbreak of purple field scabious, an excellent illustration of a weed as flower in the wrong place.

On this darkening afternoon it is a delight. Grigson names it clodweed in Buckinghamshire, which is where I am on this bank. This name doesn't seem fair. He himself doesn't like scabious at all: 'A sad name for one of the most obvious, abundant and pretty weeds of the cornfield.' He suggests gypsy rose, which would also do for a boat name, although I never see one.

Dorney can do better than weeds. In 1665 the first pineapple in England was grown here by the gardener Rose. He gave it to Charles II. A local pub, the Pineapple, marks his triumph.

Boaters keep strict hours. Around one o'clock they share a common problem. Where do they stop for lunch on a busy river? *Whispering Water III* is preoccupied with the hour: she probes the indented bank for a likely spot, severely inconveniencing a number of craft. Within about two minutes I hear the tap tap of consumation, as stake is driven into bank.

My first sight of Windsor Castle is from three miles away, over flat fields. Once, most of the great buildings of Europe offered this far-off visual introduction over a vast, empty expanse. A treasured few, like Chartres Cathedral, still do.

Huge aeroplanes are being flushed out of Heathrow, like birds off a grousemoor. On the water, *Gay Cavalier* speeds past and detonates a muddy underwater explosion. At this point Thames Water is relying on a Saxon defence of interlocking sticks to hold its river in place.

A dog on *Eight of Clubs: Little Venice*, barks at me from midstream in some confusion over the extent of its territory. A wren tumbles across my path. I have reached the best moorings on the River Thames. On this bank, any boater's camera pointed east will unfailingly take in not only the boat but also the Queen of England's favourite abode.

Windsor has been very firm with the motor vehicle. All through traffic which strikes the side of Windsor is deflected harmlessly. The bridge over the river to Eton is closed to all but the pedestrian. American men in deep red jumpers, but without the baseball hats worn at lesser locations, stroll with wives who carry the shopping bags of the most select shops in London. There are shrill mid-European girls with frizzed hair.

I walk up the hill, with the castle on my left and McDonald's, who sell hamburgers, on my right. This juxtaposition may sound shocking, but to be fair to McDonald's, it has sewn its fast food outlet into the most refined civic settings with some grace. And it sponsors the Civic Trust's award scheme, of which this very street is a past winner.

The castle is the largest inhabited castle in the world. At the Conquest in 1066 there was no castle in Windsor, only a rudimentary defence on a high chalk hill over the river.

The site had been used for centuries before. Palaeolithic hand axes, neolithic flint picks, Bronze Age swords and spears, an Iron Age broach and amber glass beads have been found. But the riverside with its heavy clay soils, flooding most winters, and dense undergrowth would have given little comfort.

However, for a confident king's castle, Windsor – twenty-five miles from London, a day's march from the Tower – was just right, up a steep escarpment, with no need for man-made defences. It became one of William I's protective bastions, together with Berkhamsted, Hertford, Ongar, Rayleigh, Rochester, Tonbridge, Reigate and Guildford.

While the others are now crumbling relics, Queen Elizabeth said this of Windsor, nine hundred years on: 'This town, whose name my family bears, is very dear to me. Indeed I regard it as home in a way no other place can be.'

In a bookshop in the town I find a remarkable picture, set before the castle, just after the start of the 1908 Olympic marathon. Signor Dorando is dashing in sprightly fashion down the hill. Remember him? He is the very man immortalised in a creaky old film being helped, more than two hours later, half collapsed, across the finishing line where he was disqualified.

Windsor, the model of civic cleanliness, is wearing its early-closing look. A French couple is pushing a chic pram. The high-level railway station, this being Windsor, is also a museum. A cranky old diesel judders off to Slough, about which John Betjeman was so unkind.

The town's lower railway station ticks quietly over like a waiting ocean liner. Trains shuttle emptily in, as if by royal command. The stations offer separate routes to London: they could still be running some Victorian inter-company competition. I walk back to the riverside. A kestrel idles down channel. At 2.45 I hear the muffled certainty of Eton Chapel's bells, calling from across the river.

All the old books agree that the river is the best place to behold Eton College, founded in 1440 as Henry VI's contribution to our system of education. It is full of architectural dignity – Lupton's Tower, the fine Perpendicular chapel, the Upper School arcade by Wren.

At the outset it accepted ten priests, four lay clerks, six choristers, twenty-five poor scholars and twenty-five poor men, educated free. The Lower School was built in 1443 and for two hundred years was the only classroom. The Upper School was added in 1694, its desks and panelling marked by the adolescent Walpole, Shelley, Gladstone, Macmillan and Eden. There are boys' names everywhere – six thousand on the stairs and a further eight thousand in the Long Room. Today there are eighty masters and more than a thousand boys.

The most famous flogging headmaster was Dr Keate who, dealing with 100 boys after a rebellion in 1832, entreated his charges thus: 'Boys, you must be pure in heart, for if not I will thrash you till you are.'

The boys used to cleanse their spirits and bodies at their private bathing spot, Athens, a little west of Eton, jumping in head first from the high ground, naturally the Acropolis.

Cyril Connolly, a pupil here, wrote that public schools intensify 'the glories and disappointments' of experiences, so that they dominate boys' lives and arrest their development. The Playing Fields certainly prepared men for war. One thousand one hundred and fifty-seven died in the Great War, when nine hundred Eton boys were decorated and thirteen won VCs. At the Battle of the Somme, a platoon was led into battle by an Etonian subaltern kicking a football. This Grammar School boy, who never went to war, walks on.

6

To the Editor of *The Times*.
Our land is now suffering from serious flooding. But this is nothing
new. Areas such as the Thames valley are age-long evidences of
these facts. I suggest we ought now to embark upon a national
scheme of flood prevention by means of widening of river banks
and the building of four feet high embankments for many miles in
all vulnerable areas. With bull-dozers and other modern machinery
the whole scheme could be executed in a few years. The cost would
not equal the cost of flood damage to people, cattle, health,
property, farmlands etc.
     – Signed, S. P. Venables, The Vicarage, Minsterworth, Gloucs.
                                              29th March 1947.

IN THE NEXT twenty-five miles the Thames meets its biggest challenge
yet. Will it be be swallowed by London? Once the white spaces on each side
of the river were so wide, the Ordnance Survey couldn't find names enough
to put in them. Now the suburban pincer is on the river. It has smothered
the green fields of west London What has it done to the Thames?

I'm going to discover that such hallowed Thames-side places as
Runnymede are under greater threat from the motor vehicle than the
rampant builder. As the river gets bigger, so does people's enthusiasm for
it. The river still has the power to enchant.

Today, my seven miles walk to Staines will take me past the most
vulnerable part of the entire river, and a place of high consitutional
significance the Americans would dearly like to dig up and replant across
the Atlantic, if they could.

I am still in Eton and I find this in *The Times*: 'At midday yesterday (the
17th) the head master of Eton closed the college and sent the 1,100 boys
home until the floods had subsided.'

The story of the 1947 flood is told by newspapers of the day with a
restraint which is remarkable, compared to today's compulsively detailed

115

View of Eton, from Romney Lock.

'Education: during the holidays from Eton.'
  – Sir Osbert Sitwell's entry in *Who's Who*.

reporting of great events. Anonymous reporters sent spare despatches to newspapers, restricted by rationing, with little space to report one of the twentieth century's biggest environmental disasters in inland England.

This was the weather forecast for March 17th, 1947. 'A vigorous depression over the Irish Sea is moving rapidly north-east while another is approaching the British Isles from the south-west.' Yet more rain after many Atlantic depressions and rising temperatures unlocked vast reserves of water in melting snow on the high ground where the tributaries rose. The banks of the Thames could not contain the increase.

On March 19th *The Times* reported that below Chertsey bridge the Thames was three miles wide. 'There was a great lake stopping all traffic between Shepperton and Chertsey. At Walton Bridge the river was a mile wide. On parts of the Thames Valley the record levels of 1894 have been passed. No trains ran from Windsor and Staines. Wraysbury, Runnymede and Datchet were cut off by road and rail.

'The floods which were six feet deep in places extend from Windsor to Walton. The floods extended yesterday to the village of Dorney near Eton. Troops built a wall at Hampton to keep flood waters from a pumping station there, one of the largest serving the London area. In parts of Maidenhead, waters were nearly six feet deep.'

In Reading, a thousand people had to leave their homes. The mayor, Alderman Mrs Phoebe Cusden, described the floods as the greatest disaster in the town for three hundred years.

A special correspondent wrote. 'To turn in many districts towards the river is to be drawn to "unpathed waters, undreamed shores". What were once green fields and wide roads were today unbroken stretches of water, leaving inhabitants marooned. There is a grim monotony in the flooded landscape, dotted here with houses, bungalows, inns and hotels, their signs only two or three feet above the water. In many places it was confusing to define where rivers, roads and fields began and ended.'

Andrew Brooks of the Thames Water Authority shows me a hazy, soundless river pageant, which turns out to be rare film of the 1947 flood. People punt easily about, ladies are helped into army vehicles, small boys earn sixpence for pushing stranded vehicles, postmen hand up letters on sticks, a baker in horse cart leads a convoy at Eton. There were vast resources of residual camaraderie left over from the war. It was not a community in mourning.

What I find terrifying about floods is not the depth of the water, but the speed of its flow. I am transfixed by the sight of water surging at a sprinter's pace past such familiar landmarks as the arches on the Eton to Slough railway line.

People's perception of flooding changes as memories of the last big flood

117

recede. There had been no major flood for over forty years from 1947. Thames Water experts meet people living in the flood plain who do not know what a flood is and what damage it can cause.

Those who ask the experts will be told that, statistically, there *will* be more big floods. The predictions are based on changing flow records. Andrew Brooks says that a flood of the 1947 magnitude, a one-in-sixty years event, *will* occur again in the future but he doesn't know when. Certain areas have been protected and some areas will not flood anyway, but substantial areas would still be affected. These floods might even get slightly worse because of the development that has taken place.

'A chap came round to my office and told me "My neighbour said I wouldn't get flooded because Thames Water extracts so much water to its reservoirs." That's a poor conception of flooding.'

Conventional flood alleviation involves digging a deeper river. This can be ecologically damaging, especially when it involves felling trees. Embankments would confine the waters splendidly. But they are sterile and unsightly. Besides, in many places they could not be built, since houses have been set on the very lip of the river. The truth is, floods of above a certain level cannot be prevented.

Andrew tells me why this area is so prone to flooding. First, some scene setting. For the last few thousand years the Thames has not moved far from its present position. In fact its route has remained fairly stable over the past 300,000 years.

Before the Ice Ages, the Thames followed a north-easterly course through Watford, Ruislip, Rickmansworth, Finchley, St Albans, Ware, and out into East Anglia where it discharged into the sea.

London would not be where it is today if the Thames had remained on that course. Since then, it has taken a number of different routes to the sea, before settling for its present position.

In glacial times most ice sheets came down to just north of Oxford. The Thames was on the glacier's southern edge. Only in the last twenty-five thousand years did the river take roughly its present course, when a further slight advance of the ice pushed it south.

During the last retreat of the ice the rampant river, cascading off the glaciers, brought thick layers of sediment down to clog the river valley in three well known geological terraces, Boyne Hill, Taplow and the Upper Flood Plain Terrace. Subsequently the river eroded these deposits, exposing conspicuous layers.

The Thames eleven thousand years ago was a number of watery threads, with beads, the islands, scattered loosely among them. That River Thames carried four to ten times the water in today's river. It could have spread across the entire valley between terraces, as it might today in floods.

Only within the past eleven thousand years has the river reverted to a meandering single thread channel. And it has changed substantially in that time, in the way it works.

It is normal for rivers to build up flood plains, which every so often they annoint with a mighty spill. But historians believe that there was no major overbank flooding on the Thames until quite recently. Many of the late Neolithic or Bronze Age settlements were actually on the gravel deposits laid down in earlier floods, yet there is no evidence of regular innundation during their occupation.

So something has changed in the way the Thames works and the burden it carries, within the past two thousand years. The obvious factors are climatic changes and the increase in yet another, finer, deposit carried down by the river. The conclusion is that this fine sediment is the result of recent major deforestation throughout England. The felling of trees, rainfall and major siltation are linked. The Thames became a single thread when its outer channels were clogged.

The geologists' warning runs like this. It is natural for the Thames to flood on to its plain. Yet, still, people build on the flood plain, particularly around Maidenhead, and the area between Wraysbury and Staines around the M4, M3 and M25 motorways. As a frenzied corridor of development, there is hardly anywhere in Britain to compare with the expansionist Thames Valley. A repeat of the 1947 flood would do heavy damage here.

Development has done another dangerous thing. It has reduced flood plain storage. Building, the excavation of gravel pits, some of which are then filled and capped with clay, Heathrow airport – all take land out of the flood plain. Waters in times of flood then have a restricted area into which to flow.

I walk out of Windsor and Eton on the south bank, pondering this stark prognosis of an untameable river. Across the river is the site of an extremely ancient riverside enterprise. A few yards back from the opposite bank, at Kingsbury in Old Windsor, in a meander of the Thames, archaeologists unearthed remains of the only Saxon mill found on the river.

The mill was served by a leat eleven hundred metres long. It had three wheels, glazed windows, a tiled roof, and it was destroyed more than a thousand years ago, in the early tenth century. The site may have been occupied for six hundred years before the Romans.

Any river walk is a series of glimpses, mostly from flat low ground. I look back over some quiet pasture land and catch sight of the castle. Ahead of me is a most emphatic barrier, which looks likes that stylised portcullis on the old threepenny bit, standing across my path. Behind it royal Jersey cows graze royal sward.

I have to follow the river on a set-back road, through the fringe of

Datchet. Two miles later, I recross on the Albert bridge, so called 'By permission of Her Most Gracious Majesty the Queen and His Royal Highness Prince Albert in 1851.'

It is time for modest suburbia to claim its place on the river, in the form of little pre-war bungalows with ornamental tables and upturned boats on their lawns, slipped through before the introduction of stricter planning rules. Pinned to a sycamore, there is an appeal for a lost Amazon parrot, green with blue, yellow and red feathers. 'Makes some shouting noises or wolf whistles.'

Arentum and *Enchantress IV* drift out of Old Windsor Lock. There is a riot of floral colour. 'We used to have a best-kept lock competition,' says Frank Bird, assistant lock keeper. 'They stopped that. The same three always used to win. But we still have the flower allowance and our own nurseries.'

Frank grumbles about land theft on the river bank. 'People pinch a couple of feet here and there. The next thing you know there's a wooden building on it.

I return to cynical decadence. There is *Life O'Reilly*, flagship of the idling classes. 'Magnificent river views,' promises a board at a new Thames-side development, The Moorings, (with moorings). It does not advertise the merits of the busy A308 Windsor to Egham road to the rear.

The road changes from light to dark grey as I step into Surrey, the sixth county of my walk, after Gloucestershire, Wiltshire, Oxfordshire, Berkshire and Buckinghamshire. There is an old boat with Gothic and Doric arches, the *Nuneham*, which is being renovated by French Brothers – logo, Mr Toad in a boat, rowing. How often did the indolent Mr Toad exert himself to row?

In the Magna Carta tea shop, they are serving an exquisite cup of tea, with a choice of walnut or cherry cake. There are various photos and plaques, and framed letters from Mrs John F. Kennedy, Senator Robert Kennedy and Windsor Castle. The Kennedys were the nearest thing the United States of America ever had to royalty, and they are celebrated appropriately, if a little unctuously, with a chunk of England here.

A short walk from the tea house, I am on American territory. This is, as far as I know, the only American territory in Britain outside the US Embassy at Grosvenor Square. Unlike most bits of expatriate America it does not bristle with guards.

It is, for its function, an inspired choice. I am quite alone on a low wooded slope, three hundred yards south of the river. I climbed a causeway of cobbles enclosed in a border of smooth flints. The sun seeps through the canopy of a young oak. There is a hawthorn sprayed with red berries.

It is received wisdom that everybody of sufficient age knows where they were on November 22nd, 1963. I was watching BBC television at home

120

when newsreader John Roberts broke in, lifted a black telephone and with sombre but matter-of-fact voice announced that President Kennedy was dead. The BBC then reverted to a comedy programme by Harry Worth.

'This acre of English ground was given to the USA by the people of Britain in memory of JFK, President of the USA. 1961–1963, who died by an assassin's hand,' reads a plaque.

'Let every nation know, whether it wishes us well or ill, that we will pay any price, bear any burden, meet any hardship, support any friend, oppose any foes in order to ensure the survival and success of liberty,' it continues, quoting Kennedy's inaugural address.

This is a generous monument to a foreigner. There is an aura of perfection, deserved or not, which sits over no other modern statesman. It seems inconceivable that any other western figure, apart from Churchill, would be granted such a sacred memorial by another country.

The Kennedy monument stands in a comforting enclosure of trees – hawthorn, yew, oak. There is an open shoulder on the right. A robin, twenty yards away, delivers a cool, plaintive lament. A respectful line of trees stand at the brow of the hill, forty yards higher up.

I find this setting suddenly disturbing. On this serene afternoon, the hill behind the monument recalls the grassy knoll, behind the road at Dallas where the slain Kennedy sank into his wife's arms.

Kennedy's memory lies over Runnymede like a colour photograph double exposed on a black and white film. Before it was associated with a president, in his time as perfect as unchipped porcelain, this place was first famous for an unloved king making a big gesture.

'In thesse medes on the 15th June, 1215 King John at the insistence of deputies from the whole community of the realm granted the Great Charter, the earliest constitutional documents whereunder ancient and cherished customs are confirmed, abuses redressed, the administration of justice facilitated, new provisions formulated for the preservation of peace and every individual perpetually secured, to the free enjoyment of his life and property.'

The word 'property' is a bit eaten away. I suspect strong-minded socialists or anarcho-syndicalists take exception from time to time. However, few will read these words, on two monuments framing a fast road which dashes across the sacred meads, in any comfort.

We afford the president's memory quiet solemnity, but we set a race track through some of the most hallowed terrain associated with our constitutional development. Ironically it stopped being a horse race course in 1886 when the police refused to supply the men to keep order.

It ought to be a matter of some national embarrassment that the first monument to the barons' achievement was set up by secessionists. The American Bar Association erected a monument in a grove close to Kennedy's in 1957 – a star spangled dome resting on eight octagonal pillars. Many genealogically-conscious Americans claim descent from the barons appointed to uphold the agreement. They regard it as the highest hereditary honour they can hold.

The third attention-gripper on this south-bank ridge facing the Thames, a few hundred yards on from the American Bar's memorial, is the Commonwealth Air Forces Memorial at Cooper's Hall, quite the most staggering war memorial you could come across on British soil. There, on upright stone pages flapping open for ever in the contours of the hill, are 20,455 names of airmen lost over Britain and Europe.

Designed by Sir Edward Maufe, the architect of Guildford Cathedral and built in 1953, it is timelessly aloof from any watery disturbance in the plain below. I stand with this huge silent chorus behind me and survey the Thames.

I walk the short distance down the hill to the river, which switches north away from the busy A308 which has so recently defiled Runnymede, and then strikes south-east into suburban Surrey.

On my right is Egham. The Victorian philanthropist Thomas Holloway built his Royal Holloway College here in 1879 as a safe place for women to study for any university course. As an inspiration to the toiling ladies he modelled it on the Château de Chambord.

There is another French connection. The last duel on British soil was fought over some obscure point of honour by two exiled Frenchmen in 1845 at Englefield Green close to here. M. Cournet was mortally wounded and was carried to the Barley Mow where he died. He is buried at Egham.

In 1205 the Thames froze here. In January 'began a frost until March 20, so that no ground could be tilled and frozen wine and ale was sold by weight.'

Three quarters of a mile along the bank, just before Staines I seem to have been diverted into an underground car-park. There is a forest of heavy concrete pillars, and the most unedifying graffiti of the entire walk. I stride quickly through this dispiriting void and do not look back until, a few hundred yards on, I realise I have walked under Britain's busiest road, the M25. The structure is so massive that not a whisper of traffic disturbs the river below it. If London is to begin anywhere, it might as well be here.

*   *   *

A Walk Along the Thames Path

KEEP alive our lost Elysium – rural Middlesex again.
— *Middlesex*, John Betjeman.

I have almost left the grassy Thames bank behind. From now on the most casually-shod can take up this path in twenty-minute offcuts and, apart from one or two boggy bits, keep their feet dry from here to the Barrier.

Today I will hurry on for sixteen miles into Kingston, past some of the grandest of all the river bridges, christened in one afternoon jamboree of royal opening. I will meet a man who has done more for the standard of living in the middle of the river than anybody, and another who has done much to keep the bank in good order. I will pass pre-war bungalows, Midas-touched by the property boom, reservoirs and disputed Roman crossing points and 'Appy 'Ampton, the cockney's favourite west London excursion.

I had expected to be depressed by the suburban river, but I am not, perhaps because the momentum of interest is so great – I have to find out what happens next. And as London becomes busier, the river, as a silent band to left or right, is an increasing comfort and refreshment.

Staines was an important place on the Thames almost two thousand years ago. It was a settlement on the London to Silchester road in the first and second centuries AD, set on a small raised area of gravel. The town took its share of the through traffic on the river. Red painted Pingsdorf ware from Europe has been found around the sites of eleventh and thirteenth century wharfs.

There were two bridges here, one of them over the river Colne which wiggles down through Staines Moor to the north, between King George VI and Wraysbury Reservoirs. But today the river is only a damp dribble in the life of Staines compared to the vast flood of Heathrow Airport, three miles to the north-east.

Today Staines is a presentable west London town, convenient to the entire world through that nearby star-shape of runways. The Thames is now tightly gripped by suburbia.

Three miles past Staines, in his house by the river, I meet Bill Gardham, who in 1952 saw an advertisement for a new body dedicated to the care and welfare of the Thames. He set off for London, found the meeting hall and walked around a bit before deciding to go in.

As with many people who attend inaugural meetings he was immediately elected to high office. He has served the River Thames Society ever since.

'People looked at the Thames from a narrow point of view. They say "You can have a bridge anywhere you like, except here." We wanted to look at the whole river, and keep it as enjoyable as possible for people.'

Bill Gardham, former RAF officer, has lived on or around the river all his

123

life and in this riverside house since 1948. He was born and brought up at Staines, where his family have lived since 1805, making bathroom taps and showers.

On the river outside is moored his boat *Thamesia*, built at Lawsons, Sunbury in 1963, in traditional materials, with a Perkins diesel engine. It wears the Air Force Yacht Club's ensign, albatross wings on navy blue.

Bill serves me biscuits and coffee in a chubby mug. From his study window he watches, in his old age, the river roll endlessly past in a grey slab. 'Up to my landing stage now. About a foot higher than it should be. But they control it very well these day with their electric weirs. It flows much more quickly than it used to.' It lapped up to the beginning of his garden in 1947.

'Twenty or thirty years ago the river was not a particularly desirable place to live. You had to be very river minded. But people were sociable. In the old days I did a lot of visiting by dinghy from one bungalow to another. Today that doesn't go on at all.

'A lot of people living on the river really don't want to know anything about it. It might be Timbuktu on the other side. If they came over this side I'd be only too pleased to talk but I don't take any notice of them over there.'

Away from a bridge, the river is an isolating force. To cross to the house on the other side of the river to Bill's, less than 100 yards away, would take me an hour's trudge. I would need twenty minutes to drive there. The demise of the ferry twenty-five years ago had the same effect here as the withdrawal of a rural rail service in the countryside. It snapped a link. Look on the map and there it is, the obsolete Ferry Lane running up to the south bank.

Even these custodians of the river's spirit cannot find a way across. 'We offered to run a voluntary ferry, but if somebody doesn't turn up on Sunday morning, everything goes phut.' A shame. There may have been some form of crossing here since Roman times.

He once met the disappeared Lord Lucan's father, who owned the nearby abbey. It was very high church. The builders, Barretts, bought it and converted it into four luxury dwellings, with an unusual restriction: no car parks are allowed.

Nellie, coloured ochre, is moored on the other bank, its boiler bubbling pleasantly. Two coots try to beat upriver against the flow. They think better of it and submit, joining a pair of mallard racing with the river, like boys on bobsleighs.

There is a line of yellow and blue boxes, Portakabins on water, stretching down towards the M3. The tide is surging into Chertsey lock where the maintenance vessel *Wey* is tugging at a branch.

Chertsey, like so many Thames places, is a one-bank-of-the-river town.

I feel the vandalism of the Reformation most keenly here. Once it had one of the most important abbeys in England, founded in 666. There survives not a trace, unless you can spot a brick or two in Hampton Court.

Today it is just another of the uniformly smart and affluent West London towns, but, unlike Windsor, not firmly enough on the river to exploit it.

I leave by Chertsey's tawdry edge, past factories, debris, hissing power tools in oily forecourts, canisters, used oxygen cylinders, long rows of parked cars. Then, snap. Green fields break back abruptly, in the map's empty white floodlands of Chertsey Meads.

I chart a tentive route for a mile or so through grazing fields, to a select Thames-side domain of long pebbly drives which lead to names pickled in Thames water – River's Edge, Moorings, Kingfishers. In truth I am hopelessly lost in an exclusive cul-de-sac. The river Wey blocks my route. I retreat and follow the road into Weybridge. Down a by-road, past a school for decorous daughters and I'm back at the river, on the other side of the Wey.

There is a claim that Julius Caesar crossed the Thames here in 55 BC. But the town still takes its name from a tributary. The river Wey navigation is owned by the National Trust. It offers the most attractive diversion off the Thames, nineteen and a half miles down to Godalming Wharf.

Just outside Weybridge I meet Peter Chaplin in his house close to the river. 'I paid thirty shillings for this.' Peter gives a chuckle of recollected triumph. 'I tried to appear uninterested before they said "Sorry, we made a mistake." '

We are studying a map dated 1770, by Thomas Jefferies, geographer to the king, showing the Thames diversion line proposed by Brindley, the Brunel of his his age, cleaving its quick way west through Middlesex and Buckinghamshire. If it had been built, most of the Thames would have become a backwater.

Peter Chaplin extracts another bargain from his shelves to make a precise historical reference to one of the river's biggest problems. 'Wash from boats. I can tell you when it all started.' He opens 'The Report of the Select Committee, Thames River Preservation, House of Commons, 4 August, 1884.' 'I bought this for a pound. Could you believe it?'

'It is also urged,' says the report 'that the presence of steam launches of late years in increased numbers on the river has increased the wear on the banks and therewith the destruction of the waterplants that edge the river.'

This paragraph greatly exercises Mr Chaplin and his son Tom. Their working lives have been devoted to arresting erosion of the Thames' banks and strengthening the river's edge.

'Most of the erosion is the result of wash. People in their motorboats

125

treat the river as if it is beyond the delimit sign on the M3.' He depicts, with rapid hand movements, the assault of water on bank. The first wave strikes the bank, is drawn away and slurps back, undercutting it secretly. The bank looks safe, then the winter floods rush down and exploit the weakness. Another chunk of Surrey heads downstream to Essex.

But things are improving and Mr Chaplin has played a part in it. In the 1970s he deplored the decline of the traditional boat. There were lovely boats hanging up in boatyards, neglected. He felt they ought to have been out, being used. He offered a prize to the Thames Society and that was the start of the Thames Traditional Boat Rally.

'Owners of old boats are more likely to be careful sailors. The old boats, parading gently along the river, were designed to make as little wash as possible. They set an example. Now other people say "I want a boat that is really built for inland waterways and not a wacking great gin palace." '

Mr Chaplin has a touch of sympathy for the bank-breakers. 'I was in coastal waters torpedo boats in the war. We used to come up to the docks in London in those high speed craft, devils to handle at slow speeds. Some of these big fast boats have to get up speed to stay up in the water. If there is a cross wind, it must be hard work to keep them on course.'

The Chaplins, a Hampton family, have had business with the Thames since 1907. Mr Chaplin is as close to the river as any working man. 'I sleep out a lot in the summer, under the stars. I have done so all my life, in a sleeping bag. But the right colour sleeping bag – none of these garish things. I have watched a kingfisher eating its breakfast as near to me as you are.'

The river bank is in many hands, private, local authority and institutional. Mr Chaplin grumbles about some of their husbandry of this great national asset. 'People with private property or gardens running down to the Thames forget they are part of the living landscape. In a street it doesn't much matter what they do, but this is the public highway.'

Much of the renovation work is carried out by civil engineers. Mr Chaplin finds some of them careless on matters of aesthetics. He runs easily through the technology of keeping the Thames within its ordained course. It has not changed much over the centuries. The corrugated sheeting is driven down into the river meadow, below the soft, slurpy mud to whatever firm base is down there. Rods are tied every eight feet and anchored into the bank.

Banks are given a robust protection with yard-square wire-mesh containers made into matresses twenty feet long by six feet wide, filled with large stones. 'It really does look lovely. We won a countryside award. A minor one, but an award.'

Mr Chaplin finishes his work with a scatter of tender colour. His own seed mixture contains herb bennet, meadow sweet, dropwort, purple loosestrife, tufted vetch, common fleabane, smaller cat's tail, devil's bit scabious, and tall goat grass. 'We seem to be losing so many of our small flowers. I remember plants in profusion when I used to scull.

'Things are definitely better on the river. We hear very romantic talk about the good old days. But imagine the later part of the eighteenth century, with barges hauled by gangs of men walking along the foreshore. That must have been ruddy grim. Or later with a team of fourteen horses pulling sixty tons and then having to change sides and be ferried across. That must have been tough. And when people took their livelihood from the river and it froze.'

Back to the river. What would Mr Chaplin have made of the artless, dull banks of Desborough Cut, which was opened on July, 10th 1935? The usual plaque honours Lord Desborough, the Thames Conservators, and Middlesex and Surrey county councils. The cut has snipped off the bottom of Pont Meadow, a piece of public open space. A little grebe slips silently into a fold in the water and is discreetly spat out, about fifty yards and half a minute away.

Desborough Cut has marooned Shepperton on a very pleasant little backwater. I picnic on a gale-toppled willow. Within a minute I am joined by the most fearless of wildlife companions, the speculative robin. The tree is still warm, taking life from the earth.

There is room on this cramped little isthmus for the posts of the University Vandals Rugby Club, the pitch between them and not much else.

I retrieve the main river where the water is sitting up in little slabs in the stiff easterly. Three swans head for me, with high hopes of yet more lunch, followed by a long line of Canada geese. It will take the loaves part of the Biblical miracle to satisfy them all.

I pass Walton Bridge, probably the ugliest bridge on the river, linking Walton and Upper Halliford. Spars and girders thrash about in disorder. But they must be obeying some prime rule of civil engineering as there are cars and people crossing. Two barking geese switchback over the slapping river. Grey wagtails hop and flit.

I lean into a hard east wind in this dwindling afternoon. There is not a murmur of a boat on the water. The river seems twice as light as the sky: it has captured all the available and uncertain light of a drab day, enhanced it and transmuted it. It sparkles like dull gems, a steely, pulsating grey.

There is a straight course of three quarters of a mile, past the Thames Valley Skiff Club. On the north bank, coming out of Walton, cranes swing and strain over large flat barges. They are a commercial link with the wider

Thames beyond the last lock. Another cut tidily breaks through an irritating wiggle in the river. The footpath gives me no alternative but to follow this diversion.

Hampton church perches on a hill high enough to guarantee immunity from flooding. It is one of the most commanding riverside churches. An island of shacks huddles in its shelter like a medieval village under a castle.

I have reached the edge of Dickens' London. Mortimer Lightwood and Eugene Wrayburn from *Our Mutual Friend* had their bachelor cottage in Hampton. There is a big cathedral of a waterworks, its stones recently scrubbed. From here on, every bit of land along the north bank has been claimed and shared out. There is no more to spare.

I peer into the miserable cavern of Molesey Lock, the second largest Thames lock after Teddington, then conjure life and colour into it with a breathless paragraph from Jerome's *Three Men in a Boat*. In the lock he found a: 'brilliant tangle of bright blazers, and gay caps and saucy hats and many coloured parasols and silken rugs and cloaks and streaming ribbons and dainty whites. When looking down into the lock from the quay you might fancy it was a huge box into which flowers of every hue and shade had been thrown pell mell and lay piled up in a rainbow heap.'

This is reservoir country. An endless Victorian brick retaining wall wraps around Molesey Reservoir. Fierce illustrations warn of the type of canine terror to be encountered beyond the wall. In Hurst Park, now mostly devoured by the builders there was once a beautiful meadow, 'as hard and smooth as velvet'. On what little greenery is left a lady launches a red Frisby which an Alsatian plucks infallibly out of the air.

I cross to the river's most flourishing inhabited island. I could not see a TV aerial on Tagg's Island. Nor was there any washing line. Gerry Braban keeps high standards in his tiny kingdom.

In about two and a half minutes I have walked from one end to the other on a spruce, hard road where until recently I would have squelched and slithered. The swollen Thames slips past on both sides.

I press the bell on one of the best appointed offices upon the Thames. I mean, you understand, *upon* the Thames. During our conversation a boat passed. Gerry Braban's office, linked to his design team in the Midlands by computer, gave a little apologetic shudder, as if acknowledging a distant earthquake.

Gerry is a man of purpose and achievement. He sits in an expensive, green leather chair, high-backed and plushly upholstered. He is expecting a call from Dubai.

'Small as we are, we are the leaders in the technology of building afloat. The Arabs want a complete floating town built out there. They want us to fly out this weekend, but I'm not going. I'm fed up with travelling.'

Gerry is one of these energetic men who make things happen. He owns a Rolls-Royce and a 1920s facsimile of a car in the style of the Great Gatsby's. He is the man who saved Tagg's Island.

In the course of our interview people ring up to discuss Gerry's various floating hotel schemes. Two swans glide up to his office's patio windows as if paying their respects to a benefactor.

He is soothed by the changing views from his patio window. 'Winter is the best time – the lighting is so different. There are cormorants, geese, herons, Aylesbury duck. You name it, we've got it. We are constantly rescuing swans with beer cans stuck round their beaks, that fishermen keep chucking in.'

This is what Gerry has done for the image of living afloat. The houseboat was considered, and still is on many parts of the river, an inferior form of abode.

The houseboat can be chirpy and homely, cluttered with the cheerful marks of the nomad, but it is marred by its impermanence, its TV aerials and its washing, hung by defiant individualists. Gerry is a defiant individualist himself, but he will have none of their clutter.

'I have turned the houseboat into a very desirable place to live. But I'm not prepared to sacrifice standards. I've got one of the largest houseboats next door. It's on two tiers, with sunken baths and jacuzi pools. This boat we are on has two bathrooms, central heating, patio doors.'

The residents in his community live in a smart, controlled environment, on the restored, once-derilict Tagg's Island, with their buried TV cables feeding four channels from a single aerial, hidden in a tree. 'We build in clothes driers and washing machines. There is no need for lines of washing. There is street lighting and a vacuum sewage system. But we let people express their individuality. They can plant their own flowers.'

Once residence on Tagg's Island was a mark of social inferiority. Gerry demonstrates the stock grimace of the landbound. 'People were taking old barges and converting them. They were fun sometimes, but they were neither a boat nor a home.

'Then there are some very attractive conversions that do give a lifestyle. There were some massive boats with five bedrooms near here, with servants quarters, butlers and pantries. They would cost a fortune today. But we can't go back to building like we used to in the 1920s.'

Tagg's Island was created out of old osier beds, which once fringed the southern bank. The river meandered through on the north side. Gypsies used to camp on Hurst Park and cut the osiers for basket making. When the beds were filled in with the tailings from Queen Mary reservoir and the artificial island created, the dispossessed gypsies are said to have laid a curse on the perpetrators by wagging bones at them.

This is the 'Appy 'Ampton, destination of the Victorian Cockney's excursion to Hampton Races, although they were actually held at Molesey. In the 1800s the impressario Fred Karno bought the island and set up his Karsino, a watering hole for smart London society.

Gerry has read that the crowned heads of Europe came here to gamble and cavort and drink the night away. 'The police couldn't get here without a boat. Somebody would shout "Cave, boys" and everybody would be drinking gin out of teacups.'

There were famous and gilded patrons – Lillie Langtry, Vesta Tilley and Charles Chaplin, who was employed here for a time by Karno in his theatre and casino. Laurel and Hardy served their apprenticeship here.

Then the gay young things bought cars, roared off to Brighton, and Tagg's Island slumped. Six consistently bad summers bankrupted it by the mid 1920s. Local people recalled the gypsies' bone wagging.

For a time the island was owned by the Tagg family. Gerry and his wife keep bumping into old Taggs. Tom Tagg ran a boat-building business from the island. Two large steam yachts were built here, for Queen Victoria and Czar Nicholas. The AC car factory was built here in the 1930s over the tennis courts. Later it was a chain factory, then a factory for light machine guns.

The Brabans came for a short stay in 1968, renting a houseboat. The casino had become an Indian restuarant. Scenes from Stanley Kubrick's savage, brilliantly moralistic and misunderstood film *Clockwork Orange* were shot in the ballroom. 'There was a beautiful painted ceiling. We tried to save it but vandals got in and tore it down.'

Gerry saw potential under the rubbish and the rotting hulks. Hacking through the undergrowth he found the old Italian rose gardens. 'I decided to buy it.' His wife Gillian told him not to be silly, noting that they could scarcely pay the rent on the boat.

The age of the Jumbo Jet was dawning. The then owner wanted to turn the island into a hotel complex, with a plastic dome over the river to accommodate the huge influx of tourists who would otherwise be reduced to sitting on suitcases for want of sufficient hotel rooms in London.

Gerry formed a committee, threatened litigation and fought planning appeals. Meanwhile the jumbo jets began to land. No passenger was stranded. Gerry negotiated a legal labyrinth, bought the island and instituted a phased programme of development. He dug a lake in the middle to make it difficult for a future developer to build a tower block.

The island complete, Gerry waits for the nation to grasp the potential of living on water, like some Oswald Mosley of the Thames. He sees water as the new terrain for a nation short of land. 'We are awash with water, hundreds of thousands of derelict acres of it. I've never met anybody yet in my life who doesn't find water attractive.'

It is a short step from this bulwark of free enterprise to the first of three 1930s monuments to public works. Hampton Bridge, with its wrought iron lamps and smooth concrete was opened by Edward, Prince of Wales on a hot, high summer day, July 3rd, 1933, together with the Chiswick and Twickenham bridges.

The Times marvelled: 'The Prince has been associated with a remarkable range of public ceremonies, but when he opened three new bridges across the Thames in the course of an hour yesterday he performed a task which had never come within his own experience or that of any other man.

The Prince wore a light grey lounge suit with a dark red carnation in the buttonhole and a boater. The third bridge opening was intended to be the principal ceremony. There were fifty thousand to see him on the two banks. This was the fourth bridge crossing at Hampton.

The Times continued: 'A pavilion was erected in the middle, which although it hid the parapets, gave a striking impression of its width and a view of the curve of the river and the red brown roofs and chimneys of Hampton Court Palace.'

The Prince arrived at half past five, greeted with loud cheers. He proceeded to inspect the guard of honour. 'While he was thus engaged, about fifty cars bringing the mayor and other guests from the other ceremonies "gate crashed" the bridge, which had yet to be officially opened.

'For a few minutes there was a traffic block, but by the time the Prince of Wales reached the platform the cars had been cleared and officials had spanned the river with a length of tape.' More presentation of dignitaries, who included the architect, Sir Edwin Lutyens.

The speech was broadcast through amplifiers erected at various points on the bridge. The Prince said: ' I do not think there is any precedent for the inauguration of three bridges across the Thames in one day.' He spoke of the high value attaching to 'these great schemes of public improvement.'

'All these things are cheerful signs which add to my gratification at being with you this afternoon. I am just about to cut the ribbon. It is good luck that this has only just been put up because I have already crossed the bridge no fewer than ten times.' (Laughter and cheers).

I am on the bridge, more than fifty years later, which is a short time in the life of a Thames crossing. Under it a grebe approaches a prospective mate with a fish and the two intertwine their necks, as if in some ritual Oriental dance. Canada geese swim up and down in a domineering way. A man sends a stick cartwheeling through the sky inches ahead of the jowls of a bounding black wolf.

I walk on the north bank, past the place where monarchs disembarked for Hampton Court Palace to lock out poisonous London winter, and whence Sir Thomas More took boat to The Tower. Wysteria shines on the red brick. The river gates are marked by harps, roses and gryphons and the royal crest.

Hampton, built in 1526 is the most westerly palace on the river; Greenwich the most easterly. Wolsey built it, Henry VIII liked it, and the cardinal did the correct thing, begging to be allowed to present it to his monarch who graciously accepted. It was the favourite royal palace for two hundred years.

Centuries of processions set off from here. Until 1855 the Lord Mayor's show started here: the 1919 Peace Pageant revived the tradition. Sir Christopher Wren lived for a time in the Old Court House. One bleak February day in 1723, aged ninety-one, he was taken by water to sit in St. Paul's for the last time. He died shortly after.

Initial Concept is moored, surely not on royal business, without any competition. As I drink my coffee it is joined by *Shadowfax 2*, formerly *Graylag*, then the *Admiral Creighton*.

Now every sailor knows that you ought not to change a boat's name. Concerned that such frequent name changes was adding hugely to the potential for bad luck, Malcolm Bonnar, who restores vintage cars, decided to hold fast to the latest title. He is delighted to be told for the first time Shadowfax was Gandalf's steed in *Lord of the Rings*, a name brimming with compensatory good luck.

Two coot beat across the river like ageing dreadnoughts towards the *Titanic 2*, surely the most providence-tempting name I have come across, the *Wolf, Endeavour, Aphrodite* and *Dutchboy*, whose two ends turn up and slightly back in the nationalistic flourish of a floating clog.

Gulls are setting to work on a large chunk of bread. A black backed gull, indifferent to the prime source of the food, chooses to pursue a smaller gull, like a bully determinedly running down a younger boy in the crowded school yard. The smaller dives and darts and jinks and swerves until it concedes to the unshakeable pursuer and drops the prize.

Raven's Ait, where beer kegs are stacked many deep outside a boathouse, lacks the cachet conferred by gin drunk from teacups. Kingston-upon-Thames looms up. Troubling the background are two power station chimneys topped with black bands. On the bank there are new offices in obligatory red brick with grey mantle.

* * *

IN the forepeak of the vessel, Growltiger sate alone,
Concentrating his attention on the Lady Griddlebone.
— *Growltiger's Last Stand*, T. S. Eliot.

It is mid-morning. The shoppers are surging in a mechanised tide over Kingston bridge. The flood waters are licking to unusual heights under it.

Today I am going to walk the four and a half miles from Kingston, a solid overdeveloped place with Reading's indifference to the river, as far as shining Richmond, with its lost palace. In between I will discover how Thames acoustics served the early film industry, and how they made the river flow backwards.

First I enter the newly restored wheel house of Gordon's boat, in a glass cockpit. There is a brass wheel, which is never used because this vessel never moves – except a few feet up or down on a hint of a tide echoing up from beyond the next, last lock – and a 1920s model of a naked lady emerging from green and blue tulip leaves. Gordon and Sue hold dinner parties here, in full view of thousands. In winter it is a fairy grotto, open to public gaze.

There are no curtains at the top of his houseboat, but he doesn't feel threatened. 'We don't mind people looking at us. We look at them. They look at us.' He is right. After a time the throng on the bridge, the cars nosing around Hampton Wick for a parking place, become like the picture on a television which has been left on but which isn't being watched.

There are twenty-six boats here with alliterative names, such as *Serene*, *September* and *Sea Cow*. Although the river is big enough to allow space, they are all pressed together like Hong Kong harbour, or a watery version of the Mad Hatter's tea party. But, as Gordon will explain, this is a mutually beneficial togetherness.

His boat was once owned by the actor Ian Hendry. It was an old admiralty pinnace, a harbour boat. There used to be hundreds on the river. He runs a solid fuel boiler made to an 1820 design. 'People always assume you freeze to death on boats but when we shut everything and open this boiler up, we roast.'

The cockpit has four views, but he doesn't use them all. We sit facing the north bank, diverting our gaze from a surly concrete pile, like an eastern European disco, on the south bank at a point near where Jerome K. Jerome's Three Men must have taken to their Boat. It obscures lovely roof tops and a church.

Gordon is a carpenter, who designs and builds kitchens and bathrooms. He speaks with genial contempt of a building separated from him by a slab of shifting water. 'I call it the garrison. It is an absolute bloody eyesore. We watched it go up and I thought it might mellow after a while. It never did. It used to have eyelids, little awnings, but within weeks they were full of holes and vandalised. They could have used soft yellow brick to blend in with the church. The lovely old Victorian boathouses are disappearing in favour of buildings that don't deserve to be on the waterfront.'

We sneak a glance over our shoulders at other excesses. There is a supermarket over there: it has a canteen with *no windows* over the river. Could I believe that? Would not a consideration of the river make scampi and two veg less prosaic? And yet that very building won a design award.

The river enticed Gordon to its bosom by degrees. His initiation was a one-foot-on and one-foot-off affair. You don't take to living on the river as you enter the priesthood, full of commitment and serenity.

He stayed a few weekends on a friend's boat. Then his family broke up. Briefly ashore, he lived in a flat and hated it. He bought his own boat, then another. He has owned four boats and he has been tied up here for a long, long time – twenty-seven years.

Gordon and Sue never go away because the river is a destination, still fresh after so long. Even in the winter, they are out on deck drinking coffee. 'It's like being permanently on holiday. Boats are very characterful. You get a feeling for a boat you don't get for a house. All the boats I've lived in I've been in love with.'

It is Mole's spring cleaning, without the temptation to push up and out. 'Buy a boat, hang it all around with new curtains, paint the outside. A dowdy hulk becomes a shining temple of self indulgence. Everyone has this little love affair. But usually they move on.'

It is time to praise the neighbours. 'We've had wonderful neighbours over the years. I can honestly say we have never had any undesirables.' Problems are talked out, whereas suburbanites retreat into recrimination. He has heard strange things from on land, of wronged neighbours popping anonymous letters through doors, concerning an aberrant dog. He might be describing the brutish ways of a backward tribe.

The open air has something to do with this. 'A nice life. Any pretext, if the weather is decent and we all go swimming. The human race has an affinity for water. It must be something do with the ions. It can be the most boring, flat nothingness and yet it is still attractive.'

We shamelessly discuss the passers-by, many of whom have to step across Gordon's prow to reach the shore. 'He's an ex advertising man, David. He gave up the rat race. Now he's a motor cycle messenger – no pressures. And he's a computer wizard, Martin, in the music business. I don't know anyone on the dole, we're all hard working people here.

'We get a lot of divorcees. Marriages break up. The husband gets half the house. He's fed up with life. He looks for an alternative lifestyle and ends up buying a boat. Then he is embraced by this little community. We go out of our way to make newcomers welcome. We have them to dinner. Then the daughter comes to live with Dad. Girls find the river affordable. They manage.'

There are no more old salts on the river. Living on boats has become dainty and comfortable. 'We are clean and conservationist. And not only do we keep the river nice, but we save people's lives from time to time.'

The only bill he receives through the postman's hand is the telephone bill. Everything else is bought day to day. But there is a heavy price to be paid for living on the river. He is a man without the lifebuoy of an appreciating property.

I cross the bridge to search in vain for the point of embarkation of that most illustrious river journey. Jerome's Three Men, having bribed the engine driver with a half crown to change his train from the 9.32 for Virginia Water into the 11.05 for Kingston, arrived on the river somewhere here, if only I could find the spot.

There is more proof of the bridge that is no longer there. Kingston bridge, one of the greatest civil engineering constructions of its day, survives as some careful draftsmanship in Geoff Potter's office. He unfurls the plan, about five feet across, and shows me four boat-shaped island piers, seven metres by two metres.

For centuries Kingston bridge and London bridge were the only permanent crossing of the downstream Thames. 'Consequently when there occurred one of the frequent commotions in which our ancestors delighted, there was a good deal of competition between the two sides to get Kingston bridge destroyed first, and so prevent communication between Middlesex and Surrey,' notes *Royal River*.

What little is known about Kingston Bridge is more than is known about any ancient bridge above London. How can something which stood for five hundred years be so utterly gone? The bridge strode across the Thames, then thirty-five metres wide, broader and shallower than today, from a sloping foreshore. The stonework of the bridge was visible in the old river bank until recently when the site was smothered by a department store.

It was built in about 1170, a little before London Bridge. There is no evidence of an earlier ferry. But Kingston was already a place of distinction. There are references to Saxon coronations in the tenth century.

Geoff Potter tells me what the few shattered stones told him. How far upstream the tides penetrated before locks and weirs were built he does not know. High tides might have banked up the fresh water as far as the bridge. They certainly found great spreads of clean, yellow fine-grain silt, anything from a few centimetres to half a metre thick, indicating deep floods with water standing for long periods.

The excavated remains speak of a well constructed bridge. The boat-shaped islands were built without benefit of pumping facilities, probably with some sort of ram. One island is mysteriously out of alignment with the others.

I leave the din of Kingston's rebuilt waterfront. A man in a parcels delivery van is feeding the ducks from his seat. A riverside house garden contains two rescued red telephone boxes. A party of goldfinches, dandyish red faces and yellow striped wings, tickle over the riverside vegetation.

On the other bank, a group of teenage pupils have conspiratorially removed from the hubbub of the school yard to a secret place behind a tree, thick with cigarette smoke. They think themselves hidden, but are perfectly visible from my side of the river.

Two miles on I meet John Ryan. He and I are perched high above one of Thames Television's film sets at its Teddington studios, a few yards from the river on the north bank, like those two technicians in the film *Citizen Kane*, during Kane's wife's excruciating operatic debut. John, a soft-spoken Irishman in a sweater, is the studio's unofficial historian.

We crept into this high gallery, our footsteps deadened, our whispers hushed by green wire mesh soundproofing on silent concrete floors. We had passed men in rooms sitting in front of TV monitors, in high-speed pursuit of ephemeral images.

'You can see how TV can so easily deceive,' John notes ingenuously, as white gloves and shoes begin a ghostly disembodied pirouette in the blackness below. A gutsy rendering of 'My Home Town' skids to a halt, then whirrs forward in a demented screech to a concluding, lingering 'There's no place like London townnnn . . . '

The lights rise to reveal chorus girls in black leotards, and masks, wearing permutations of odd white gloves and shoes on various feet and hands. A floor crew is engaged in what people who work in film and TV studios by reputation do very well, which is waiting around. But when the cutting is complete these sirens of the Thames will bewitch the world's audiences.

John leads me past general props, bits of wood, brick walls, sylvan backcloths and Doric temples, to visit the car park wall. In its bricks, on John's initiative, are preserved three rams' head gargoyles. They come from the outside of the old Warner Brothers' construction shop, built fifty years ago, and represent ancient history in the film business. When John heard of the rebuilding he confronted the architect and secured the heads. There they protrude – trophies, or rock climbers' foot holds.

We climb to a roof. This is peripheral London. John points east to Richmond Hill and deep into the south, to Weybridge and Guildford. The company's token presence on the river whose name it has taken, is the Sir Thomas More hospitality boat and floating restaurant for guests.

136

How did the studios come to the quiet of the Teddington river bank? Flash-back to 1912, to those delirious enthusiasts of slapstick comedy, the Kellino Brothers, with artists from the Kingston Hippodrome, shooting silent pictures with cameras made from tin cans with holes in them. Their studios were the glasshouses of the mansion that stood on this spot.

'They didn't know a damn thing about films. They taught themselves everything.' It was an inspired improvisation. They had neither set, nor lights. So they built a circular stage with which they could chase the sun as it toured the garden, and capture maximum light.

The house's last occupants were Mr Henry Chinnery, prominent member of the Stock Exchange, and his wife, Marion. Only the Weir Cottage survives from their handsome domain. John Ryan tracked Chinnerys well back into the 1700s in his researches at the Cork county library, in the Republic of Ireland.

In the early 1930s Warner Brothers took over the studios to circumvent a protectionist home film industry which insisted that foreign companies produce films in Britain. Their Teddington output was described as 'quicky quotas', rushed out to meet the regulations.

Warners liked Teddington because it was quiet. There is still little traffic with no major road through it, or industry, and the river soaked up rogue mechanical noise. Their Studio 1 included a façade which looked like a grand hotel, with a big revolving door. Warners did not build anything without giving it shooting potential.

In 1944 a German flying bomb fell on this inoffensive studio. A studio official, Bob Salmon, who had insisted in remaining at Teddington during the war, died in the explosion. The studios were rebuilt but Warners soon retreated to Hollywood.

In the late 1950s, ABC TV, the independent television company contracted for the North and Midlands, took the studios as a London production base, to save artistes appearing in the West End the long day trip to Manchester. In 1968 ABC and Rediffusion were fused, but senior executives did not have to ponder long over a title for the new station. Thames TV virtually selected itself.

I leave these busy, thriving studios and regain the river edge. But I cannot pass Teddington Lock without considering that famous occasion when the river had shrunk to such a size that the river engineers made it flow backwards.

The details are at the button-pressing fingertips of Mel and Dennis of Thames Water. I'd better not call them the Flood Control Unit because they don't control floods. Dennis recalls an irate gent ringing from Marlow demanding to know why all the local fields were flooded when those around Windsor were not.

'What were we doing special for Windsor, and not for Marlow? I told him there was nothing we could do for either place, but with a dry spell we hoped it would go down soon.

'Well, the next twenty-four hours were dry and the floods did go down. I can imagine that chap going into the pub and saying: "They told me they couldn't do anything but I gave them a mouthful, and isn't it funny that the water did go down." '

Belief in Thames Water's ability to conjure away the torrent is not confined to the pub bore. 'We have a flood seminar here every year and a lot of well-informed people come over to us and say: "You have all that telemetry. Can't you just push a new-fangled button and get rid of it?" We can't. All we do is monitor.'

In the flood monitoring operations room there are buttons and lights and a radar picture of the weather over Southern England and another of the Thames valley. The first shows moping clouds off West Wales and a breakaway group moving into Gloucestershire like a line of eager girls advancing on to an empty dance floor. East Anglia is under a saturating mantle.

Yellow lights interrogate green lights and convey to Mel Sligo the water situation at important places. He can punch a button to tell me the rainfall at X and the height of the water at Y bridges or weir. He can tell me the severity of the showers, and I suspect even the diameter of the raindrops. It hasn't rained much over the main Thames today but he has a good example from the night before where there was a cloud-burst at Guildford.

This is the degree of precision in the warning he can issue from his plush seat. A few more thousand gallons into the Wey above Guildford would have produced the sort of level in the town where the unit ring the police and tell them to warn the patrons at the Yvonne Arnaud Theatre that the car park is likely to flood. Warning people is what the unit does well.

The anger of the Thames can best be measured at Teddington Weir. Five thousand to 5,500 million gallons a day is a bank-full, or typical low winter flood, not doing anyone any real harm, once or twice a year. (The season of potential floods for about three months around the turn of the year.)

But even that is beyond Thames Water's powers to control. They can only contain the river by opening the weirs and at four thousand million gallons a day at Teddington, they would all be wide open.

Dennis is beginning to sound like my old maths master, building an edifice of bigger and bigger numbers to prove a point. On a day of near-flood at Kingston last winter, its severity recognised with a broadcast flood-warning, 7,650 million gallons a day were surging over Teddington, well over the wringing-of-hands threshold, where the authorities are powerless.

'It only needed one bloody good downpour and there was no space for the water to go.'

In the 1947 flood the daily figure reached 13,572 million gallons at Teddington. But, and Dennis finds this remarkable, in September 1968 there were 11,404 million gallons at Teddington. You would only have been aware of where this huge flow came from if you lived in the Mole or Wey valleys, saturated by a slow moving storm.

'Lock keepers draw their weirs and keep water courses clear,' says Mel. 'All we can do is try to say when the high water will peak and hope to give sufficient warning of an impending flood.'

I recall the stories that intrigued the popular press in 1976, the year of the Great Drought. Did not the authority perform a miracle by making the river flow backwards? It is true, Dennis admits, that they effectively stopped the flow over Teddington weir by back-pumping water over the next weir up-river, at Molesley, so it could be abstracted for Londoners to drink. A modest water engineer's trick: hardly a miracle.

The volumes in the London reservoirs fed from the Thames fell that wizened summer from 42,000 million gallons in May to nineteen thousand in August. Mel shows a blue line taking a deep dive on the year's graph, like an acrobat missing the trapeze, eventually being caught in the safety net, which was the rain that eventually fell.

Did they panic? They were called up a lot in the night but they were sanguine about the future. 'We knew bloody well it was going to rain some time,' says Mel. 'It always rains here.'

Many people believe at the time that rain came through the intervention of a reincarnated rain god, Denis Howell MP, a junior minister in the Labour government. Mel points indignantly at a plaque on his wall recognising Mr Howell as the man who opened this very room. 'But he was never here. He was off sorting out the miners. We had the lord mayor instead.' At this, Mel knocks over a cup of tea and expertly staunches the muddy-brown flow across his desk with several pieces of computer print-out paper.

Mel and Dennis, gregarious men, warm hosts, have a short-term involvement with an environmental problem which will last for millennia. How will we ever stop the Thames flooding people?

In some respects it is more liable to flood. There have been changes which cause rainwater to find its way into the river more quickly. The water runs faster off large paved areas in Swindon and Aylesbury into the drains leading to the river. Cultivated fields drain more briskly.

'If we want to keep the aesthetic value of the river, there's nothing to be done.' They don't think much of one brave and expensive proposal, to encase the river in a long concrete channel. They did that on the river Mole after the 1968 flood. (Mel has drawn a series of long straight parallel lines in blue felt tip on his map.) 'It smells like hell in the summer. But that's what the locals want.'

They have to balance a number of responsibilities – 'water for the reservoirs, and enough in the river to stop the boats banging on the bottom.' Between Windsor and Hampton Court the river provides two thirds of London's drinking water. There are five pumps at Datchet, each capable of slaking 100 million gallons a day.

This is the epicentre of the river's Doomsday scenario. 'If somebody punched the wrong bloody button here, we could have all five pumps going at the same time and the bloody river would dry up.' That it has never happened is a triumph of responsibility over mischief.

The radar-charted showers creep over Oxfordshire. There is rain at Cleeve. Mel predicts that my garden will be watered within the hour.

I leave these affable men, regain the river edge and walk on to Richmond, past Ham House, owned by the National Trust, with a long gallery which contains portraits of some of the bold, bad women of Charles II's time. A mile on from Teddington Lock I pass Eel Pie Island, 'once in high repute with picnic parties'.

Charles Dickens, senior, uses the Thames as an additional character in many of his novels. In *Our Mutual Friend* it is an active player in unfolding tragedy. In *Nicholas Nickleby* it is a location for feast: Morleena Kenwigs dines, as Dickens did, at Eel Pie House, on 'cold collation, bottled beer, shrub and shrimps'.

It assists Dickens at his most tender and yearning. His hero Clennan is walking down to Meagles' house in Twickenham. 'The tranquil sun shone on him as he passed through the meadows by the riverside. Everything within his view was lovely and placid.'

Daniel Defoe wrote in his *Tour of Great Britain*: 'From Richmond to London the River sides are full of Villages, those villages so full of Beautiful Buildings, Charming gardens and Rich Habitations of Gentlemen of Quality, that nothing in the World can imitate it.'

At the Orleans Gallery, on the north bank, I am allowed a rare peek at Peter Tilleman's *View From Richmond Hill*. This is an idealised vision, of sinuous river, gliding through deep green glades and meadows. I do not recognise these curves from the Thames I am walking. 'The bends in the river, with artistic licence, have undergone adjustments to create a sense of balance' explains the catalogue.

It is a work from the Government Art Collection, never normally seen by the public, but briefly on display here, and as such is an inducement to stand for Parliament or join the diplomatic service. It has been brought here from the Foreign Secretary's residence: before that it was in the British Embassy in Paris.

A short distance upstream, on the other bank, is Pope's Grotto, where the poet who put the lily on the Loddon sat for inspiration. Marble Hill House, built around 1724 by George II for his mistress, the Countess of Suffolk, which stands close by in Twickenham, is a gem in the Palladian style. It was one of many villas built on favourable sites close to the river, in this 'village remarkable for the abundance of curious seats'.

A man on the riverbank tells me an interesting story of how, to much local rejoicing, a female great crested grebe successfully raised its family single-handed, after the male had been killed by a rival. Parenthood in this species is usually a hard-working task undertaken by both parents, since the young have to be fished for until they are quite old.

A mile on from Eel Pie Island is Richmond, which was Sheen until Henry VII decided the view of the hill reminded him of his Yorkshire earldom, Richmond, and gave it the same name. Down on the river, the late summer sun bounces off the smooth water, on the edge of the tide's influence.

7

A fine scene. We've nothing like it in Scotland.
— *Heart of Midlothian*, Sir Walter Scott
(on the view from Richmond Hill).

THE NEXT SEVEN miles will take me into bustling, fashionable west London where frontage begins to command the sort of premium Mr Salisbury in Goring could only dream about.

The riverside path is the most pleasant way of entering London. It will take me past a wild island, the best garden in the world, and the once quiet, and on the Thames still quiet, fishing villages of Chiswick and Strand on the Green. At the end I will hear news of piscatorial prodigals.

I find in Richmond the sort of London village Kingston could have been if it had tried. Its royal credentials, on paper, are as impressive as anywhere on the river. The town has a claim to the best green in England and surely the finest river-facing Terrace anywhere.

After the heavy concrete of the Kingston waterfront, I am cheered to find a new office development in subtle blues and pinks on the waterfront just below Richmond Bridge. Quinlan Terry's neo-classical design, drawing on plans of two hundred year old buildings, is a pleasing, cultured contribution to Thames architecture of the late twentieth century, reinforcing the Georgian character of the town.

In the town I find mature ladies strung in long queues at bus stops, waiting patiently to be borne to the higher stations of this fashionable riverside village. They are the very best behaved of passengers but because they travel on concessionary tickets it is hardly worth the bus company's trouble to stop to pick them up. 'The thirty-three won't do. It has to be the thirty-seven,' insists a devotee of the routes.

Shene Palace was first occupied by Henry I in 1125. Edward III died in it in 1377. Henry VII rebuilt it and Henry VIII was born here and lived in it, entertaining the Emperor Charles V in 1520. Wolsey came here after he had loyally donated Hampton Court to Henry. Elizabeth, also born here,

The Thames, from Richmond Hill.

'On the idle hill of summer,
Sleepy with the flow of streams.'

– *The Welsh Marches*, A. E. Housman

found it her 'warm winter box to shelter her age'. There is now nothing left of it. However, the view from the Terrace remains, more stunning than anything in Bath.

Scott, in *Heart of Midlothian*, referred to the view from the 'commanding eminence where the beauty of the English landscape is displayed in its utmost luxuriance . . . turretted with villas, garlanded with forests. The river moved on slowly and placidly, and bore in its bosom 100 barks and skiffs whose white sails and gaily fluttering pennons gave life to the whole.'

John Ormiston, Chairman of the River Thames Society, leads me out on to his balcony to admire the view. Here through half-shut eyes, you can imagine yourself above the Rhine. The river runs to the foot of Richmond Hill, inspirationally to artists, then veers north in a graceful arc.

We tour the horizon. We can see the North Downs, Guildford Gap, the Devil's Punchbowl. John gives a loyal whoop of delight 'Look, just to the left of that plane coming in to land. Windsor Castle.' Our heads swing left, following the low spit of the Chilterns. Then the high North London of Hamstead Heath. We politely leapfrog Ealing and Acton, prosaic boroughs to be recognised by their gas holders.

This house, eighteen-feet-high ceilings, was built in the 1830s shortly after Jane Austen in *Northanger Abbey* remarked that there were some nice dwellings in Richmond. 'The only really well known person to live here was Fitzgerald, translator of Omar Kyam. No royal mistresses as far as I know.'

It is appropriate that John has both the Queen's residence and the river in view as he has to propose toasts to each in about equal measure. I ask the chairman, an engaging voluble man, how he came to love the river.

One of his first known statements was an emphatic declaration of affection for this sumptuous redoubt. When in the early 1920s the young John was wheeled up to Richmond Hill, his recorded words were: 'Nanny, I would like to die here.'

'I came to love the river. Particularly the noise the water makes on the bottom of boats. All river people know it, especially those who go in punts or skiffs.

'It's a lovely noise. I've been attracted to it ever since. This is what our members feel. They all love it for that sort of reason.'

The trouble with river lovers is that they like to dream before it, bask upon it or browse alongside it but not do very much about it. 'They say, "Here's our sub. Good luck." Ninety per cent are like that.'

The society spends most of its time and energy not on composing odes to the glorious Thames, but in trying to fashion the look of the river in its corridor of about a mile wide.

The society regularly take to a boat and survey the land from the river.

From this peculiar vantage point members built a persuasive case about where gas holders and tower blocks ought not to be.

The banks of the river is littered with 'Told you sos' from the society. 'A very bad example at Lewisham. Twenty-two storeys right on the edge of the river. We told a public inquiry it was liable to flooding. We were proved right five years later when five stories were submerged.'

'If these high buildings have to be built, they must be right away from the river.' They are skilled in beating buildings down, like a child slicing blocks off the top of a Lego tower. 'We managed to reduce a twenty-one storey block to seventeen storeys, and another from seventeen to eleven on the Embankment.'

A navigation committee puzzles over navigation bylaws (those above Teddington are very different to those below), dusts them off and suggests modernisation. Until recently the maximum penalty for throwing a brick off a bridge was five shillings.

Older river hands like John have always found it hard to bear the passing of the Thames Conservancy, and the swallowing of their river by a body enjoined by law to concern itself with sewage in Aylesbury and flash floods in Swindon. Pleas for a return to the Conservancy are a ritual ingredient in conversation with people with notebooks. 'It was a lovely thing. As boys we were told to wave to the Conservancy when we saw their boats.'

The society is passing its concern for the river downstream like a baton. Among the latest converts are the people of Brentford, 'waking up at last to the fact that they are on the river.'

John then makes a surprising admission. 'I'm a commercial man and I wouldn't bring up anything by barge if I could get it done for half the price by road.'

Walking back to the river, I distinctly hear one lady of the bus queue generation say to another: 'Who's your boy-friend then? Go on.' I thought I had touched the daring underbelly of this frightfully seemly place, when under the ancient bridge, built 1777 and the oldest surviving Thames bridge in London, Stan Peasley and Jim Springett tell me of the prevailing misbehaviour.

'You should come at the weekend and see the sort of person who visits,' said Jim, a genial white haired man, who worked for a company that developed an anti-collision device for boats shortly before satellites made it instantly obsolete.

'Hooligans. They go out with a wine box, get drunk and wreck them.' The management's solution is to provide the clientele with a type of lumpen plastic boat of no navigational scope but which is quite indestructible. I inquire about a skiff and Stan informs me that they would have to charge a prohibitively high deposit on this wonderful wooden boat. He doesn't know where I *could* hire one.

All this is a preliminary to how things were. Stan pushes out into a flood tide of nostalgia, tapping for effect a fourteen feet 1902 skiff, reconditioned in a rich burnished brown which he is completing for sale. 'There were four thousand skiffs between here and Teddington. Patrons used to really look after them. We never even took their money until they came back. Six people would hire this. It had a gramophone, soft pillows, a table, food hamper, the whole shoot.

'They all carried a rolled-up cover which could shelter the occupants against the rain or the night. Five shillings (25p) a day, fifteen shillings for the weekend, twenty-five for the week.'

The hirers offered a particular service to the early-rising, living-in staff at the big Richmond stores, Breaches, Goslings and Kempthorns. For a penny a week they could punt and skiff from this stage for three hours until 9 o'clock, and for four evening hours until 10 o'clock. Come here at six o'clock in the morning, the whole river was full of people rowing around.'

I don't know whether he took the canine metaphor too literally, but this is what he thought did for skiffing as a major pastime. 'It was dog racing that finished it off. A young man could take his girl to the track for sixpence. It was a different thrill.' (Fifteen thousand watched this 'New Sport at the White City' on June 21st, 1927, noted *The Times*.)

'You can tell how little the river is used by the state of the slipway,' says Jim. 'You have to fight your way down it.' A batallion of powerful weeds stalk off to the tide line, awaiting the kind attentions of the wine-box brigade.

But consider this, from *Royal River* in 1885. Advice, surely, to arrive early to avoid the great grandfathers of Jim's hooligans. 'If he has arrived on the spot at an hour when the rowdy element, unhappily too prominent among the dwellers in our metropolis, has not yet broken the peace of the Thames by those simian howlings or that loud-voiced blasphemy, which is deemed expressive of pleasure, then he will find it hard to detach himself from this stretch of the river.'

A little later I find a discreet path, a patch of beaten grass, plastic sandals and a towel. Their owner is on his back, in the river, windmilling his arms elegantly. My loitering bothers the swimmer, who is recalled by the unique suspicion of those who feel their clothing is going to be stolen.

Having failed to contact the Mao Tse-tung head in the river above Dorchester, I resolve to speak to this man, and I approach him like a market research interviewer trying to fulfil a quota. Fred is American, and with that peculiar diligence in health matters found in some of his countrymen, he has checked with his doctor that swimming here is safe. The fact that he has been bathing for eleven summers is all the proof I need that frequent immersion in the river need not lead to certain death. He has either by now acquired a resistance to all the punier germs, or there really is nothing to worry about.

Fred, a tall man, in thin, gold-rimmed spectacles, swims from May to October, even November, with his mouth closed. He stands dripping uneasily in the hot sun, but speaks with clear enthusiasm some fine words of self-justification. 'The river is immensely to be preferred to the cholorific water in our local very beautiful public swimming pool, which is also so crowded.'

He is a pioneer in the era of the cleaner, post-war river. In the late 1830s, when the river was last clean, Charles Dickens, the elder, used to swim from his rented cottage in Petersham Road to Richmond Bridge. Fred comments on the stories in the local newspaper about swimmers dying and drowning. 'If you look into the cases of those who drowned, either they had been drinking or they had no experience of swimming, or both. The most dangerous thing I can do is not take enough care on the slimy edge.'

If the tide is racing, Fred may swim against it with all his strength and still be pulled slowly back. He swims every day and follows it with a shower or a bath. He is a walking pollution monitor. 'The river is noticeably cleaner. I used to wash off brown.'

Under the railway bridge the river is beaming up an agitated, mottled, bejewelled pattern of intertwined hexagons, beyond the creativity of any computer. I proceed through a tunnel of horse chestnuts. The sweet tang of suntan lotion hangs in the air.

Richmond Lock is the last lock on the navigable Thames. It is as much a border outpost as Lechlade Lock, so many miles ago. From here you could navigate uninterrupted to the Amazon. Fierce notices warn against importing rabies.

The pleasure boat *Kingswood* barks a warning of its approach to the lock keeper. Some white haired ladies nod to me, as the Queen might. As she passes, *Kingswood* jettisons a trail of white bread. Gulls skid in and maul for the booty like New Zealand loose rugby forwards.

I picnic on the gravel, scoured twice a day by the tide, just above low water among discarded mussel shells, opposite Isleworth Ait. This is an unusual aspect of the river and the surrounding land, known only to fishermen and beachcombers. The sound is from deep in the countryside, of wheeling crows in the high trees.

On the north bank opposite, a gull torments a heron, kee-hawing in sudden circular sweeps. The heron stands stoically, then delicately lifts a large foot and adjusts its neck and shoulder by a few degrees, like an angle-poise lamp. The gull departs and the heron strains, peering into the water for some minutes, as an art critic might, intent on a fine detail in a new painting. A second heron takes up its fishing station a few yards downstream.

On the mud upstream there is a swan, a few wing beats from the swan sanctuary at Richmond, where ironically there were no swans. I cross to Isleworth Ait, tip-toeing along a line of concrete blocks. There is a fringe of osier beds on the northern bank. Snipe are feeding in the shingly mud. I scramble over huge wooden piles, fifty to sixty feet long, larded with moss and fungi and slime.

On this island we need to refer not to any mere nature handbook, but to the *Red Data* book of the International Union of Nature Conservation for details of its most important inhabitants. The two-lipped door snail and the hairy German snail are both national rarities. They are in invisible repose somewhere in the detritus.

Today planning inspectors are impressed by the presence of such creatures. Few of us see them, and their tiny distinguishing features are apparent only to experts. But they frustrate the developers. This three hectare island in the Thames in London was highly esteemed by the builders. But a government inspector in 1985 decreed that the presence of the sensitive snails was sufficient cause to keep them out.

Martin Brandon, my guide to this secret enclave, leads me past gale-shattered trees, spared where they fell as useful habitat. We don't find the two-lipped door snail but we did come across a jew's ear fungus. It looks like the trophy from a seaside gang fight, pinky brown and a disconcerting fleshy colour, springing back on its base of dead wood after Martin flicks it, like a human ear.

Elsewhere on the river, the value of protected landscape is measured in hundreds of years. On the Thames in London thirty years, the age of this secondary woodland, is considered old. We squelch through its sodden ways, among tall and spindly sycamores, pitted with nest holes for greater and green woodpeckers. I must no longer malign the sycamore. Its status is being revised.

Received wisdom is that the sycamore is aggressive and uninteresting. But like some rehabilitated Russian revolutionary, in an age of arboreal *glasnost* this inhospitable tree has been re-evaluated. Surprisingly, it contains many more species than we believed. Indeed it compares well with the beech and hornbeam.

'The aim had been to remove the lot,' says Martin. 'But the attitude to it is changing in London. We thought "Hang on, we haven't got many trees anyway." The lichen people will tell you it's one of the best trees, and its pollen is supposed to be fantastic.'

Isleworth Ait's new neighbours on the north bank are reluctant to lose any trees at all. The trust tells them they have to cut *some* trees down because they are too aged. The residents respond they have just donated £5 to the Woodland Trust. 'So we will cut them down on the side they can't see,' says Martin. 'We do it subtly, because people don't always know what's good for them.'

Back to the river bank. At Isleworth, just beyond the ait, I encounter frustrated creativity. It is a comical sight, similar to arriving at a concert and finding an elephant sitting in the seat in front. I reach a gap in the bankside vegetation, opposite the Young Apprentice pub. The village is nicely displayed. Keith Noble had intended to spend an hour or two here painting this restful vista.

However, even as I stand idly contemplating All Saints church, the *Charlight* steals upriver towing four barges, on each of which is balanced a vast, shining steel cylinder the size of a moon rocket nose cone. *Charlight* swings round in the flowing tide and the four barges drift soundlessly, feather-light, into a position where they obscure the church and half the embankment.

Enter Mr Noble, bearing easel, artist's materials and portable seat. His annoyance is great. 'Well, that caps it, that really does. Just my blooming luck. Umpteen times I've been on the other side looking here, and I come across here to find this.'

Mr Noble has hurried along the towpath with an hour and twenty minutes to paint a half-imagined Isleworth river front. The afternoon sun does a twinkling tap dance on the river, which is reflected in the bulky rocket heads, the use of which I was to discover later.

> THESE places indeed lie all to the water and to the sun, so they are open on one side to the air: and perhaps the constant rising vapour from the river helps the plants against the poisonous quality of the city smoke.
>
> – *City Gardener*, Thomas Fairchild, 1722.

When the architectural history of the twentieth century is written, the 1960s will receive few plaudits. My worst riverbank view, created in that era of functional reaching for the sky, comes on the long north-westerly stretch of river beyond Isleworth.

Beckoning me maliciously at the end is the overpowering presence of six tower flat blocks. It isn't even as if the people in those grim higher regions enjoy living there. These flats cannot last. Already we are tearing down the mistakes of the 1960s. When they are flattened, their grateful occupants will regain the ground and the river will no longer have to compete with monsters.

From here it is five easy miles to Hammersmith. The path is becoming a wide urban walkway, with unlimited fresh air to left or right, linking a dense accumulation of interesting places. Because it wiggles, the river is also developing into such a roundabout route from A to B that I can be sure I shall only meet people who are here for fun. There won't be any hard-nosed citizens in a hurry.

In places the path is still not where it ought to be, right next to the river, but as riverside buildings are re-developed, the line of the old towpath must surely be reinstated.

After walking in seclusion for about half a mile, trying to avert my eyes from the flat blocks, I enter an open stage, brightly lit by the sun. Syon House is the backdrop on the other side of the river. The audience, mainly white-haired ladies, are on my right, their seats set firmly riverwards. They are on the edge of the Royal Botanic Gardens, Kew, gazing out from a formal vantage point at this background without a foreground.

My walk-on part ends with neither bow nor applause, and I exit right. The footpath follows the edge of Kew Gardens. Parts of the gardens are defended by that most primitive version of the keep-out notice, a stockade of broken glass topping a high brick wall. Men are snipping the grass to make walkways through the fringes of Kew.

Inside I meet the director, Professor Arthur Bell, who tells me about plants as an instrument of imperialism. Kew Gardens prospered as Great Britain's explorers flourished – surgeons doubling as biologists on distant voyages were detailed to look for economically important plants. This became the clearing house of the world's transplants. For two hundred years Kew has been the horticultural capital of the world.

Royal patronage selected this west London flood meadow. One observer commented that the original ground was 'dead flat, the soil barren without wood or water. It is not easy to produce anything even tolerable in gardening. But what was once desert is now an Eden.'

Professor Bell, as if acknowledging old friends, raises an arm towards living links with Kew's founder, Augusta, Princess of Wales. 'See that big gingko and that big pine. Two of the exotics she had brought to Kew.'

There had been royal links with Kew and Richmond since Norman times, and gardens around the palaces at Kew since George II's reign. But it was William Aiton, head-hunted from the Chelsea Physic Gardens by Augusta, who brought the tradition of systematic botany to Kew.

Augusta developed the gardens with the Earl of Bute. She put up Kew's first glass house: her envoys brought in robinia pseudo acasia from North America, wysteria and gingko from the Far East and pinea pinea from the Mediterranean. By 1789 there were 5,600 species of plants at Kew.

George III inherited his mother's riverside garden and fused it with the landward garden which had belonged to George II: hence the 'Botanic Gardens'. The plural usage has been devotedly copied throughout the world, such is the commanding influnce of Kew.

Under the gardens' first official director, William Hooker, the gardens grew to their present size of just over three hundred acres. Hooker's son, Sir Joseph Hooker, opened Kew's greatest era of acquisition, bringing back from the Himalaya twenty-seven species of rhododendron. Three million people a year came to the end of the horse tram line to behold them, the wonders of London.

Kew collectors, casting their spades ever wider, were always on duty. Collectors would diligently climb ever higher until they found the desired plant in an ecotype to match the chills of Britain. Colonial administrators sent material home. Kew-trained botanists set up gardens worldwide, a guaranteed source of materials for Kew.

Kew grows ten per cent of the world's flowering plants. 'Nobody believes me, but we have such a good climate,' said Professor Bell. 'There is a relatively small fluctuation between maximum summer and minimum winter temperatures. We can grow a lot of things outside which may do better back home but don't die here because it is neither too hot nor too cold. We can grow magnolias grandifloras, natives of South Texas by using south facing walls.'

The gardens' situation he concedes is 'terrible' on the sand and gravel of the river's flood plain. The secret is in the feeding: high quality manure from Britain's biggest dung heap, the royal stables and cavalry barracks.

Professor Bell explained the contribution Kew – 'the most beautiful scientific institute in the world' – has made to everyman's horticulture. 'It has brought in from the four corners of the world and still does, interesting and sometimes spectacularly beautiful plants. These have found their way into gardens throughout the country.'

He gives me a good up to date example of trial and error. A hundred and fifty years ago Kew had a fine collection of proteas from the Cape. Over the years they stopped flowering. In 1982 the Queen opened the refurbished temperate house where they were kept. The next year the curator noticed they were in bud. They flowered for the first time in 100 years. Why? The windows were clean and the heating was better.

I walk back to the river and head east. The Grand Union Canal, which would carry me almost to my door just north of the Chilterns in three days, slips north on my left, at the most important of all waterway junctions. At Chiswick Bridge the *Vicky*, the *Nutkin* and *Admiraal Tromp* strain their lines in the rising tide. There are red and pink roses at Magnolia Wharf.

Kew Bridge links the old county of Middlesex with Surrey. Long forgotten aldermen and councillors are still honoured on the bridge merely

151

for attending the opening ceremony. But I can find no mention of the men who actually built the bridge.

On the south bank is Strand on the Green, which still has the look of an eighteenth century village. I sit on the north bank with relaxed Chiswick society, outside the City Barge pub where the lord mayor's decorative barge *Maria Wood* used to be moored. The management does not trust the tide, which here seems to be flowing two ways. There is a heavy metal door to shut out potential disaster.

Chiswick is a sophisticated sort of place. Whistler lived here. Hogarth had his 'little country box by the Thames' off Chiswick Square from 1749 to 1764. It was narrowly missed by a wartime bomb. Today it is a museum, full of engravings. Rousseau also lived here, boarding at a grocer's shop.

My guide for the afternoon, James Wisdom, a college lecturer and chairman of the Chiswick Local History Society, defines the area. Chiswick is split into two by the Riverside Recreation Ground. First, tucked under Kew Bridge, is Strand on the Green. Beyond the recreation ground, three quarters of a mile on, is Chiswick Mall.

'Two halves, and very different.' He feels the sense of village most strongly in Strand on the Green. It retains many of its older residents from when it was nothing special. Until the late 1950s they repaired steel barges there, riveting from seven in the morning until nightfall. So it became a residential area with the massive increase in property prices much later than the Chiswick Mall.

A lot of people have known one another for a very long time here. There are people who can remember the Pierces, a fishing family with roots in the eighteenth century when Zoffany painted them. You can still find the old fishermen's names, but they have moved inland.

When Zoffany retired from the service of the Nabob of Oude, he rented Strand Ait and turned it into a pleasure ground, unvisited by the common throng. His gazebos and other attractions are all gone. But a mystery remains. How did he conduct his guests across at low tide when the boats were held back by the mud? Did they walk? It has been possible: a man walked from bank to bank at Westminster in 1846.

We walk on to the Mall. This too was a riverside village with fishermen, water taxi men and barge repairers in the seventeenth century. Some of the houses on the Mall date from that time. They are timber framed buildings gentrified in the eighteenth century behind brick façades. By the mid nineteenth century, the poorer men were elbowed out.

The Mall end of Chiswick James describes as an industrial village that has lost its industry. Even until the 1930s there were two hundred ton barges moored opposite the eyot being unburdened of bricks, timber, oil, coal and malt.

We walk by the waterfront, overlooking the eyot. This is the most attractive part of Old Chiswick, thick with fine houses. People who live here must tolerate more curious glances into their living rooms than anywhere else on the Thames.

In the twentieth century, Chiswick lost its shopping street and its function to road development, and became an island, frozen in space between two massive systems, river and road.

Today the industry is architecture. 'Most of the owners are architects. They won a Civic Trust award for the way they built flood defences into their houses, as glass panels.

'Now it's a marooned place, high class residential but there is still enough evidence to show what it must have been like not too long ago.'

We pass Walpole House, at one time home of the actor Beerbohm Tree. Some think it was the inspiration for Miss Pinkerton's Academy in *Vanity Fair*. At the far end is the site of the Chiswick Press, a nest of mid-Victorian typography, and an inspiration to William Morris.

Chiswick's church is dedicated to St Nicholas, fishermen's patron saint. King Edward VII was the village's most famous resident. In 1903, in honour of his coronation, its ringers achieved a rare peal of grandsire triples – 5,040 changes in three hours. It is another of the putative resting places for Oliver Cromwell.

'We are very closely knit. Originally people came to the suburbs to get away from the country villages and made London villages in their own way. It's astonishing how small and interconnected a place like Chiswick is, not a soulless mass of suburban houses.

'The Thames connects a series of villages. The bargemen would marry their sons along the river, down to Battersea, Lambeth and Greenwich and build up their business. We are as close to Rochester as to Wembley. I'm sure they would rather take a ton of stone to Rochester than Wembley.'

He leaves me with a plea. 'Could you say something about walking the Thames at other times than fine days. On Strand on the Green, particularly if the tide is high, or a rainy, stormy day it's just breathtaking. There's such a strong connection between land and water and the elements.

'I get so depressed when the amateur artists come and paint the same chocolate box picture when the sun shines. The really exciting pictures are the ones that capture the drama of the water. It's a threatening, competitive, forceful, dangerous thing here, not a tame little river. How the old bargemen could manoeuvre their craft in the middle of the night out there is beyond me.'

I walk back to Barnes Bridge. In the recreation ground, I come across the Riverside Health Centre, a shrine to exclusive, high-price fitness. I peep

153

through a chink in the fence and spot a cluster of medical monitoring points, where patrons may take inter-lap cardiograph tests.

I pass the unlikely outpost of Northern England sport, the Fulham Rugby League Club, and cross to the south bank at Barnes Bridge. The Thames has now achieved full adulthood. It is a very big river. From where I stand this brimful river, empty of boats, accounts for a larger proportion of what I can see than anything else, including sky.

It is time to contemplate the salmon, which is certainly not the fish I would have expected to encounter here, the site of William Morris's utopian dream, as unlikely as the recolonisation of Dartmoor by the golden eagle.

Morris, in his romantic vision *News From Nowhere*, had his time-travelling hero discover a salmon fishery at Hammersmith in the early twenty-first century: 'But of course the nets are not always in use. We don't want salmon *every* day of the season.' It is one of the few prophesies in the book likely to be fulfilled.

Dr Banks of Thames Water meets me here and tells me the story. In December 1974 a salmon swam into the power station infall lower down the Thames and survived, where no other salmon had ventured for about 140 years. It was Noah's dove. It proved that the Thames, in one of its most bilious reaches, now contained enough oxygen to sustain a living fish.

For about five years salmon entered the Thames in ones and twos, mistaking its dark, writhing waters for their ancestral river, possibly the Hampshire Avon. By 1979 Thames Water began a restocking programme. The first significant return took place in 1981.

The salmon had declined rapidly in the first thirty years of the nineteenth century. The fish had certainly been abundant. A 1793 painting shows netting of salmon at Putney, where it was a daily sight. As late as 1804, sixty salmon a day were taken at Maidenhead. The last salmon is believed to have struggled up through the Stygian murk of the Thames as far as Twickenham in 1830.

The causes of the decline were the poisoning of the river, the new pound locks which drowned out spawning areas, and the dredging which deepened the channel. By 1832 the salmon were gone. From then on the river could not possibly have supported fish. It stank. Its oxygen level was zero.

It was not until the massive cleansing of the estuary and the tideway in the 1960s, that the authorities considered it might be clean enough to think again. Lord Thurso donated fry from his Caithness hatchery to Thames Water. The Hon Edward Davies put some into a Cotswold stream. Then the power station fish arrived.

The first salmon taken by a rod on the Thames was landed by motor mechanic Russell Doig in September 1983. It was a six and three quarter pound fish taken in the rough water close to Chertsey Weir. He also collected £100 from Lord Chelwood who had wagered the money against such a feat.

Now an estimated five hundred salmon swim up through London in the best years. Where do they go, when they return to the wide sea? 'We wish we knew,' he said. 'They have turned up off the north-east coast, Scotland, the Faroes, off the west coast of Ireland and west Greenland. Wherever salmon go, ours go too.'

The biggest obstacle is the lack of fish ladders at locks. The locks were built without reference to migrating fish, because there hadn't been any for 150 years. The adult salmon finds the lock and weir serious barriers to reaching its spawning ground. However, a salmon is known to have reached Godstone weir above Oxford.

The new Thames salmon will not be encouraged to pass much beyond Pangbourne. The task is to produce a slightly different kind of fish that can spawn in the chalk streams below this point.

Nobody knows where the salmon went when they had the run of the river. The evidence is only anecdotal. In prehistoric and historic times they may have spawned in the main river itself, where the gravel structure was different. But, on this river, there are many interconnections. Surely salmon once slipped through here on their way to the river Ock, above Abingdon.

I walk into Hammersmith over the bridge, splendid in its green and red lattice work, smart wooden red rail and heraldic shields. London begins to roar.

8

FRESH from the streets of London, the odours of the Underground Railway still in his nostrils, the vapour of its smoky streets still lingering in his lungs, a little heated, it may be . . . he walks rapidly for a brief space along the towing path, and then perforce halts in another and a new land.

– *Royal River*, 1885. Bloomsbury Books, 1985.

IN THE NEXT seven miles to Vauxhall the Thames becomes a fully fledged metropolitan river. William Morris lived here as well as on the Oxfordshire Thames. There is a theatre which ought to embrace the Thames, but cannot afford to, and the river's favourite ornithological service station.

I will meet a man who assures me that the Thames has no rival on Earth, pass the doorsteps of the most exclusive riverside addresses, in Chelsea; and, in Battersea, the most productive plot, in terms of nature, on the riverbank.

Today's jaunt is a mere two and a half mile walk along a bank congested with retarding meetings. I walk into Hammersmith in search of William Morris. Articulated lorries thump on the flyover. I blunder down the ninth out of sixteen exits from the Underground Station for the Metropolitan, District and Piccadilly lines. The Thames is now served from all points of the capital on the public transport network.

I needn't have looked so far. William's Morris's London residence was Kelmscott House in Upper Mall, a few yards from the river. I have come to pay my respects to this formidable Victorian conservationist, in the days when wanton destruction of wildlife was routine and opposition to this destruction was eccentric.

Once, his temper detonated by the felling of an avenue of willows along the towpath between Hammersmith Bridge and Barnes, on the opposite bank, Morris took his protest to the imposing offices of the River Thames Conservancy Board. It was a spectacular assault on the vandals.

156

The Chelsea Harbour Development.

'In architecture the pride of man, his triumph over gravitation, his will to power, assume a visible form.

– Friedrich Nietzsche.

His friend Sir Arthur Richmond records the conversation. They were ushered into a vast empty boardroom, in front of an enormous table, writes Philip Henderson in *William Morris, His Life, Work and Friends*. Enter the chairman. 'We've come to ask you savage, bloody chaps why the hell you've cut down that pleasant grove of willows,' said Morris. 'We mean to kick up the Devil's own row about the bloody affair and demand at the very least a reparation from the bloody board.' After several exchanges in equally intemperate language, the chairman unexpectedly agreed that fresh trees be planted. They stand today.

Morris was always fuming about the treatment of the river, writes Henderson. 'He took any opportunity to berate the board's representatives, in each case his own language overtopping that of the retired seamen in the board's employ.'

Near Morris's old home, the Riverside Studios, hugging the bank, hang the following accolade as a permanent inspiration to themselves and proof to any confused visitor who was about to ask in the facing corner shop on Crisp Road, that they are in the right place: 'An artistic powerhouse, the like of which exists nowhere else in London.' (Irvine Wardle, *The Times*).

So what am I to make of the two people incongruously dolled up in mid-morning, she in a shining gold dress and he in a tuxedo, primed to entertain? Well, even artistic powerhouses have to make money.

When the Riverside isn't challenging the West End as a flashing beacon of artistic endeavour in Hammersmith, it reverts to its original incarnation as TV studio.

Today it is an *Opportunity Knocks* audition. So Gold Dress and Tuxedo may yet begin a career where Tony Hancock finished his. When it opened as a television studio in 1954 it was claimed to be the most advanced in the world. They made enduring monochrome testimonies of the 1960s here: *Z Cars*, *Dr Who* and *Dixon of Dock Green*. And bearing out an evolving theory of mine that there is a royal association for most riverside halts, Prince Andrew came here in 1966 to favour the five hundredth edition of *Play School* with a visit.

If there were a river person's theatre, as there are river pubs, this would be it. The land approach is vulgar and prosaic. If funding for the arts were not so tight, river-borne patrons might glide to the front door, and pay somebody to moor their boat. But they cannot. The studios, when they were studios, faced inland, to the taxis of arriving artistes. The part facing the river has always been a muddle of storerooms.

'We have plans. No, dreams. No, plans to open out on to the river, make a glass fronted restaurant with a walkway,' says Christine Cort. 'Change all this area.' This sounds like the optimism of the person who having clawed away from the brink a number of times, imagines that on the next visit she will grow wings and fly over the void.

The Riverside Studios endures periodic financial crises. 'We always weather the storms. Last year the gallery was threatened with closure. We set up a rescue committee. Well, it's a wonderful building. Unique character.'

The Riverside wears the fashionable poverty of the artistic establishment, challenging on the strength of its ideas and its players alone. A brief tour reveals not an inch of architectural accomplishment.

However it has very serviceable, heavily soundproofed double doors, a relic of the acoustic purity of television days. There are lots of exposed ceilings and breeze blocks. 'We haven't tried to disguise them. We can't. We haven't the money. Anyway, why should we? We don't think the actors really mind.'

However the public might mind wandering around in Crisp Road for a time trying to find the way in, and then mistaking the actual entrance for a tradesman's door, down a dingy alley. It is a most unlikely way into a theatre. 'The business next door is so embarrassed with our façade that they are giving us some money to move it on to the road.'

Meanwhile the Riverside's studios are earning money. In one studio Tuxedo is crooning in saccharin tones to Gold Dress before some sceptical TV persons. In another the black reggae production, *Oh Babylon*, is in rehearsal. In a third, planners are conducting a seminar on traffic flow in critical urban situations.

Christine speaks of the theatre's spirit of adventure. 'Our difficulty is we are not on the theatre circuit. You have to really want to make the trip here. We *have* to be better.'

I find a token reference to the Thames on my way out. The designer of the carpet which leads to the theatre's new cinema achieved it by weaving a river motif of the wavy lines into the carpet. Otherwise, I might as well be in Croydon.

I cross Hammersmith Bridge and find, a few yards to my right, the second best school on the river, oddly displaced. St Paul's School used to be opposite St Paul's Cathedral where it was founded in 1509 by John Colet, Dean of St Pauls to provide free education for 153 boys. So why is it here, in nondescript blocks which speak nothing of its eminence?

On its original site, it was destroyed in the Fire of London, rebuilt in the same place, twice, and eventually moved to Hammersmith, north of the river. In the war, the boys safely decamped to Berkshire, the 11th Army was garrisoned at the school and Old Pauline Field Marshal Montgomery planned the Normandy Invasion there.

In the 1960s the school sold its Hammersmith site for £3.5 million, bought some old reservoirs on this thumb of Surrey land and reincarnated itself. What it lacks in architectural flair, the school makes up for in financial security and the very best listings in the good school guides. Today it has 785 pupils, including the original number of 153 scholars entitled to wear a silver badge of a fish signifying the Biblical miracle of the fishes, and eighty staff.

Not so many prime ministers here but an impressive trawl of past pupils includes Milton, Peypys, Chesterton, the First Duke of Marlborough, playwrite Peter Shaffer and artistic polymath Jonathan Miller.

Under Hammersmith Bridge two scullers skim up on the low tide. Before I enter the towpath I must ponder the relevance to me of this notice, full of antique proscription. 'No person is allowed to ride or drive any horse, or drive any cart, waggon or other vehicle, or ride, wheel or in any way use any bicycle or tricycle over or upon any part of the towpath.' I curse myself for not hiring a monocycle for the day, to remain aloof from these ancient, fussy conditions, and immediately come within a whisker of being thrown down by a furiously-ridden bicycle.

Here the Thames curves south-east into the second bend of its wag through London. I come upon an overgrown metal paddock pleasantly perfumed with elderflower, rusting iron gate ajar. This was once a place of easeful recreation, reserved for the employees in the large building on the right. This turns out to be the Harrods Furniture Depository.

On the other bank is Palace Wharf, another contemporary version of bankside recreation, set to curling metal staircases, slanting glazed roofs, pot plants and tables on a patio, laid for morning coffee. It was built by the Richard Rogers Partnership, having been discovered when it was a derelict oil depot by one of the directors when he took a wrong turning.

I take the hint from the easeful elegance opposite, spread my newspaper on the shingle and open my Thermos flask. Some dusky London pigeons swagger across the river, expecting provender.

I resume my walk and pass a low hedge of flowering brambles through which about half a dozen bees are dutifully working. Behind it mounted policemen attempt some low jumps in a field, next to Barn Elms reservoirs.

A redheaded lady on bicycle, with a basket and baby on baby seat, pass in sensible contravention of the aforementioned sign. I come upon a bust of Steve Fairbairn, 'Famous oarsman and coach, 1862 to 1938'. This point is exactly one mile from the start of the boat race course, (which runs from Putney to Mortlake) informs the legend. Here Fairbairn might have seen his glorious charges at full exertion. Fulham Football Club stands hard against the other bank. Its directors have the best view of all.

The Boat Race, along with every popular sporting occasion, is now sponsored by a commercial interest. This, in the view of one newspaper this summer, is a bad thing. How the status of the race has declined, he notes. But few complaints about Thames developments are new.

'The fact is, and becomes more and more plain every year, that the boat race is becoming vulgarised,' (*Dictionary of the Thames* , 1893). 'Cabmen, butchers boys and omnibus drivers sport the colours of the Universities in all directions. The dark blue of Oxford and the light blue of Cambridge fill all the hosiers' shops, and are flaunted in all sorts of indescribable company.'

Crowds were huge. Dickens speculated 'at what particular moment the mass of spectators on Hammersmith Bridge would break it down and plunge with the ruins into the river'. The bridge stayed up, and the race remains on this reach, despite the writer's suggestion that 'removal from metropolitan waters would not be lamented by lovers of genuine sport.'

Alongside this big wobble in the Thames, on my right, there is a matrix of well-ordered water, Barn Elms reservoirs. People come here to observe the ornithologically extraordinary.

In the spring, the reservoir's intersections are commanded by Canada geese, hissing menace from horizontal, extended necks, all black except for a warning white collar. Like avian traffic lights set at red in all four directions, they are defending the indefensible, nests made on the stark, flat concrete.

There have been four nesting pairs in the past five years, Rupert Hastings tells me. 'The fishermen can't stand it. They pay five pounds a day to come here.' The geese build a sprawling, untidy tangle several feet across. The female lies low while the male flails crazily at intruders. Question the Canada goose's breeding strategy if you like, but don't make light of the advance of the most successful big bird on the river.

Not quite at pest proportions, Rupert concludes, but now very common. Lawns are encrusted with their droppings. No area of short grass is now safe from this over-rich fertilising.

The goose, introduced into England in the 1600s as an ornamental waterfowl, was held in check until fifteen years ago. Now big flocks set down all along the riverside, breeding at reservoirs and gravel pits and larger lakes. For many it is the most familiar wild goose. It flies in majestic formation.

But ornithologists are uneasy about a big bird that blunders into a vacant ecological niche. 'There is the impression that it is becoming too common,' says Rupert. 'It has all happened so recently. Very small numbers up to the early 1970s, then rapid growth ever since. Just when you notice it is getting really common, in the next year there are twice as many, and it is ultra common.'

On glum winter days of roaring wind and tearing clouds, Rupert comes here in his lunch hour to train his telescope on visiting marvels. He lifts it to a skein of pochard, pelting in overhead with rapid wing beats, and tells the remarkable story of the London cormorants.

On any winter day they can be seen sitting in a formal line on the water's edge like crusty old aldermen. Virtually all of them breed on St Margaret's Island off the coast of Pembrokeshire. In the autumn they retreat east, possibly following the Severn, then pick up the Thames, hurrying through to urban sanctuary.

The cormorants spend their nights roosting on Queen Elizabeth and Wraysbury reservoirs, feeding entirely on fish which they determinedly pursue underwater, homing in with solid webbed-footed thrusts. For some reason December is a good month on this reservoir. They can often be seen loitering in the centre of London around Vauxhall and Westminster bridges.

Barn Elms is sparse, forbidding, high and exposed. A bleak place to the wintering human. To the long travelling bird on high over much of west and south London, it flashes a welcome. Anything heading up or down the river will, snipping off the corner of this promontory, find Barn Elms.

Two goldeneye struggle up to the parapet and flop over. A straggle of yellow wagtails work the water's edge. Bird life is turned over as if by some cosmic store manager. 'We never know what we are going to see here next,' says Rupert.

I coax out his finest recollections. 'Three Arctic skuas in mid September. They went straight through. A friend saw two long tailed skuas drifting over for four minutes. There are only a handful of records in the London area.

'I saw an Alpine swift over those houses,' he points towards Church Road.' Pretty staggering. It's a Mediterranean bird, several times the size of the British swift. It stayed here a few days. I've seen some extraordinary birds here. Bonaparte's Gull from America and gull-billed tern. They stayed for twenty minutes. Still the only records for London.'

Barn Elms has some of the biggest horizons in this flat part of London. A shaft of sunlight illuminates the water from the huge clouds, like a wartime floodlight in reverse.

A medium-paced airliner drawls down to Heathrow. I regain the footpath through a gap in the fence and encounter at low water some heavy litter, which includes a motor cycle engine and four supermarket trollies. I have been walking through a paper chase since Hammersmith. Nevertheless, a toddler, programmed to good works upon the pot, turns up an exaggerated nose at some horse droppings. 'Disgusting, the horses,' he remarks. The offending beasts, returning from the police jumping grounds, trip lightly in procession along The Embankment.

The child ought to be a mascot of this tidy-minded borough. 'Welcome to Wandsworth, the Brighter Borough' extols a blue and white sign. Wandsworth has marked its edge with a bold promenade, with a strong wooden rail over blue and grey railings.

There is a line of boatyards on my right. I meet Bill Colley, Thames waterman, freeman of the river, racing boat builder. He disparages his trade.

'It's a potty business to go into. Everything you want to buy to build a boat is a problem.' He opens a tin, half-full of shiny copper nails. 'Nails like that are priceless. You can't buy them. I don't know anywhere in the world. When this tin is empty, that's it. They have all gone. I've got thousands of sizes that I don't use, but the size I do use I'm down to half a tin.'

For the craftsman, the next size up simply won't do. 'These are three quarter by eighteen pins, made in Charlton down by the Barrier. A few pounds of those and I'm virtually set up for life. That firm could supply the three companies who used them forever with fifty-six pounds. The one I want just now is the five by eight, two hundred and nineteen gauge square: they just aren't there. How do I make do without? I haven't cracked it yet. I will have to find a way. Instead of five by eight, I could use three by four and when all those are gone, use one inch. But I'm talking about ideals, and they are nearly gone. So I have to lower my standards.'

Bill is secretary of the London Rowing Club in the same way that master printers are commissionaires for want of any appropriate employment to test their skills. He builds racing boats in his spare time. Strapped to the wall behind him is a single sculling boat he built in 100 hours. 'My record is seventy-two hours. That was a long time ago. I'm blowing my own trumpet, but I don't know anyone who has done much better than that.

'That one's not finished. It's maturing. I left it there because I'm fed up with it, to be quite honest.' But it's a very special boat. It contains the last of the wood he bought when an old Thames builder Edmund Phelps died in 1978. 'I bought all the stuff left, and that's some of the last of it. A beautiful piece of Honduras cedar.'

We are talking across a boat, the product of a master craftsman, 'a very interesting thirty-five year old eight, built by George Pocock of Seattle.' It illustrates a number of points: that the best and the good have deserted such fine wooden boats, for no good reason, even though these craft are as good as the plastic boats that supplanted them.

Bill believes that Pocock, who emigrated from England, was 'possibly the best boat builder in the world.' Pocock's boat is in Canadian yellow cedar, used by British builders until the 1960s. 'Beautiful: no grain, just lovely and straight. The Japanese ship building industry has discovered this wood and told the Canadians they will buy every stick that grows. So that's it.'

Yale University brought the boat to Henley in 1953, and in the usual way, rather that pay its fare home, sold it to the LRC which has owned it ever since. He guides me through a spectrum of woods: 'spruce, yellow cedar, spruce, ash, spruce, pine, western red cedar.'

He was talking to some young members of about twenty the night before. 'Cor, bloody hell. What's that old thing?' they remarked, referring to Pocock's masterpiece.

'I told them if they were to get themselves together, this thing could be entered for the Grand Challenge Cup at Henley and win. Pocock said in his book there are no fast boats, only fast crews. It's thirty-five years old but it's sound. There's not a ripple or a bend or a wobble on it. But they wouldn't consider starting in it.

'It is only used by the old men, the Irregulars over fifty. It's a terrible shame really. She's been hammered and busted and banged but she still goes. And when she is back on the water, she won't be looked after. But she could last another thirty years. Some of the features in this boat, people are only just getting around to doing now.'

He is replacing the original canvas snout, torn by some of the club's lesser navigators, with 'nasty blue plastic'. Using plastic affronts Bill's sensibilities. Plastic forced him out of business. He worked for companies in Hammersmith, Richmond and Kingston for thirty years. 'Then plastic comes along and out you go.'

Plastic and wood are the difference between a suit from a High Street store and one from Savile Row. 'There are bespoke suits. Well, I do the bespoke boat. It will cost a lot of money. I was always too cheap, all my life. Then the plastic people came along and built boats. They didn't build them: they put them together somehow. And they charged more money than wooden boats which is very wrong. Now if I do anything, I make sure I charge more than plastic.'

I do not suppose I reveal anything the insider doesn't know, but the University Boat Race boats are made from plastic. 'And not only plastic, but foreign plastic.'

Upstairs in the club, Bill leads me along squeaky wooden corridors. He defines the club's atmosphere by comparing it to a well-appointed boating centre that has none. Hurst Pierrepoint, the National Water Centre in Nottingham, new, well-equipped, but no atmosphere. Henley and this club have no fittings but an abundance of illustrious spirits recalling past achievements. A craft, slung from the ceiling, was used in the 1936 Berlin Olympics. 'I just resurrected it. It won a silver in front of Hitler.'

A painting of Henley Reach is stained with beer. Several times a year club members meet for dinner and as they become exceedingly drunk beer sploshes over this famous interior. The money raised goes to a good cause, this year to restore the besmirched painting.

The club, once one of the finest rowing clubs, has been in shallow decline for some years, eclipsed by the Thames Tradesmen, the Tideway Scullers, and the Lee Rowing Association. There is no fresh paint on the achievements boards. The club has not entered a team for the Grand Challenge Cup at Henley since 1976. Until then it had entered in every year since 1856.

'There is a nucleus of fifteen or twenty top oarsmen, who flow from club to club. We have not been fortunate to have them. Right now we have a good eight, but it's anyone's guess whether they will stay. A lot of rowing is fashion. It's the same with the places they buy their boats from – it's a bit like the smart place for ladies' clothes.'

Outside the club, small boats hang in the tide like obedient dogs on leashes. On the pavement of The Embankment a traffic warden and a Metro driver are soundlessly acting out a familiar scene. Traffic warden: (by means of a look of disappointed puzzlement): 'I am surprised at you.' Embarrassed parker (by means of a sickly smile): 'The open door, it means I never meant to stay. I'm leaving this very moment.'

A hundred yards on is Putney Bridge, the destination in the Ramblers Association guide to the Thames Walk. I pass it, and venture on, as a batsman might, reluctant to throw his wicket away at 150 when 200 beckons.

> TWENTY bridges from Tower to Kew –
> (Twenty bridges or twenty-two) –
> Wanted to know what the River knew,
> For they were young and the Thames was old.
>   – *The River's Tale*, Rudyard Kipling.

At Putney Bridge, developers have conspired to force me away from the river's edge. But I must be bold. There *is* an alternative route.

I descend past the church, down on to the foreshore. This is an odd, slightly unnerving experience, descending into a nether world of furtive riparian ghosts. I pick a way over unsavoury, slimy, odorous stones, mindful for the awkward angle of surface which could fling me sideways into the mud.

I struggle on in this manner for a few hundred yards. At last I am defeated by the evil glue. A police launch hovers in mid channel, in routine suspicion. I climb a stout, iron staircase and emerge in Wandsworth Park.

From here it is five miles to Vauxhall Bridge, on the edge of Central London. 'Farewell to the characteristic scenery of the Thames, farewell to all natural beauty. Its waters have now become a great highway of commerce,' wrote *Royal River*.

165

I am now entering the London of awful reputation.

'Dank and foul, by the smoky town in its murky cowl;

Foul and dank, by wharf and sewer and slimy bank,' wrote Charles Kingsley. Grim warnings.

I misdirect myself into a little backwater of bright and ephemeral light industry, out of which useful small items will emerge in bubble-packed plastic. A lorry-load of raw materials, used to make this efficient packaging, blocks my way.

One man in a suit is holding up earnestly for another's inspection an artefact which might strike a primitive Amazonian tribesman as the most amazing thing he had ever seen. The man to which the object is being demonstrated is also marvelling, as if at some rediscovered truth. The object is a conventional, old-fashioned tap, clearly destined for some exciting new marketing venture.

There is no crossing at Bell Lane Creek, where it joins the Thames in a dull concrete channel. I am thrown out as far as the South Circular road, a few hundred yards inland, in order to bridge this sullen water, and finally regain the river close to Wandsworth Bridge.

Beyond the bridge, a West Indian man in blue woollen cap, his lady companion clutching a bunch of yellow flowers, is trying to attract the attention of a lady who is gardening on the deck of the *Queen Philippa*. The lady does not reply. Her garden has no front gate. The Queen has been here for a long time. I have seen her in old photographs. Those who dwell on her exclude the world by the simple removal of the gangplank.

Behind St Mary's Church, Battersea, there is joyous animation, lit by the high afternoon sun – playgroup of dancing children, and seated mothers at ease.

Battersea bridge, is another of London's iron bridges, metalwork picked out in blue and orange paint, with a whale's white underbelly. A number 19 bus driven by a black lady hurtles over it.

On a marble plinth is an eloquent intertwining of figures, depicting hope. A man and a woman are launching in their upstretched arms a child, which in turn is releasing a dove. A plaque identifies it as John Ravera's *In Town*, commissioned and on loan from Wates Built Homes.

I and the statue stand alone in a low amphitheatre with several low tiers, in a herringbone pattern of red bricks. A lady in a floral dress and white cycle helmet freewheels in at a slant.

Over Battersea Bridge Road a commissionaire is the only visible figure in a five storey office of dark, reflective glass, which conceals enterprise and indolence. On the opposite bank is Chelsea Wharf, with its imitation Kew Pagoda rising to a gold cap. I cross the bridge and investigate.

The Belvedere Tower that looks like Kew's pagoda has at its point a large computer-controlled ball which rises and falls with the tide. It is the sort of extra that the residents of the eighteen flats contained within the Belvedere might expect and can afford.

The Chiswick Harbour Development, designed by Moxley Jenner, is as exclusive a place to live as anywhere on the river. And why not. People who tidy up derelict coal wharves which clearly are not going to handle coal ever again can afford to build as expensively as the market will bear.

The lady in the sales office reels off fabulous prices for over four hundred apartments and forty town houses, served by their own shopping centre, marina and health club. There are also offices and light-flooded studios. Almost as an afterthought she mentions what is to me the best reason of all for living here. You need never encounter another traffic jam. Fifteen minutes, non stop by boat to Westminster Pier, twenty to the City, thirty-five minutes to Docklands – surely the most trouble-free commuting prospect anywhere.

A few hundred yards east, along Cheyne Walk, Mrs Gloria King, who speaks in a soft Bostonian accent, introduces me graciously into the society of Chelsea boat people. The boats are pressed together like bananas on a stem, but it is more like a village High Street than Aberdeen Harbour in Hong Kong. 'Everybody knows everybody else. There are a lot professional and theatrical people here. The actresses Claire Bloom and Dorothy Tutin were residents. There is somebody at the other end who did something so brave they made a film of her.'

Mrs King leads me aboard *Joseph Conrad*, built 1892, a working clipper barge sailed over from Holland. A painting of a clipper barge in its working life, full of sail and energy, hangs in the saloon. Mrs King's late husband had her converted ten years ago by the Chelsea Yacht and Boat Company. He died shortly afterwards and Mrs King decided to stay on. 'My husband didn't live to see her completed. It took a lot of courage to go on with it, but I'm glad I did.'

The *Joseph Conrad* projects further out into the Thames than any other boat here. 'Very few kitchen sinks with a view like that.' She can clearly see the Battersea, Albert and Chelsea Bridges, and the Chelsea and Battersea old churches.

'I see swans and cormorants. There is a wonderful dance in the sky every evening from the starlings. The most beautiful choreography. They roost under Battersea bridge.'

Mrs King has taken the highest refinement of life ashore on to the *Joseph Conrad*. She is a pianist. Her piano and harpsichord were lowered through the hatch into her study, which was then composed around them.

In the high tide the boat can rise by as much as twenty-five feet, a steep walk down the gangplank to the Chelsea Embankment. Is her river life disturbed by tempest? 'The boat rocks when the tide is high. The chandeliers are secured in four places.' Objects are secured, hinged or settled on non-slip plastic.

In the dining room-cum-study is a gypsy stove, with glowing fire, ('my delight enhancer'). In front of it basks the riverside cat, loosely owned by the entire community. It recently presented Mrs King with four kittens. 'The river is a wonderful place. I'm up at the crack of dawn and I rejoice in it.'

In 1520 Sir Thomas More built his country house at Chelsea. By the sixteenth century it was 'the village of palaces'. The Duke of Norfolk and Earl of Shrewsbury all had splendid homes here. Later Swift, Addison, Carlyle, Leigh Hunt, and Rossetti gave it character.

There is a long established and illustrious artists' group, the Chelsea Arts Club, close to the river bank. Its members have included Whistler, Steer, Brangwyn, George Clausen and Sickert. But there was never a 'Thames school' to compare with the Seine's. No Monet, Sisley, Seurat and Morisot who made the Seine just west of Paris world famous by 1900. However there are some fine works, including Monet's *Waterloo Bridge*, and Whistler's *Chelsea Reaches*.

I set off east along Cheyne Walk. Once near here a Chelsea pensioner asked me the way back to his Hospital. He went on his way 'with his scarlet gabardine, flaming along the ways like a travelling fire,' in the words of an old guidebook.

The Walk's Queen Anne houses are a long list of famous addresses. George Eliot at number four; Whistler at 98; Sir Marc and his son Isambard, that constant influence on the Thames, lived next door at 98; the prodigous walker Hilaire Belloc at 104; Steer at 109. The artist Turner lived under the name of Booth at 119.

Rossetti, not content with distant Kelmscott kept a small zoo here, including peacocks. Later leases prohibited the keeping of this noisy bird.

At intervals along the riverbank there are statues. Sir Thomas More, his cross picked out in gold, and other figures, comfortably seated in timeless repose. The body of More, without the head, was interred in 'Chelsey Church, near the middle of the south wall.' I pass F. Derwent Woodra's (1871-1926) *Nude*, which has stood here, inspiring the taxi drivers for fifty years, and recross on the Albert Bridge.

A notice carries what surely is the most bizarre prohibition on any bridge across the Thames. 'All troops must break step when walking over the bridge.' This might suggest it is also the flimsiest of the major Thames bridges.

The din on the north bank is slightly absorbed by a line of plane trees, the very trees which the Victorian writer Edmund Ollier hoped 'every season' would make 'thicker and more umbrageous'. I enter Battersea Park. Two women in jungle fatigue hats are painting the view opposite. Once this was one of the more unsavoury waterside locales. It was here that the Duke of Wellington fought a duel with Lord Winchilsea in 1829. Both men compromised their reputations as marksmen by firing wide and high respectively. Nobody was hurt, unless a pigeon caught it from Winchilsea's shot.

There was further decline. The place was filled with wide boys running Sunday fairs in the low marshes. The builder Cubitt suggested to Queen Victoria's Commission for Improving the Metropolis that a royal park be built. The government bought 320 acres, setting aside 198 for the park. The surface was raised and the park laid out by Sir James Pennethorne and opened in 1853. It became fashionable as one of the first venues for bicycle riding in 1896 when the new craze was banned in Hyde Park.

The Festival of Britain Gardens, within it, were laid out in 1951 by John Piper and Osbert Lancaster. In November the Veteran car run to Brighton starts from here.

At the far end of Battersea Park I find Brian Mist. He puts away his gun in deference to me. 'I thought you might have been a squirrel lover. I hate squirrels.' He has been shooting them, properly licenced and with the blessing of the Battersea park police, on a part of London named after him. Few people get such an opportunity to defend personalised territory.

You cannot on any part of the Thames bank find a purse fashioned from such an unpromising sow's ear.

First, the welcome. Brian, a fit fifty-three with rimless glasses, and swinging binoculars, was waiting for me at the portals of his pitch. Behind me, buses thunder down Queenstown Road, tugging vortices of dust, past the Marco Polo building, a glassy coated temple, home of The *Observer*. In the background is Battersea Power station, designed by Sir Giles Scott and opened in 1937, and off which workmen were noisily knocking bits before turning it into a stately pleasure dome. There is a fine tradition for fun on the south bank.

In 1968 Brian gave up his last job, as a roofing contractor: 'I was a bungling businessman.' He is now the apparently indispensable, unpaid proprietor of Mist's Pitch, a fragment of Battersea Park which in 1985 the GLC decided to fence off and declare a nature reserve.

Why 'Pitch' and not 'Patch'? 'Not my decision. I looked it up in the dictionary. Think of a stall in the market, a place where a man has his business, where one is active.'

The pitch is famous. It has been on television, in the national press, and in Wandsworth council's own newspaper. Brian is disappointed that the media takes so much and gives so little. 'Out of all the publicity, with TV crews spending hours here, I received just thirty-five pounds, and even then I had to wring it out of them.'

The money is for his winter bird feed fund. Blue and great tits and greenfinches scrummage gratefully over three hanging feeders. Like a tantalised tabloid reporter, I pay Brian a certain sum, not because I believe in cheque book journalism but because I think his cause deserves it! However this means he will now tell me his story and let out previously unpublished secrets.

He is cautious about what people write about him. One book referred to the pitch as a 'dump'. 'I phoned them up and corrected them. Does it look like a dump? There are winter aconites, wild daffodils, genuine snowdrops. It isn't a dump is it? I have even read that my family name is Nordic. The first I knew of it.' He does, however, endorse an opinion that the perfume here is like nowhere else in central London.

Battersea gardens are a by product of the Thames. Until 1836 it was marshland. 'There were swallow tail butterflies and marsh harriers here then. The flowers must have been marvellous.' It was filled with spoil from the excavations of Victoria docks. The pitch is on a man-made hill.

I listen to a list of noteable visitors: hoopoe, firecrest, pied flycatcher, wheatear, reed warbler, lesser whitethroat, turtle dove, hobby, tree creeper. 'I'm one of the few people to record the wood warbler in London. I could go on and on.' His naming of birds is touchingly old-fashioned: yellow buntings for yellowhammers; blue tits become titmice; the tawny owl is the brown owl.

This was not a test but when did he see the hoopoe, a bird that normally finds France a perfectly acceptable northernmost limit for its migration? 'The twenty-first of October nineteen eighty-four. It sat on that tree, then went south.'

It is a pleasant, vaguely self-congratulatory business, swopping accounts of rarities. I have but one claim to offer, of clouded yellow butterflies near my doorstep in 1983. This was the year of an invasion by this rare Mediterranean butterfly, the best for many years.

His clouded yellow story, from the same year, is a wonderful study of the sane man in the healthy grip of enthusiasm. He was showing a colleague a speckled wood. Then a male clouded yellow danced into view. 'It settled on that ragwort. I said "See that. I can't believe it, Les." I couldn't get him to understand.

'I rang a friend at the British Museum. I had to tell somebody. At ten o'clock it was off like a rocket. Than a second bugger flew in over the elm and landed on the scentless may weed.' He rang his friend again. 'Might it have turned round and come back?' inquired his friend. 'Now I ask you, *do* clouded yellows come back?'

We arrive at Brian's black plastic lined pond. It cost £222. He paid for it from his 'pittance'. Last Sunday vandals made nine perforations in it. 'It nearly broke my heart.'

He peels back a fringe hanging untidily over the water to reveal two frogs and tells me the story of the broad bodied chaser, a dragonfly. To his 'utter delight' one turned up, lured by uncolonised water. 'But he needed a female.'

Then, to his further 'utter delight', a female turned up three days later. With a stabbing finger he shows how it dropped its eggs, stab, stab, stab around the pond. To his 'great elation' it was shortly followed by a back tailed darter.

We walk around Mist's Pitch. It takes five minutes. Brian hurries through a well rehearsed list: eighty-eight species of birds; 143 of wild flowers; twenty-four butterflies; eleven dragonflies. 'The only place in London where there are three species of hoverfly, four species of bees and wasps, various grasses.' There is a spindle, wild irises, and giant puff balls.

He thought hard about telling me the next bit, but decided that as another writer had already let it slip, who hadn't contributed to the winter bird fund, and I had, he would tell me officially. It is the white letter hairstreak butterfly, whose pupae he hoped had slept through the Great Gale and would shortly cheer his summer.

'See that big tree there. That's a Huntington elm. Next tree to the right, upswept and rather dense, is an Exeter elm. Next to it English elm. There are lots of suckers of English and Cornish elm.' I tell him that the hairstreak can feed on non-flowering elm suckers. He seems elated by this.

A branch of his Huntingdon elm lollops drunkenly down, split by the winter gale. It destroyed his wych elm, two of the few surviving elms in London. A bow maker asked to use the wych elm wood. Brian refused. 'The bow is a weapon of violence.' He negotiated its use down to a park bench.

Brian, a naturalist since early youth, knew Battersea park well. He saw an opportunity in this three quarters of an acre corner, fenced for 100 years as a leaf dump. In the 1970s received wisdom on improving such a place was to tear down the fences, smooth out its furrows, manicure it and integrate it smoothly into the bland civic sculpture of the park.

Brian would have none of it. He wrote to the newspapers complaining of 'gross vandalism'. Nobody took much notice. Fortunately he knew the head of the parks department, and a few people in the town hall who accepted his then revolutionary proposition: an *urban* nature reserve.

He and his wife cleared rubbish, an old car, bottles, concrete. Birds and plants took triumphant possession. All he did was plant some buddleia, as an extra inducement to the butterflies.

171

Brian saw me off with a little litany of despair, which is really an appeal for no more than £1,500, a modest sum to guarantee his continuing attention to the 'pitch'.

At least one member of the House of Lords and many civic worthies told him: 'We can't let you go, Brian. We won't let you go.'

'Perhaps I'm looking at the blackest end of the rod.'

A brown rat scampers along his chestnut palings. 'I do like rats.' He says he is better disposed to rats than some people. How does it feel to have a bit of central London named after you? 'It doesn't mean a damn thing, unless people come to see it.'

I cross the Chelsea Bridge, opened on May 6th, 1937 by W. L. Mackenzie King, Prime Minister of Canada. Why he, and not the usual member of the Royal Family? Could, I wonder, the task have been assigned originally to that great three-in-a-day bridge opener, the former Prince of Wales, later King Edward VIII, who had abdicated five months earlier?

There is a cool breeze off the river. On the north bank, past the Lister Hospital on the corner, I enter the City of Westminster. 'Welcome to the heart of London,' says the blue and white sign.

On my left a line of slumbering trains from the Victoria line is parked off the road. This is a favoured place for waiting conveyances. I pass a coach ready to depart to Shrewsbury, linking Thames and Severn. A uniformed hostess replenishing a drinks cupboard looks up like a startled mole.

There is a succession of enterprises on the south bank – Battersea Power Station, the Royal Mail, the Western Riverside Waste Authority. The vessel *Blue Circle Venture*, no more than a floating line of concrete filled vats bound together, buzzes upstream.

The north bank is an idler location. A Rolls-Royce with Arabic registration plates stands in River Lodge. A man measures carpet for the covered porch of the Elephant on the River restaurant. In Pimlico Gardens is a statue to William Huskisson, statesman, 1770 to 1830, in toga. And a rarity, a drinking fountain which delivers a strong jet of sanitised Thames water from an inaccessible valve.

In his office close to the riverside, Max Hobbs greets me with a fierce handshake and the blazing gaze of commitment of a man who is setting out to persuade people that London has a river called the Thames running through it.

Even Londoners don't know where to find their river. 'How many people know where Westminster Pier is? Precious few. Only a few hundred thousand people use it, yet twenty-two million people a year hover around the Big Ben area. Londoners are not selling the Thames to themselves, or to their visitors. If you go to Paris or Amsterdam, the locals will tell you to go on to their river.'

Max, a senior Thames water executive, explains his vision of Thames as consumer item. It could become one of the most profitable attractions in London. That bit of the river which 100 years ago was a commercial highway is being turned into a leisure and pleasure highway by Max.

Then there is a night river. People behave themselves on night boats, he claims. There were fourteen thousand people on the river on New Year's Eve. They were not there just to escape the licencing laws.

Our conversation turns to comparison with other rivers and crunches up against the brick wall of Max's loyalty.

The Seine? 'The Thames has far more history than the Seine. It breathes or circulates the air twice a day, something fairly rare for a capital city's river. London breathes through the Thames.'

The Thames is a less kind river than the Seine. It isn't a river for amateurs. It has other features that make it even grander and more magnificent and more difficult to tame. 'Perhaps it is a little more difficult to appreciate the Thames than the Seine as you sit sipping champagne on it. Here you are on the Thames in a boat: one minute you can see a beautiful lion's head mooring ring. The next minute the tide has taken you down ten feet.'

The Thames carries more people than the Seine. Not many people know that, says Max. The Thames is a lot more magnificent. The Seine is narrow – you get a cricked neck from looking up. In the Thames there are such large vistas: you can see up to St Paul's, down to the Tower, round the sweep of the bend to Kings Reach. 'Magnificent views. Different river. Bigger scale and much more successful river, provided people know where it is and we get the boats to match it.'

After debunking the Seine, Max bears down on the Hudson. 'No history. Americans will shoot me down for this. It has pier nineteen, but it's a bit more like the open sea. It doesn't flow through the capital.'

The Far East can hardly muster a challenge. 'Their rivers are like the Thames in the 1920s. They will get their comeuppance when their labour costs rise. The Ganges is, well, a rather more functional river.'

He believes the Thames is under-used. A hundred years ago, there were twenty million passenger journeys across the river alone. Not many bridges, so there were a lot of people in rowing boats. The wherry man could row you across for sixpence. Ten million tons of cargo came into the Pool above Tower Bridge, and most of that in sailing ships.

There was fair confusion. Sailing ships, difficult to steer at the best of times, with people in rowing boats sneaking across their paths.

Last year there were seven million tonnes passing upstream of the Barrier, with about a million tonnes to the Pool, in easily steered diesel-powered ships. 'So if we increased that by a factor of ten, the river would be no more busy in terms of confusion than it was 100 years ago. And it would be more manageable and safer.'

Max identifies part of the Thames's spirit in her peculiarities. A royal navigation, with a company of waterman, the only non-liveried company in the City to be controlled by acts of Parliament.

'There's a brotherhood on the Thames. It's very thick. I often hear it said that Thames water is thicker than blood. You don't find it on the Severn or the Mersey or the Clyde. I know those rivers as well. But you find it on the Thames. There's something about being a waterman on the Thames. It's bigger and better than being a member of a trades union.'

But doesn't this watery brotherhood belong now in a museum case? 'Yes. We must create something new: an awareness that the river is now, in terms of its quality, like it was hundreds of years ago, possibly when the watermen started their business in 1500. We've gone back to that. It's a nice place to be and to visit. It has a spirit again.'

And even in the 1500s it would have been liable to flood. So virtually for the first time in modern history the Thames in London is both relatively safe and a pleasant place to be. The selling of this truth, packaged by private endeavour by a public utility newly sold, is an appropriate challenge in the final years of the century, in a commercial framework erected by Thatcherism.

The river is a vibrant commercial ambassador. 'A clean Thames states our purpose. It doesn't matter how many billions of pounds worth of pipes we put underground, they are unexciting. But the Thames: everybody can see it, walk beside it, swim in it. It's a river worth facing. Once overlooking the river was not very salubrious. Now people pay a premium, my goodness me.'

9

ROUND the great curve go the lamps and the lighted trees and the lighted, lumbering trams; and at the end the calm clock of Westminster hangs in the sky.

– No Boats on the River, A. P. Herbert.

FOR THE NEXT three miles, from here to the Tower, runs the Thames everybody knows. It is the foreground to postcards, the backdrop to the teeming trudge to the office. It accompanies towering buildings and poetry which is hackneyed yet still great. Trains from all parts burrow under it and rattle over it. Open-top buses stop upon it for the view. The best free display of art anywhere by a famous son of the Thames lies alongside it.

There is no warmer, more reassuring vista in England than the Embankment by night, lit by glowing lights with the river rustling below. It returns to me from my first visit to London as a ten year old, an intense memory, this trusty old location for innumerable black and white B films. Alas, there are no longer any bootlace sellers.

There is a tremendous study by the Port of London Authority which shows the London river when it swarmed with trading boats – many of them, on both sides, to be sunk in the war – at a thousand wharves, piers and jetties, one continuous line of photographs continued overleaf, the entire length of the waterfront.

I will meet men with almost two hundred accumulated years of memories of the river when it was the busiest in the world. I will travel with the officers of the oldest police force and delve into the mud which contains the evidence of the birth of London.

From now on the river bank collects historical associations like fallen leaves in an autumn lane. Just beyond Vauxhall Bridge, on the north bank, I find this point of lamented departures: 'Near this spot stood the buttress at the head of the river steps, from which until 1867 prisoners sentenced to transportation embarked for the journey to Australia.' Opposite is a line of empty lions' heads mooring rings, awaiting river revival.

175

The Tower of London.

'Is not this house as nigh heaven as my own?'

    – Sir Thomas More on The Tower,
        where he was executed.

Next door to the Tate, and a few yards from the river, I walk into the Turner Clore Gallery, where there is a fabulous free display of art.

J. M. W. Turner, son of a Covent Garden barber, sometime Professor of Perspective at the Royal Academy and dedicated artist of the Thames – he lived close to its banks in houses at Twickenham, Iselworth, Hammersmith and Chelsea – was 'a short stout man, somewhat sailor-like with great colour in his face.'

In 1840 he brought his Margate landlady Mrs Sophia Carlone Booth to look after him at his house in Cremond Gardens, Chelsea, later Cheyne Walk. He was known as Puggy Booth by the streetboys; his more genteel neighbours took him to be a retired admiral.

He took pleasure during his closing days in climbing on to the flat roof of his house and watching, wrapped in a blanket, the movement of the river, and gazing at the dawn, the flushing and paling of the morning sky.

A biographer wrote that the very hour he died in 1851, his landlady wheeled Turner's chair that he might see the sunshine mottling the river and glowing on the sails of the passing boats.

Turner ranged the Thames with his brush. He painted *Dorchester Mead in Hazy Light*; *Shipping at the mouth of the River*; *Windsor from Lower Hope* – with a refreshing disregard for the fashionable location the title of another 'Windsor' painting was changed to *Ploughing up Turnips near Slough* – the *Thames near Walton Bridge*; a *House beside the river with trees and sheep*.

Turner's England: Richmond Hill on the Prince Regent's Birthday is described as 'quintessentially English' by the Tate. The Thames is one twentieth part of the painting, the rest is trees and sky, but without the river the painting would have been quite empty.

Back on the bank, I see the ribs of old London exposed on the foreshore at low tide. Opposite, the offices on the Albert Embankment are a forlorn triumph for bleak 1960s functionalism, built without any grace and style.

Lambeth Bridge has metal towers, like an old French railway station. 'Perhaps, on the whole, the ugliest ever built' notes the younger Dickens. An urban revolutionary identifies it as a strategic target. 'Take the Bridge' exhorts his slogan.

My behaviour in Victoria Tower Gardens is constrained under twenty-six headings of the Royal and Other Parks and Gardens Regulations 1977. I may not feed or touch any deer or pelican; carry on any trade or business; solicit persons to be passengers in a hackney carriage; wash or dry any piece of clothing or linen; skate or otherwise go on any ice.

Sensible rules. But not 'engage in any form of sport or exercise'? The closing stages of a 180 mile walk clearly put me in contravention of that edict. But it is hard to strike the pose of relaxed stroller with heavy shoes and a backpack. An androgynous couple pose for each other's photographs, and they could as well have been dressed in each other's clothes, in front of the *Burghers of Calais* statue.

My way is blocked by a high security fence. Inside, Sir Charles Barry's honourable and learned figures gaze down from their alcoves in the wall of the Palace of Westminster. I press on through the teeming, international forces in front of the Houses of Parliament and Big Ben, to Westminster Pier.

A greying man in his late forties, wearing a red T-shirt, and pushing a yellow bike sensibly fitted with green reflective bands to his panniers is behaving very strangely. Where a front light is normally attached, he has fixed a radio which blasts out pop music at the full blare of the High Street boutique.

Runners pad past on Victoria Embankment in shirts proclaiming 'I ran the world' and 'Sweatshop'. Open-top tourist buses rake the throng with commentary. Heavy lorries grumble past in low gear.

There is a clamour at ticket booths for distant destinations – Hampton, the Barrier, Richmond. 'They are on strike' reports a thwarted father. 'Oooh' exclaims a small girl in a bowler hat, banded by continuous Union Jacks.

I take my picnic on the Victoria Embankment, on a raised seat partitioned by classical winged creatures, in order to take in a spectacular cityscape.

The Embankment is one of the nineteenth century's most impressive riverside improvements, the work of Sir Joseph Bazalgette. 'He placed the river in chains' proclaims an inscription of his memorial which finds a place here with Gilbert, and Sullivan, Burns, I.K. Brunel – resident engineer for the first tunnel under the Thames, among his many other achievements – a member of the Imperial Camel Corps and Cleopatra's Needle.

Why should the Defence Secretary have unveiled the stainless steel information board which guides me through the panorama of riverside buildings in silhouette? Perhaps Boadicea is the link? 'When the Gauls invaded she put swords on the wheels of the chariots and cut all their legs off,' a man informs a foreign visitor. 'Ees terrible', comes the reply.

We marvel at Wren's St Paul's and praise Sir Giles Gilbert Scott's Waterloo Bridge (1939), but the names of the designers and architects of the other buildings on the horizon have still to enter the tourist's conversation. What of Shell-Mex House – Joseph and Partners, 1930; the Royal Festival Hall – Sir Robert Matthew; Ralph Knott's County Hall; the new St Thomas' Hospital – Yorke, Rosenberg Narfall, who created a box worth a second glance.

On a large flagstone close to where I sit, the artist Jonathan draws a large plastic veil over Virtue, for about the fifteenth time today, to shelter her from a shower.

Heavy rain on its own will not erase his chalk and pastel pavement art. It will dry, mistily. Feet are the main threat. A line of chalky boot prints step guiltily away from Virtue, whom Jonathan is copying from a postcard of Raphael's allegory, *Vision of a Knight*.

'And there's another interesting thing about the rain.' Sometimes the ghostly form of a work he completed three weeks ago reappears. Then there are eery tricks of the light. Once he returned to his pitch late at night with a friend who wanted to photograph Westminster Bridge and found his chalk drawing glowing at him. 'Wow! As if it was back projected.'

Vision of a Knight is a three-day project. Soon Passion will take her place, a few slabs to the left of Virtue, leaving room for the knight to recline just above the river wall. It is his fifth attempt to complete the work after repeated interruption by rain and boots.

Jonathan, who wears a broad brimmed black hat, from the rim of which little fists of red hair protrude, has learnt that the public do not like impressionists. He has tried copying Degas, Renoir and Pissarro and hardly made his bus fare home. 'They like the old masters. Rosy cheeks and cow eyes. Innocence . . . '

His finest creation in this most ephemeral of art forms, was Peregino's *Madonna and Bambino Jesu*, which he drew in a Florence piazza. It took him three weeks, just before Christmas. Then he ringed it with candles.

Benefactors betray themselves through their shoes. Women in high heels never stop at his drawings. An American couple in sensible brogues halt and drop a coin. Large police boots no longer presage an instruction to move on. This is a wide pavement and Jonathan's sublime subjects are not an obstruction.

Jonathan has no training. He was spurred into pavement art while unemployed, after wandering through Covent Garden and seeing 'some work that was so bad'. He found this riverside territory, which includes the unusually large slab on which he depicts Virtue, with its scope for the expansive theme.

His technique is to make a fuzzy image and gradually consolidate it with colour. Colleagues use different methods. One artist he knows starts in the top left-hand corner and invades the entire slab, with full, complete colour.

This is the true pauper's art. Chalks cost fifteen pence the box: on this painting he will expend thirty pence. He says he must go shopping for some Renaissance blues and reds.

'I get very meditative. It seems to affect people. I often sense a crowd of children standing around, all saying "Shhh".' As I leave him he thrusts out a chalky handshake.

On Westminster Bridge, which through the agency of the London Marathon, has now become one of the most crowded finishing lines in the world, a lady wearing a cowboy mask of a red spotted handkerchief pedals past me.

Here Wordsworth, a man of the open air and out of town, gave the world the most famous urban poem:

> Earth has not anything to show more fair:
> Dull would he be of soul who could pass by
> A sight so touching in its majesty:
> This City now doth like a garment wear
> The beauty of the morning: silent, bare,
> Ships, towers, domes, theatres and temples lie
> Open unto the fields and to the sky,
> All bright and glittering in the smokeless air.

Today his 'Ships, towers, domes, theatres and temples,' are obscured by a squall. And there are no longer any fields. But, remorselessly, the poet's river 'glideth at his own sweet will.'

From here I can proceed on either side of the river. I take the South Bank, because it is the quieter. A piper in green kilt approaches from the south and plays a lament to the Houses of Parliament. An alert tourist standing in the door of a well-appointed coach from Boostedt in West Germany ('*Vom Nordkap bis Sizilien sind wir uberall zu Hause*' senses a photo-opportunity.

Several Japanese teenagers and a Scandinavian man in a thin face-framing beard stop and point their cameras, oblivious to the upturned tam that indicates this piper is at work and they are part of his public. A lady in black, who could be a peeress or a piano teacher, opens his account with a coin.

There is panic as another shower billows up river. The piper is hushed but stands stoically into the wind, rain drops flicking off his tam. The predominant colour on the open-top buses retreats to the dingier end of the spectrum, as passengers throw on water-repelling garments of blue and grey.

A big slab of wood swings down the river. First lady with ice-cream: 'I saw a cow floating in the river once.' Second lady with ice-cream. 'A cow?' First lady 'Hmmm.' Second lady 'There are supposed to be fish in the river now.'

There are further delicious outbreaks of melody by solo instrumentalists along Albert Embankment. A violinist commands the top of the steps at Hungerford Bridge. The bridge itself is the ugliest of an ugly family, leading the old Southern Railway line out of Charing Cross. Victorian writers were greatly distressed by the railway bridges which were thrown

180

---

insensitively across the river, often spoiling the effect of the more tasteful river bridge built alongside.

In the middle of the river is a petrol pump. The vessels *Lady Phymor*, *Abercorn* and *Bertram Rose*, stand close by, in reserve against a rush at Westminster Pier.

Some of the most extravagant studies of the river, such as Canaletto's *View of London*, about 1746, of great gilded barges rowed by toiling teams of oarsmen on huge slabs of water, are set on the river here. There is something very strange about that huge eighteenth century river. It is much wider than it is today, constrained by embankments, and, in many of the paintings, there is not a single bridge.

On July 17th, 1717 a barge of musicians 'to the number of 50' was stationed alongside the moving barge of King George I, on the river near here. A contemporary account read: 'The concert was composed expressedly for the occasion by the famous Handel, first composer of the King's music.

'It was so strongly approved by His Majesty that he commanded it to be repeated, once before and once after supper, although it took an hour for each recital.' Musical historians doubt, however, that the *Water Music* had its première on such a convenient and appropriate occasion.

It is odd, that a river which inspired so much poetry, art and literature, had comparatively little to say to composers. Vaughan Williams' *London Symphony* is one of the few works to directly quote the river.

This is the site of the many water activities in the annual summer Thamesday. But nothing will ever match the popular pull of the Thames frost fair, never to be repeated – the river is now too warm to freeze.

John Gribbing in *Our Changing Climate* describes the freezing of the Thames, and its reduced flow in times of drought as an indicator of the changing British climate over the past thousand years.

In October 1114 the flow was so low that men and boys were able to wade across the Thames. In 1325 and 1326 the low level allowed salt water to pass much further upstream than usual.

In the Little Ice Age, between the 1400s to about 1860, the Thames froze frequently. In the first thousand years after Christ the Thames froze at least eight times.

In the winter of 1149/50 it froze so hard that men were able to cross on horseback. This is the first reliable account of a Thames Frost Fair.

In 1204/5 it froze again. In 1209 London Bridge was built. The bridge appeared to encourage the freezing. It took a less intense cold to freeze the river. There was more bridge than there were gaps for the water to pass through. The bridge acted as a dam: water built up upstream, and poured through the arches like a waterfall. If ice formed up river, it piled up against the bridge. The arches were blocked with ice and the floes consolidated.

In 1269/70 the river froze so far downstream that goods had to be sent overland from the Channel ports. In March 1282 it froze hard enough for people to walk across it. It froze in 1309/10. Between 1407 and 1564/5 it froze six times. Horses and carts moved about on the ice when Henry VIII visited the frozen Thames in 1536/37 or 1537/38. Queen Elizabeth, in the winter of 1564/65, took regular strolls on the ice. Her subjects played football there.

The first Frost Fair is recorded in 1607. Booths sold food, beer and wine. There was bowling, shooting and dancing. There was another Frost Fair in 1620/21. In 1662 the king watched the new sport of skating on ice. The greatest Frost Fair took place in 1683/84. Stalls were arranged in streets. A printer produced notices 'Printed on the Thames'. The ice was eleven inches thick, the Thames was frozen for two months. (This was the severe winter mentioned in *Lorna Doone*.)

Another Frost Fair took place in 1688/89 and another in 1715/16 when the fair attracted so many shops the Thames was like a separate town. The Prince of Wales visited it in January when the high tide lifted the entire community fourteen feet without breaking the ice. There was so much activity on the Thames that London theatres were almost deserted.

In all, the Thames was frozen ten times in the seventeenth century, and a further ten times between 1708 and 1813. The 1813/14 occasion was a poor affair. After a few days the ice broke, on February 6th. Many booths were destroyed, and people drowned. Loose ice caused £20,000 of damage to London Bridge and in Westminster.

It has never been completely frozen since, because of the warming effect of industrial and urban effluent. Tributary streams were put into pipes and new bridges were built, allowing the tide to reach further up river, making it even less likely to freeze. Between 1894 and 1940 in only two winters, 1916/17 and 1928/29, was there ice on the Thames in a few places.

Why was there no Frost Fair on the Thames in 1963, the bitterest winter this century. Measurements by the vessel *Discovery 3*, sailing from Plymouth in the depths of that winter, throw some light. It found temperatures of 9.8°C to 10.3°C in the sea. These levels fell to minus 0.2° in the mouth of the Thames where ice belts along the shore were up to a mile wide.

At the same time explosives had to be used to release ships in East Anglian ports, and ice floes restricted the use of the port of Cardiff.

Yet the *Discovery* found water temperatures rising to between plus 8°C and 10°C in the Thames, all the way up from east Tilbury. There was no sign of ice as far up river as the power station at Kingston. The ice did not begin until Hampton Court, where it was possible to walk across the river.

Meteorologists conclude that artificially high temperatures due to the then warm water flowing from factories prevented the icing over of the river. By the end of January 1963, the frost already exceeding for severity the frost of 1895 and 1925 when there had been a lot of ice on the river in central London, not a speck of floating ice was found in London. Instead the river was often to be seen *steaming* to a height of three to six feet.

I walk on. Further along the wide, paved South Bank I find pigeons basking in the dust behind the British Columbia flagpole, which stretches endlessly up, like Jack's Beanstalk, to a postage-stamp flag. A man on a seat is methodically re-counting the plastic bags which contain his belongings, spread in a circle before him.

We are several years into the loosely-focused programme to make the South Bank more like Paris's Left Bank. There is already as great a concentration of music and theatre, and works of displayed art in the National Theatre, Hayward Art Gallery, and Festival Hall as in any western capital. Occasionally the muse escapes from behind the dense concrete walls. I once saw a memorable performance by Brian Glover playing God from the top of an electricity board lorry's extended arm, in an offcut from the National Theatre's *Mystery Plays*.

The young men of the borough clatter and leap on the low inclines in the South Bank's concrete underbelly. Hard against the river wall, I find, at last, competition for the Red Lion team at Castle Eaton, so many miles upstream. South Bank Boules is played in little raised gravelly beds. Detailed graphics depict the correct flight of the balls, stage by stage. Mislobs would fly over the water's edge, but I'm sure the resourceful young men of the borough could be engaged to recover them at low water, when the Thames subsides to expose a fringe of soft sand.

I am opposite Shell-Mex House, about which the Press said some delightful things when it opened in January 1933. 'That dominating structure which has caused many a gaping bargee to shoot through the wrong arch of Charing Cross Bridge, ' said the correspondent of *Light Car and Cyclecar*.

The building, (212 feet high, twice the height then allowed under the London Building Act) was a practical demonstration in its day that tall buildings need not dominate riverside architecture and overwhelm their neighbours. It stands there now, a convenient timepiece for guests taking inter-act refreshment at the National Theatre.

Close by Shell-Mex House stood one of the most remarkable of all Thames-side developments, disgracefully destroyed in the 1930s. As an architect, Robert Adam bestrode his age. He and his brothers were the smart operators of the optimistic 1760s and 1770s. Their Adelphi development, a multi-level complex of houses and shops on the river, was a combination of architectural and daring speculation. (Adelphi was a play on the Greek for brothers.)

I reach Waterloo Bridge, where Eric Mahoney indicates the preferred angle for rain for the dry conduct of his business. Today's wind-assisted showers are penetrating to the fifth or sixth bookcase along, under the bridge. The difference between the Rive Gauche's *bouquinistes* and his Londinium Books, Eric tells me, is that the prints here are authentic. Those sold in Paris are copies. A first edition Edgar Wallace is on sale for £8.50. I manage to find an original Penguin 1937 *Tarka the Otter* for £1.

Inside Denys Lasdun's National Theatre, I detect the atmosphere of a slumbering airport lounge between landings. It is that time of day and week (Monday, 4.15) when there never seems to be a theatrical performance. Outside a chauffeur sleeps at the wheel of a Rolls-Royce Silver Shadow.

I walk on to Gabriel's Wharf, and the Coin Street Development where, on a large sign, proletarian victory is being claimed, with the appropriate key words – 'sheltered units', 'work-shop', 'child care', 'homes for people'. The bounty on the river's edge here includes, in addition to the ubiquitous trollies, litter bins.

Gone is Dickens' vista of 'quickset hedge of masts and rigging, with ragged buildings upon the shore, overhanging tavern bay windows, ship builders' yards, steaming factories, smoking chimneys, soaring warehouses.' Sea Container House is built in bricks of the soft, sandy colour of a freshly exposed beach, smoothed by the tide. Behind smoked glass windows, men stretch shirt-sleeved arms in wide Vs and yawn. A remote camera studies me.

At Doggett's Coat and Badge, the pub, cigarette buts bob in storm water-filled ash trays. Thomas Doggett's race is still rowed, from Chelsea to London Bridge, by watermen in the first year of their freedom, according to the bequest of 'the well-known actor of Drury Lane.'

> THERE was an old person of Ems,
> Who casually fell in the Thames,
> And when he was found,
> They said he was drowned,
> That unlucky old person of Ems.
> — Edward Lear.

At Blackfriars Bridge the wind comes hollering in from the east. The tabloid Press was forecasting a hurricane for about midday. I escape into the Dark Ages and earlier, through some subterranean doors under the northern portals of the bridge. The basement where Gustave Milne works would be one of the first places to flood if the Thames Barrier, nine miles downstream at Woolwich, malfunctioned.

Gustave, archaeologist, reminds me of the wonders disclosed on the riverbank in Central London. Only three Roman wrecks have been excavated in Britain. They all came from the river, within a few hundred yards of the Museum of London's bunker at Blackfriars where Gustave is masterminding a hectic rescue of whatever remains.

One wreck came from the site of County Hall in 1910 when it was being built out over the south bank creeks. Another was found on the Dyers House extension creek on the South Bank. The third was on this office's doorstep.

One was a merchant ship; another was a lighter or bargette; the third was a working river barge for coastal and river work. 'Three quite different types. If we found another it would probably be different again.'

This stretch of river from Blackfriars to the Tower is the cradle of London, the historic heart and ancient harbour in the Roman and medieval period. In post medieval period the harbour moved, from 1800 onwards, downstream to Docklands where London fought its last stand as a riverborne commercial centre.

The professional archaeologists in this room are responding to permanent crisis. It is due entirely to the City's growth and constant change, manifested to the outsider by the frequent tearing down of old (twenty years) building, and the erection of new, (designed to last, say, twenty years). These buildings are identified by their acres of plate glass and dark reflective surfaces above ground, and dungeon car parks beneath.

Basements and car parks destroy the clues to how London was put together. 'There is unremitting development of the waterfront,' says Gustave. He scribbles on a piece of paper. 'In the past eighteen years no two years have passed without an excavation on the waterfront. If you include the South Bank as well, no single year.'

Rescue archaeology is a furious, incomplete business. Archaeologists find lots of wonderful things, because they have to, not because they want to. In normal circumstances, which hardly ever apply in urban archaeology these days, they would not wish to find all the treasure at once.

In this period of great enforced excavation along the river, what have they found in the past eighteen years? 'In terms of the river and harbour, everything. There was no plan of the Roman harbour. No one knew where it was. We, the department of urban archaeology, found it in the mouth of the Wallbrook, ' (near Cannon Street station.)

'We didn't know what the Roman quays, the Roman warehouses

looked like, we didn't know how long the Roman harbour lasted, where the river was, how high it was. The answer is nothing. Everything we found was not known. It has been an incredibly successful programme.'

Gustave then surprised me by launching a bitter attack on a long dead civilisation. He accused the Romans in their days on the river of being a wasteful, blundering, imperialistic power. He has original proof.

'The Romans wandered over England exploiting the woodlands. Roman quays are built of massive great pieces of wood for no other reason than that they were in charge and would exploit the land if they wanted. The medieval quays in contrast, built of timbers often less than seventy years old, show far more sensible managing of woodlands.

'There was no point in building a quay which was going to collapse in seventy years and needed to be replaced unless the timber had replenished in that time. The Romans built a quay with two hundred year-old timbers that lasted for twenty years. That's wasteful and that's what the Romans were all about.

'Their quays were only about weight. They were using timber as if it was reinforced concrete. Their civil engineering projects have the stamp of their general attitude. They were here to exploit everything, people, slaves, silver, lead, wheat: they were here to exploit and that's what their quays looked like.'

He compares the heavy footed Romans with the medieval builders, emergent conservationists, reusing timber. 'Their quays were reinforced with reused bits of old boats. Their timber structures were far more intricate and more intelligently built. Medieval quays are much slighter but just as successful in civil engineering terms, and less exploitative.'

He shows me photographs of an excavated quay built in 1380. 'Much slighter construction than those ponderous great Roman slabs of oak, using whole trees.' The quay included a fish tank, fixed below low water, to keep fish fresh.

'Let me show you how subtle they were. We are talking about a mere timber quay at Trigg Lane. These are rubbing posts to stop barges moored against the quay demolishing the warehouses. They project above high water mark.'

He shows me how the part of the rubbing post below high water, which shrank and swelled twice a day with the tide, was carefully replaced to fit on to the top piece so that it lasted 100 years. 'This structure is designed to have a replaceable second storey that is a damn clever structure. And this is not the king's works, just a private owner of a fish wharf.

'This is the level of thought and ingenuity in the medieval mind, compared with the dull but efficient Roman technical mind. This is how you understand people, by looking at their civil engineering. They were a damn sight cleverer than those great lumps of wood that have no artistic merit other than weight.

'If you look at all the medieval quay structures on this stretch of the river, each one is subtly different from the next. Owners were constantly trying to improve on the structure of the one before. In this structure they reached the most complex and ingenious resolution of all the problems they faced: how to build a quay with as few timbers as possible.'

The unit is also studying the historical changes to the river. The highest tide in Roman times was a lot lower than it is today. Today there is a difference of 7.7 metres in this part of the City between high and low tide. It was only a metre and a bit in the Roman period.

There are a number of reasons for this. South-East England is dropping; the sea level is rising worldwide; more water in the river; constriction of the river through bridges, weirs; massive encroachment and reclamation – for instance the council estate on ground reclaimed from the marshes at Thamesmead prevents the river from flooding there.

The river was a relatively minor backwater in the Roman period. The port of London was thereafter one of a series of Saxon harbours. Ipswich and Harwich may well have been more important. However by the tenth century London had eight mints, which made it one of the top five towns in England.

By the nineteenth century London was the largest port in the world. The Thames was a means of transport servicing a burgeoning city. There was the endless passage of hay boats from the country; coal from Newcastle; grain, fruit and vegetables in barges and wherries. And unless the river was frozen, huge consignments of fish for fast days, high days and ember days. Fish Street Hill, Fishmongers Hall: the clues are everywhere.

Before the Docks Act of 1799 there were some dry docks and the occasional wet dock for ship building and offloading at Rotherhithe, Deptford and Woolwich. But there was no enclosed water for offloading, although such docks had developed in Liverpool generations earlier. Ships were maintained against the quayside until the 1800s.

Gustave believes there are probably a number of sixteenth and seventeenth century ship building sites yet to be found. Henry VIII's tragic *Mary Rose* and many other ships were built on the river. And they don't know where Roman and Saxon and the earlier medieval ships were built.

But the changing course of the river and the reclamation of marshes has moved the river. These early shipbuilding sites may now be buried inland. They will be hard to find.

Today's foreshore stands over where the deep water channel was once. If they dug deeply enough underneath today's foreshore, they would recover the wrecks which were discarded on the then foreshore. But they will not look until they are forced to, which means when the banks are threatened.

When that happens, the prizes will be rich. In the 1970s, during the construction of a road along the north bank, a coffer dam was built on the foreshore from Blackfriars to Trigg Lane. The dam cut through four wrecks in that short distance, one Roman, two fourteenth century and one seventeenth century.

One wreck they found was a barge carrying building materials to reconstruct London after the Great Fire. How it came to upturn is an unanswered question. It might have been a freak wave or a storm surge. Or it might simply have been offloaded in a haphazard way. Such are the mysteries pondered in the Blackfriar's Bridge basement.

I recross Blackfriars Bridge and walk on east to Bankside Reach, where the local hero is the Labour politician Roy Hattersley, who in 1980 opened modest houses where today there might have been sumptuous penthouse flats.

I pass the site of Sam Wanamaker's proposed, outrageous and wonderful Globe Theatre on the very ground where Shakespeare's original theatre stood. Excavators are pawing at the ground behind firm board defences on which there is stencilled the huge likeness of the bard's head, with exaggerated pointed beard.

On the opposite bank, churches peep over a bland façade of dull grey. 'A rag bag of breathtakingly ugly and mediocre buildings' accuses George Nicholson in the design manual *Thames-Side Guidelines*.

St Paul's, once the arresting backdrop in so many paintings of idealised river pageants, has been concealed from much of the river and the South Bank, which is a shame upon those who allowed it. But at Cardinal's Wharf, there is a concession. The offending riverfront buildings draw back to allow a brief, clear view up several flights of steps, directly to the cathedral.

Sir Christopher lived at Cardinal's Wharf on the South Bank at the same address where Catherine, Infanta of Castille, the first wife of Henry VIII first stayed after her arrival from Spain. Their old house is for sale. 'A rich medieval house. Viewing by appointment only.' No appointment needed to stand outside and marvel at the good fortune that such a house, green curtains drawn back, with crest and flagpole, survived the battering to this part of the river in war and peace.

I am patiently charting a course along the South Bank which has struggled to regain a positive identity in recent years. It may have inherited its uncertainty from an early geographical imprecision. Once there was a series of small islands from Surrey Docks to Waterloo Bridge.

There were extensive marshes in prehistoric and Roman times. The wide river spilt like a slobbering drunk overe North Surrey, flowing in interlocking rivulets. Islands were intersected by channels, creeks and streams. Gradually all of this wetland was drained and reclaimed.

Little inhabited islands stood above the uncertain flow in flat, low, marshy land, Rotherhithe, Bermondsey (Bermond's isle or eyot), an area around Borough High Street, and, south of London Bridge, Horseye. There may have been more islands, not yet identified.

This topography of the South Bank inhibited early developers. At high tide many of those islands were under water in intertidal marshes. Only Bermondsey was high enough to peak above the tide, and even it was reached by a causeway across the creeks. The north bank with its two hills and an area of dry land was the clear preference for invaders, conquerors and settlers.

On to Southwark Bridge, 'rebuilt without burden on public funds out of monies derived from the Bridge House Estates Fund.' North Southwark was one of the most important areas outside the City, a town in its own right and a southern suburb of the city of London from Roman times. There were notorious slums here in the eighteenth and nineteenth century, in the Jacobs Island area around St Saviour's Dock.

Notorious Bankside was at other times important and elegant, with ecclesiastical residences. Around St Mary Overie's Dock, which overlies part of a Roman settlement, are the remains of Winchester Palace, a medieval residence of the bishops of Winchester. The bishops, crossing to the City, were spared the inconvenience of woefully congested London Bridge. They had their own private boats.

Down at St Mary Overie's Dock, where the parishioners of St Saviour's Parish could, and for all I know, still can land goods free of toll, a man is working atop of the main mast of vessel *Kathleen and May*, a West Country topsail schooner, built in Bideford. The wind which flaps its furled sails brings in the first tang of the sea.

Next to the permanently imprisoned boat is a pub with a curious notice. Its patrons are asked to wear smart casual clothes, 'preferably with hair of a human colour.' This is rehabilitated riverside. The pubs have been reclaimed from the natural run-down state of the riverside hostelry, which welcomed hair of any colour, and have been transformed to evoke a carefully composed, but utterly synthetic, romance of the sea and ships.

There are new cobbles and flagstones and a token buddleia. As I retreat, in search of anything genuinely old, a customer who fails to find somebody to sell him a ticket to the *Kathleen and May*, goes below decks, regardless. A voice calls from 100 feet up, at the top of the mainsail, to a colleague arriving too late. 'Chap down below, wants a ticket. This is a waste of time, isn't it.'

I remind myself that those remote Thames-side churches, way back up river belong to the same Anglican communion as this most-hemmed in and

189

overwhelmed of all church buildings, Southwark Cathedral. One flank is assailed by the old A3, London to the south road; another by the Charing Cross and Cannon Street to London Bridge Railway; a third by the river Thames, now largely silent.

This everyday torment is exactly what such places are constructed to withstand. As I pass the front door the glorious sound of choral music seeps out. Red-sashed attendants stand to attention in the aisles.

It is here that the police had agreed to help me with my inquiries. Within the hour we are proceeding upriver at a stately rate, behind the *Margaret G*, inhibiting the swift, in an unnamed police launch. There is no offence of speeding on the river, but culprits may be charged with causing a dangerous swell. The transgressor is run down with impressive seriousness – blue flashing lights and siren. It is a public entertainment.

I had resolved not to open the subject of bodies. Sergeant Gordon mentioned it first. He said the attempted suicides most likely to survive were old ladies with abundant petticoats. 'Their petticoats act as a parachute. They hit the river and float. Their top half stays dry. We had one who could have floated all the way to Southend, no problem.'

Then there was the medical student who trudged despairingly to Waterloo Bridge, with a haversack full of medical tomes for added weight. He jumped, he sank and he floated up, his books imitating the properties of wood. The river police saved him.

At the riverside station close to Waterloo Bridge, a river police boat stands on permanent alert to pluck the foundering jumper from the water. Expect an audience if you leap from here. This is one of the most public places to commit suicide. It is not like cutting your wrists in the privacy of your bath.

The police launches carry oxygen and officers are very good at bringing people round. But in the winter, time is short. They must try to reach the victim within two minutes. Thereafter the river's deep chill immobilises muscles and deadens the will to survive even in those who didn't intend to see it through. Within five minutes the jumper would be dead.

The river may appear calm on the surface, yet underneath it is a relentless conveyor belt, moving at six miles an hour. The person who falls in has an evens chance of being asphyxiated by the slap of water on his chest. Then he plunges eight or ten feet underwater. Only then can he begin the fight back, if he wants to.

The force give victims a warm bath and sends them off to hospital. 'So it is galling to see them back again the following week, trying it again,' says Sergeant Gordon.

Rescuing suicides is a branch of the river police's work for which they are rewarded with little gratitude. Even those with no self-destructive intent are less polite than they might be. Sergeant Gordon recalls the night they rescued a sodden Lazarus. They had received a report of a man in the river near HMS Belfast. They arrived and made three sweeps around the Belfast, seeing nothing. They made a final sweep and spotted something white in the water. A man's underpants. Inside them was a man, hanging in the flow like a jellyfish, head down.

Three river policemen hauled out this immobile burden and found he had indeed stopped breathing. Apparently dead. Brisk application of oxygen, and within minutes he revived. Deeply drunk, he had tried to swim to the Belfast. Unaccountably he was very ungracious to his rescuers.

Then there was the man who jumped in three times and was duly rescued by the force three times. One evening he appeared again at the Waterloo Bridge station, dripping on their doorstep. 'He played hell with us because he had jumped in a fourth time and nobody had saved him,' says Sergeant Gordon.

The sergeant and his brother officers tell these stories with the protective humour of men for whom the identification of corpses blanched by months of tide and river is routine work. The line from T. S. Eliot's *Waste Land* comes to mind – 'A current under sea, Picked his bones in whispers . . . ' Much police time is expended in this task. 'People go to considerable lengths to conceal their identity, cutting makers' tags off clothing and so on. Those already fingerprinted and tattooed are helpful.'

People die in tragic circumstances on the river. Sergeant Gordon recalls eight heroes who have died, diving into the river to rescue others. It is the ironic rule of the river that the police boat makes for the victim and not the rescuer. Others have perished as casual victims. One man died after jumping through the window of a pleasure boat to escape from a fight. Another fell to his death walking along the outside rail of a boat in an attempt to beat the queue for the bar.

The cruiser is a relic of Victorian liberality in the licencing laws. The bars are always open once it leaves its moorings. Crowded cruising inflames passions. Even 'respectable' people carousing on the river, trouble the police. Say a building society hires a boat for its staff, and somebody touches somebody else's girl-friend. Riot. A police boat will not itself try to placate passengers in ferment. The boat will at least be in the charge of a responsible man, a licenced Thames waterman, who steers it to land where larger forces await.

The police launch is an ideal means of spiriting important people of high security risk, such as NATO generals, through London, to the bafflement of waiting terrorists. The times of their departure are totally unpredictable. Sergeant Gordon is carrying a First Sea Lord this afternoon.

Plaques in the galley, in no order of prominence, record some of the launch's passengers: the FBI, the Torres San Pedric Pilots, Russian admirals, John Wayne, the Nineteenth Purley scout troop, Hungarian magistrates, the crowned head of Qatar and the Duchess of York. A fellow passenger on this trip is a novelist who seeks to test a theory: can a person jump from Waterloo Bridge, faking suicide and be lifted from the water by an accomplice hiding under the bridge? Can boat and occupants disappear without the person on the bridge, who is the intended victim of this subterfuge, realising it?

With a devotion to the river and its tricks, Sergeant Gordon drives the novelist under Waterloo bridge to test this stategy, which if it worked would be partly at the expense of his force.

We pass under Blackfriars Bridge. Sergeant Gordon, who polices the beat from Blackfriars to Dartford, was in the boat whose officers cut down here the body of the highly insured Roberto Calvi, the Pope's banker. ('The Hanged man, Fear Death by water,' – *Waste Land*.)

'That one's hit everything' notes the sergeant, pointing to a certain ship which regularly plies this reach. 'She's hit HMS Wellington, Charing Cross Bridge, the Thames Barrier. She was off to Raynham Marshes with rubbish, her engines cut out and three thousand tonnes of towed boat is swinging over the river. We have to be the AA and the RAC.'

Most river accidents are a matter of exchanging names and addresses. But the river punishes those who don't respect it. At this point in the 1970s the sergeant took out the body of the master of the *Nova L*, who perished after he had returned into the cabin of his sinking craft to rescue the ship's money. On the south bank close by, Boy A pushed Boy B into the river in retribution for Boy B pushing in Boy A's bicycle. Boy B's body was found a month later at Erith.

Sergeant Gordon and his colleagues claim to be, as policemen, no different to their land-borne fellows in the Metropolitan Police, but I conclude that the pace of human evil has slackened on the river. It *is* a depository of cut-up bodies and implements of crime. But the crimes are committed on land.

Yet there is surprising news of piracy on the non-tidal river. Young men are jumping on to boats from bridges – Walton's is a favourite – robbing the occupants and making off before they can raise the alarm. It couldn't happen in London: the fall from bridge to boat would kill or cripple the robber.

Could a man swim across the river to escape a crime? Sergeant Gordon doubts it. The greatest progress he can recall was made by a car thief who took to the water at Greenwich and swam half way across before he was caught.

Policing the river is the water equivalent of patrolling the M1, but with

192

the road traffic of 1920. It is not easy to be anonymous. You cannot slink in unobserved. Take a boat approaching the river-mouth laden with contraband. Gravesend Radio's computer positions a cursor over any suspicious incoming craft and computes its port of origin. The river division has ample time to apprehend it.

A river policeman's navigational skills match those of the river waterman's. And the policeman is probably a better swimmer. The test is two laps of the swimming pool with clothes on. Sergeant Gordon has never fallen in, in twenty years service. Recently a colleague of his fell in three times in a week.

We turn to the benefits of the job. 'Lots of people buy boats for their own pleasure. In this division the commissioner supplies them.' He recalls a day of stifling thundery heat, the river low in oxygen, a salmon gasping near the surface. They took the fish easily, without a line, and served it up, cooked in the mess microwave. Was it in season? I dare not ask.

> BUILD it up with stone so strong,
> Huzza! 'twill last for ages long.
> – *London Bridge is broken down*, Anon.

It is a mile from London Bridge, the world's most famous river crossing, to Tower Bridge, which, together with The Eiffel Tower, may be the world's most immediately recognised piece of engineering. But first there was The Tower, Britain's most famous piece of military architecture, begun by William the Conqueror in 1076.

A few yards downstream from London Bridge at Fennings Wharf I found one of the many bold, smooth, pink marble offices of the dynamic business Megalopolis.

This is the building that finally obliterated the London bridge which fell down so many times in the nursery rhyme. There is now nothing left of the old London Bridge. There was a chance to save a large chunk of it, and we lost it.

We must be clear *which* London Bridge we are talking about. The bridge eagerly bought by the Americans and transported as many stones to the desert, some say on the mistaken assumption that they were buying *Tower* Bridge, is the Victorian replacement.

It is worth recording what Roy Dennis and the members of the Museum of London's urban archaeology team found when, in a great hurry, they excavated the massive abutments of the old London Bridge in 1983, shortly before the pile drivers and the bulk cement mixers moved in for the final destruction of a folk memory, gouging out and filling a ten metre deep foundation to a new river wall.

The old bridge's abutment went down to seven or eight metres below modern ground level. The outer casing of ashlar masonry had been repeatedly repaired and altered. Some masonry blocks had been set in pitch and clamped together with iron bars. It was high quality construction.

The casing had been filled with enormous pieces of chalk and ragstone to give it solidity. At the base of this structure, what did they find to stop London Bridge from falling down for over six hundred years? A foundation of vast oak sleeper beams driven into the old foreshore. They dated one of these original beams, which contained a piece of bark and traces of sap indicating it had been felled for the job, to the year 1186. This was the precise clue that they had indeed discovered the foundations of London Bridge, built between 1176 and 1209, and not some fake.

London Bridge, built by Peter of Colechurch, who now has an office block here named after him, was the first non-timber crossing of the river. It took over thirty years to build, and in its day would have been among the wonders of the world, matched in those times only by the great cathedrals. But unlike the cathedrals it was annointed four times a day by the advancing and retreating tides.

The bridge was much more than a crossing. It ran alongside six hundred years of history: 'Knights, citizens, men at arms, priests, apprentices, beggars, ruffians, fugitives, the rich, the poor, the mighty, the humble, the downcast – all this wealth of human action, suffering, despair and hope, furnished such a record as few other buildings can parallel,' said *Royal River*.

We think of the Forth Bridge as the symbol of that which is unendingly maintained. But for longevity it is only a minor successor to London Bridge. Generations of young craftsman who embarked on the constant repair of London Bridge, to prevent the river washing it away, had a job for life.

Frost etched into the bridge's cladding. But the worst damage came from its unplanned function as weir. It had twenty piers which slowed the retreating tide, creating an enormous dam. As the ebb tide surged down, torrents of water cascaded through the arches in waterfalls six or seven feet high. For young blades of the day it was a conspicuous adventure to shoot these rapids.

There is evidence of a major bank collapse in the medieval period. A thirty metre section of bank was bitten away by the river, swollen as it backed up behind the bridge. There was another lake on the south side during the flow tide.

The line of the south bank remains much where it was in medieval times. The present river wall on the south bank is built just in front of the medieval abutment. On the north bank, however, the greedy City was continually pushing its frontage out into the river. The first few northern arches of London Bridge were subsequently incorporated into the land and were discovered in the 1930s under Adelaide House, an elegant block on King William Street. This land grab on the north exacerbated the erosion problem on the south bank.

The medieval bridge piers would have been boat-shaped, pointed at each end, surrounded by massive sets of timber piling starlings, to prevent them being torn away by the furious surge. The designer seems to have underestimated the force of the river but he may be forgiven for this. He would have been working to the limits of civil engineering technology.

Roy Dennis is still indignant over the loss of the last of London Bridge. 'We have not accepted in this country that what is buried underground is part of the nation's culture, heritage, history and property. We still believe that it is part of private land that can be dealt with by a private person as he chooses. The entire bridge structure could and should have been saved. By the time redevelopment was under way it was too late.

'I wish this new building well. But it is painful to relate that structures built these days on the banks have a short span, which scarcely justifies the destruction they wreak.' He and his team are already probing underneath demolished buildings which were put up in the 1960s.

There were earlier crossings than London Bridge. The Roman bridge probably had stone piers with a timber superstructure. Where was it? The river and tide have washed away the Roman bank for some distance inland, so archaeologists cannot identify a certain site. But the original roads point roughly to the site of the second London Bridge, built between 1824 and 1827 by John Rennie, and the medieval bridges. And there was evidence of a timber and stone bridge beneath the medieval bridge. Indeed there may have been several bridges in the late tenth and early eleventh centuries.

The present, 1960s, bridge was erected in the same place as Rennie's structure, which in turn was built upstream of the medieval bridge. Then London Bridge was finally and irretrievably knocked down.

This redeveloped area, between London Bridge and Tower Bridge, overlies a big moated house associated with Edward II which was later the residence of Sir John Fastoff, Shakespeare's model for Falstaff. This was once a vibrant neighbourhood, an important red-light district. There were pubs, brothels, theatres, bear baiting rings.

I cross to the north bank and in the hall of the Company of Watermen and Lightermen, at St Mary-at-Hill, just north of the river, I meet a group of men with vivid, and sometimes bitter, memories of working on the river, when it was one of the world's most vibrant commercial centres.

I recalled that glib simile, that river water was thicker than blood. Bill Woods confirms it. 'There was great cameraderie among the men. They would never let you down.'

Bill, seventy-five, who started at fourteen as a tug boy is a large and serious man. 'Many times in the bad old days the governor would give you a job which you couldn't do on your own, and a chap who wasn't working for your firm would come over and help. He wouldn't see you struggling your eyeballs out and yet he was cutting his own throat really, because there was three thousand lightermen and one thousand of those was out of work at the time.'

The waterman's day went something like this: 'When I lived at Rotherhithe, I used to go to Braithwaite and Dean, and shape up [look for work] there. If no work there, up to Halls at Waterloo, walking all the way, because I never had the fare. Then I'd come down to the City, where all the big lighterage offices were – Humphrey and Gray, Whitear, Perkins. They all had different times of coming out.

'So you would be on the corners from five o'clock in the evening till six-thirty. When you saw the foreman come out looking for hands, you'd nip over there. Sometimes twenty would put their names on the list. He'd come up and take two men. That's how you started.'

A docker, a less skilled man than the waterman, might have to look for work not once, but twice a day, at half past seven in the morning, and quarter to one, to be called on for half a day's work, until the war when the National Dock Labour Board did away with casual labour.

'I was single. I used to see the married men: they was in trouble, they had no money, all they got was dole. It didn't matter how long you had worked for a firm, you was always liable to be put off. Even men who had worked for a firm all their lives, the governor might put them off "owing to slackness". They'd never know when they would start again.'

The waterman and lighterman's was a nepotistical, admired trade. A boy was apprenticed to his father, grandfather or uncle and taken to Watermans Hall at fourteen. Bill joined a firm and 'did a lot of rowing about.' After two years he went to stand before a court of master lightermen who questioned him on his trade.

'It was like "When did you last see your father?" A favourite question was to ask the names of the river bridges, and the bearings at different reaches, or "What bridge hole would you aim for at Waterloo?" ' If these august men were satisfied, he was competent to take a barge of up to thirty tonnes on his own, row it about any part of the river. He could also handle a waterman's skiff and carry fare-paying passengers.

After a further five years he became a freeman of the river, a full-blown waterman and lighterman, competent in the handling and loading of cargo

196

in the flat-bottomed lighter, and in a locked-down barge. He could take cargo to a bonded warehouse or clear it on a ship, and cover up the cargo on the barge.

'There were so many different types of cargo. Frozen meat, butter, bails of wool. All kinds of cases, transhipment jobs, working out of one ship into another. You never knew where you were going the next day until the governor gave your orders. The trouble was, you never had the right gear. The governor expected you to do it with or without the gear, or pinch it. You never had a line, so you stole a sling off the cargo.'

His licence allowed him to work all the wharves up to Chiswick, to Teddington, Brentford Dock and Cut. It was a bustling river. 'A hell of a lot of traffic. Trawlers used to fly up to Billingsgate. Tug captains had to keep out their way, they was always in a hurry. Dozens of ships in the Pool; ships at Butlers, Hays, Irongate Wharf. Big ships would leave on the high water. They would come down over the tide, and tugs and various craft would be going the other way, so there was a hell of a lot of congestion. But things went all right. Mostly they went unbelievably well.

'Sometimes the *Ascania*, a big Cunarder, fifteen thousand tons, would run into Surry Commercial Dock. She was big for that part of the river. She would come up head first up river, then would have to swing so as to get head down upon the tide.

'She would swing across the river, so every tug, each with a half dozen barges behind, would have to chuck round, head down the river until she was clear, then swing up again and proceed. All tricky stuff for the pilots. If she didn't judge it right, her stern would catch the opposite shore.'

He evokes the smell of the docks. 'I remember walking down by Tower Bridge, by the spices and pepper. They used to discharge rum and stow it in cellars. Then there were the ivory warehouses. I wouldn't say romantic, but it smelt well. But some of the places you smelt were terrible. And the mud.'

The barge was a supremely cheap form of transport for cargo. The master lighterman knew precisely how to handle any cargo. 'Say a ship came up with three thousand tons of lead for Lovells Wharf. It couldn't get there, not enough water. So it would go in barges.

'We would go to the West India Dock for Fielder and Hickman, discharge it into barges, only two or three lightermen. We'd load all those barges one after the other. The same three would tow them over to Lovell's Wharf, moor them up, and that was it – three thousand tons with three men.

'Apprentices could do that work at seventeen. A couple of freemen around ship and two or three boys. You couldn't get it no cheaper. The governor would have as many boys at work as he could and sack the freeman. As soon as we became freemen we would get the sack. We used to call it our out-of-work papers.

197

'Once you bought the barge, you paid very little tax on the river. The owner could put a dozen barges round a ship and leave two men to get on with it. Then the lorry came in. The lorry only does twenty tonnes, with all those men on them. Yet the river lost the work.

'It was all put down to restrictive practices and that they murdered the job, which at times they did. But a lot was brought on by the governors themselves, so when we got the chance we tried to stop it. The dockers did overdo it a bit, but they were really taken advantage of.

'I've done a bit of docking when there was a date ship up. Everybody went, dockers, stevedores [the men who stowed the cargo in ships], porters, to get eleven shillings and twopence [50p] a day. To work you had to get a tally. There were so many people, he would throw them all up into the air, so we would fight like dogs to get a tally for half a day's work. This was going on all over the port, so you can understand them being a bit militant.

'You was out in all weathers, with no restriction on hours. The governor could work you seven days and nights and he very often did. The unfairness was that, at the same time there was one thousand men out of work.

'The foreman ran the job. Some was rats, some was better. They might say, "You've got one at Tilbury tonight. Hop home and have a change." Or another guy would keep you hanging about.

'But there was a great deal of pride working on the river. We were part of this continuing history. It was different to working in a factory.'

The river did not grip Bill Woods as fiercely as it did some. He went to South Africa, returned and finished his working life as a tug captain at the Barrier. Well paid work. It made up for his missing bus fares.

Another old waterman, Jim Smith, is wondering where all the cargoes have gone. All along the wharfs, from Brentford practically to Tilbury was stowed 'every commodity you could name. Where it's gorn now, I don't know. It must be inland I suppose.

'It was a hard life but it was an 'appy life. You was never in the same place for more than a couple of days. Erith one day loading logs from Nigeria. The next day British and Foreign Wharf near Tower Bridge with casks of brandy from France. Then along to the Clyde boat for Dundee.

'We would be trading up and down the creeks – Barking Creek, Dartford Creek, up the canals, Limehouse Cut, Regents Canal.' He was towed by horse up past London Zoo in Regent's park.

Once he unloaded a bouquet of imported roses locked in a block of ice for some glittering occasion. Sublime extravagance.

'I can remember the river, from London Bridge to Tower Bridge, nothing but ships unloading, crowded with merchandise. They used to call it the larder of the world. I can remember when I was still at school, walking over London Bridge and what was going on there was terrific.'

198

He started when he was twenty-four, apprenticed to the man next door, John Wheeler, in Boscawen Street, Deptford, 'to learn his art and with him to dwell and serve upon the river, from the day of the date hereof until the full end and term of seven years.'

'I used to be called "linen draper's son." I was an interloper into the industry.' Imagine, then, this interloper sailing up to the Normandy beaches in a Thames barge with two eighty horsepower Chrysler engines at the back, one of 100 Thames watermen in the 1944 invasion.

'I was on loan to the Yanks for ninety days. Great pride though you didn't think so at the time.' His cargo was nothing more than water. 'I never knew how important water was until I had that barge. You couldn't make tea or wash wounds.

'We lost some men going over. We had to leave a few hours before the main shipping because we were so slow.' Mrs Smith interjects: 'Bill Shaw, Alice's husband, you lost him.'

Syd Huntley, waterman and lighterman, tells a story to illustrate the demands of his former job. He had been out working for two days and returned home at six in the evening. At eight his wife Violet said: 'Syd, I'd better get to the nursing home. I think the baby is coming.' Syd said: 'Can't you wait a bit. I've got a terrible headache and I've got to be back at work at midnight.'

Thames water is thicker than blood, so Syd left for work at midnight. 'I never saw him for four days,' says Violet. 'That really is the truth. I'm telling no lies.'

Syd and Violet's combined telling of this story is an example of the state of almost permanent toil the waterman found himself in. Syd has just said this: 'Good old days? Terrible old days. I don't know what the others have told you, but I worked fifty years and I didn't enjoy one day of it. No, I must be honest. I never had a regular job all the time I was afloat. You was pitched from pillar to post.'

'You never had a holiday,' interjected Violet.

'Never had a holiday,' echoed Syd. 'It's all altered today. You know that, don't you? Oh dear, oh lor, it's a lump of cake today.'

Syd is an exceptional waterman, as he has shown in this little commentary on his working life.

Violet: 'They are very proud around here. You are the only one who isn't proud.'

Syd: 'I'm not. I try to come down to the truth of the matter. We thought we was a very proud lot and I think that was most of our trouble. Really we was cheap labour.' He refuses to display his certificate celebrating his freedom of the river, framed or unframed.

I feel Syd was entitled to his complaints after fifty years of the following

199

sort of thing: 'You would row a fifty ton barge up to Wandsworth gas works, load fifty tons of sulphur ammonia, carrying all the sacks on your back, then get on the phone to the governor. He would say "Take it down to Albert Dock tonight, Syd."

'He said "tonight". See what I mean, not "next day". "Tonight". Exactly. We ought to have been ashamed of ourselves. So after working since eight in the morning, at five p.m., on the ebb tide, you would take the barge down to Albert Dock.'

Syd, over eighty now, started work in 1926, following his father and grandfather, which puts him within two generations of the great Victorian beginnings of the London docks.

'Fifty years, rowing the barges up and down. Never had a regular job. You might be with one firm for two months and then somewhere else. You had to get what you could. You worked night and day: you would go out Monday and might not come home till Friday. You couldn't turn the work down. The master lightermen got away with murder. They didn't supply us with nothing.'

Violet: 'You used to get soaked. You had nothing to wash your hands and nowhere to go to the toilet. Unbelievable that it was allowed to go on.'

Syd: 'We carried some terrible old stuff at times.' The worst? 'Guano, bird muck from this island somewhere. We would unload it at Greenwich Buoys into the barge for manure. But we got no extra. Today they wouldn't stand for it. We thought we was the kings of the river. Funny idea we had.'

His youngest son was on the river for a time. 'Have a guess what he is now. A hairdresser.'

And the decline of his trade? 'You could see it coming. You could really see it was old fashioned, although I didn't think it would happen so quick, but I did say "This can't last." '

Violet: 'That's what did you. Containers. Straight out of the ship into the lorry.'

Syd, the last waterman in his family, having shorn his trade of all false sentiment, surprises me with a contradictory image. It is a photograph of a punt, a fifty tonner, the sort he and his father used to row, starting away with hope and diligence to catch the tide under the pink early morning sky. 'That could have been my dad and me.

'But it's dying out; it will die out and I can't see no hopes for it.'

I leave these fading recollections and cross back to the south bank. At the side of the office built over the old bridge, Number One London Bridge, there is a riverside walk put in at additional cost by the developers for pedestrians. Along the entire bank, I have never set my foot on such fine stone. There is a tubular bar to conduct me down.

A short way along a group of secretaries are eating wholemeal bread sandwiches inside the huge, mirrored atrium of the Cottons Centre, next to an imitation Lake District rocky outcrop, flowing with recycled Thames water and greenery. For a time I wander in unchallenged, on moving walkways, pink-carpeted, mirror-lined corridors, past waves etched in glass.

In this same, smart riverside complex a pub is dedicated, incongruously, to a tea baron. John Horniman, who personally welcomed the tea clippers bearing in his fortune, was said to have been the first merchant to sell his tea 'unadulterated, in sealed packets'. For this he was known as Honest John. On my polite request, the barman cannot immediately tell me where I may purchase a cup of tea.

A little further on, opposite the permanently moored HMS Belfast, the onward rush of South Bank development falters. Once this was a lorry park: then an urban wildlife park, where naturalists proved the ability of the fox to invade any environment, by photographing it with Tower Bridge as a backdrop. But, the developers promise more sparkling new edifices here. One proposal for this site is a neo-classical creation which, in a mist, will look like the Houses of Parliament, and could persuade an airline pilot that he is flying the wrong way down the Thames to Heathrow.

I eat my picnic on a rampart next to the river, overlooking the Tower, in the company of about twenty well-behaved children from a Kent school. We are doing the correct thing. 'It is from the river, and not from Tower Hill, that the first inspection of this venerable edifice should be made,' advises *Royal River*.

A fashion model in denim dress is posing in front of Tower Bridge while a photographer in grey raincoat, legs split like a novice ice skater, struggles for the indefinable camera angle and facial composure in his subject that puts photographs into *Vogue*.

On this old river, Tower Bridge is an outstanding innovation. 'O cloud cap't towers: O spanking spans' exclaimed Father Thames in an 1894 *Punch* cartoon.

'The opening of the Tower Bridge on Saturday was a picturesque and stately ceremonial,' recorded *The Times*, July 2nd, 1894. 'The decorations were brilliant and profuse, while the brilliant sunshine brought out in full relief the many beauties of the noble river which all true Englishmen love with a proud affection as the chiefest glory of their ancient capital.' It was opened by the Prince of Wales, whose grandson was to do such productive service at bridges upstream.

10

THE cottagers of Rotherhithe knew something of his fame.
                    – *Growltiger's Last Stand*, T. S. Eliot.

I AM REACHING the end of my walk. Once in the early 1980s this section
of the river was so drab, with so many derelict wharves, piers and jetties,
that the pleasure boats running down to Greenwich used to turn on an
audio-visual display to take their customers' minds off the view.

This is the Thames Gaffer Hexham worked in *Our Mutual Friend*,
helping himself from the pockets of the drowned. 'Down by where the
accumulated scum of humanity seemed to be washed from the higher
ground, like so much moral sewage.'

The change is startling. Today this is the most vibrant and commercial
section of the entire river. It is a land of portable telephones and offices of
plate-glass Eiger faces. The planning rules which villages in the Green Belt
hold as holy writ have been boldly set aside to make the miracle work. The
London Docklands Development Corporation can do what it likes.

It is also a triumph for common sense and architectural conservation.
While twenty years ago it would have been routine to flatten the old
warehouses, today they are refurbished as penthouses.

A short distant downstream in Wapping is the shrine to the printing
industry's biggest step forward since Caxton, the headquarters of Rupert
Murdoch's controverial News International empire. Subsequently, almost
the whole of Fleet Street decamped to the Docklands.

The path will take me past the best of the palaces at Greenwich, my walk
for today, and ultimately down to Britain's only real candidate for the
Eighth Wonder of the World at the Barrier, nine miles from here. I will
meet the last of the old proprietors and hear of scuttling, river bed relics.

I walk on, under Tower Bridge, to Bermondsey, past the sliding, silent
river and down tight streets. The old books would not have drawn their
readers past this point. It was a sour land of strange tribes, and rituals, of

The Thames Barrage, Charlton.

'I have fought a good fight. I have finished my course.'

— 2 Timothy, 7.

violent attack on the outsider. Now, only a lingering resentment to incomers remains among some local people.

The docks are dead but their aromas linger. At Cinnamon Wharf the smell of spices is still as pungent as a Christmas cake factory. The transformation of mean, artless warehouses into flats is something which would have amazed the old watermen more than any innovation along their river.

To them, technological innovation outside their environment, such as jet aircraft trundling down the river line to Heathrow, would have made more sense than heated towel rails and high quality ceramic disk chrome-plated mixer taps throughout, which are standard fittings in Cinnamon Wharf penthouses.

BMWs nose through the cramped streets of converted warehouses in this alien world behind Jamaica Road and the familiar focus of Hassan Brothers Kebab House. 'Build your heliport in your back garden' taunts a slogan.

'The crowded shipping of the Pool, the steamers coming and going, the vessels lying at anchor here and there, as if the river were a huge dock, feebly represents the vast tonnage which is borne on our grand and historic river every day of every year. Behind the great piles of warehouses – towering over the house-tops, ornamenting the sky with a curious fretwork of masts and spars and cordage – lie scores and hundreds of the vessels of all nations, crowded into dock beyond dock, making a line of rigging, of glittering yards and masts of furled sails and flaunting canvas on either side of the Thames for mile on mile,' wrote *Royal River*.

At the Old Justice pub, a man with a radio telephone is summoned back to his work. The few yards between the pub and the river, where houses are to be built, have been derelict since the war. Eileen, the barmaid, remembers the steamers plying down to Southend, Clacton and Margate, a comfortable day-trip from Tower Bridge.

On a wall outside, there is a lively interchange of ideas by the sloganisers. '75 more local jobs lost for an ultra modern apartment,' informs one.

Draw back to the middle of the river at Rotherhithe, and you see an amazing thing. Braithwaite and Dean's premises, a thin three-storied building, standing proud and alone like a single tooth in an empty bottom gum. Peter Braithwaite is the only man left in a wasteland qualified to speak about the return of fat times.

There is nothing to his left for a hundred yards and nothing to his right. All around are bright new, glassy dwellings with sloping sides and flourishing pot plants on balconies.

This is his bleak prognosis of the Thames as trade route: 'I can tell you as a professional man who knows his bloody business that the ships are not coming back.'

Managing director Peter Braithwaite conducts himself, as the last general carrier on the river, according to a searing commercial logic, uninfected by nostalgia.

'Nostalgia? I don't see the Thames in a nostalgic light. Some spend hours swinging the lamp about what it was like. I don't know about that. You can drown in buckets of tears. Some people live and breathe the river, but I have other interests. It's always been a nine to five job for me on the river.' He lives in Catford and travels in.

Mr Braithwaite is a practical survivor. As a general carrier, he only has specialists left to compete with. 'We are available to do what there is to do. How long it goes on for, I don't know.'

He survived by remaining sharp in a diminishing pack of hunters. As one door closed, another opened. Every time a competitor went out of business, it left a certain amount of work which the survivors snaffled up.

He knows he cannot compete directly with the roads. Lorries always win. Even refuse, lugged in fistfulls of barges down river, is cheaper by lorry. He claims it is only carried on the river for environmental reasons.

From his high office Braithwaite has surveyed (without Dean, a long-dead sleeping partner) the inexorable decline of the river. 'Lots of things we could do economically have gone into containers.'

They can compete with bulk grains. Easy to handle, pumped in and out. And they have the competitive edge in carrying cargo in large quantities from Tilbury Dock to riverside destinations such as Gravesend Reach.

But most of their work is below the barrier. They have taken pressure vessels for the Reading Courage Brewery, up as far as Walton on Thames, and occasionally to Rank's Mill at Battersea. It was their burden that blocked Mr Noble's view of Isleworth Church. 'Other than that, we don't do anything up river.' His tugs work mainly from Swanscombe, in and out of Tilbury Dock.

'We don't have the right to expect a single tonne next week from anybody, but we shall get it, provided we give a service.'

This stretch once bustled with vessels carrying the produce of Empire. Commercial traffic can now be summarised in this little list: boats carrying London rubbish; tripping and party boats; Thames Line; the Bow boats carrying aggregate to Wandsworth; Blue Circle boats; Hall's ballast; Charrington Oil; the Port of London Authority; the River Police; Tidy Thames.

He repeats his proprietor's prospectus for the river. 'Nobody wants to establish wharves or factories here. But they do want money-broking floors and they do want to live here. Some of the planners are thinking instead of gold, frankincense and myrrh.

'The area is going up now, oh yuerrs. And does that offend local people. They say, "We can't afford it. How scandalous, these wealthy people coming down here." They stir up antipathy to anybody who has got a couple of bob more than they. They say this is a working class area for factories and docks and not for money broking. Money broking is quite unworthy of their children. They want to reserve wharves for when the ships come back. But they won't come back.'

He believes that if the overmanning of the Dock Labour board was cut out, the river might become competitive again. The former employees of some companies, who have told me grim stories, might disagree.

Mr Braithwaite has been in business on the river since 1942. His grandfather Charles Thomas Albert founded the company, but the family had been working on the river for four generations by then, descended from a Braithwaite who walked down from the north of England.

The family moved through Stepney, Wapping, Bow, the Adelphi, handling all sorts of produce except the demanding coal and rubbish, and specialising in oil seeds.

His grandfather had a fleet of small dumb barges. After the war, they built their own, the *Chastim, Hurricane, Charlock, Regard, Charlight* and *Leonie*. They worked in and out of all the docks, but not much above London Bridge. Once they carried marble chippings to Pimlico.

Using the tide, their men rowed forty ton dumb barges up and down river. They stopped that in the 1950s. 'It was causing too much damage. They kept hitting things. It was very difficult to damage a dumb barge, which is very strong, especially right forrard. They could be undamaged themselves but put a ruddy great dent in ships' plates. It was antisocial. Less skilled men were on the river, and perhaps less careful men.'

These Dickensian chambers are a living anachronism. Mr Braithwaite conducts his business as he speaks, searching in neat ledgers. I can understand how the players in a story he tells me rifled the company's name, assuming it was part of history. This is the story.

Mr Braithwaite saw his company name in a newspaper, attributed to an estate agent. He went along and asked to speak to Mr Braithwaite, or in his absence, to Mr Dean. The proprietors had to confess there were no such gentlemen. The real Mr Braithwaite decided recourse to law to win the sole right to his own company name was too wearisome.

He shows me a pre-war photo of his premises, then just another tooth in a full set of South Bank dentures. They were dining rooms then, next door to the Case barge builders. 'A bit of a gambling den.'

We repair to the Angel, the first building across the wasteland. 'A dirty little beerhouse when I first knew it.' He was consulted, as a regular, about what he wanted in the new Angel. 'No plastic sawdust; no musak; no fruit machines. And get rid of them horrible scruffy unshaven barmen.' They satisfied him on all points. My beer was pulled by a gentleman of impeccable facial smoothness, of indeterminate mid-Thames accent. The old proprietors are still men of influence.

Outside the pub, in the oasis of cleared waterfront, I meet Anna who works in a nearby office. She is painting 'a strangely nutty view' which takes in towers and cathedrals, the new riverside palaces, bridges, the City, Wren's St Paul's, and the Post Office Tower.

At the Mayflower, whence Captain Christopher Jones set sail in 1620 in the Mayflower to America, they are selling Jolly Jack Tar Chicken, Force Six Steaks and Keelhauled Plaice. I walk back down Pumping House Street and Brunel Road past the Underground station to the north bank, which uses the tunnel built by Marc Brunel, father of Isambard. In the station there is the sound of constant (cold) running water.

No sooner have I reassured myself that bustling everyday London is a tube ticket away, than I plunge into one of those deep narrow alleys between old glowering warehouses. High up there is a smart sign painted like one of those magical old circus posters, advertising a man whose work is finding things. I ring at a secret door I cannot pass. He bids me enter.

Ron Goode's showcases are all bodge-up jobs on account of the money situation. His spelling may be eccentric, his guided tour unconventional. But the legends to his finds have been carefully researched, and he is as keen to instruct his visitors as any more polished museum curator.

Take his River Fencibles' button. Caption reads: 'This button could have been lost on January 8th 1816 during the river funeral procession of Lord Nelson, when they rowed up from Greenwich to Whitehall. There were a considerable number of gunboats and rowing boats and the London River Fencibles took part in the procession.' He doesn't guess at anything or make it up.

A big piece of whale bone? Simple. Surrey Docks was once a whaling station. The Museum of London keeps asking him if he has found a harpoon yet. He produces another bone. 'Don't know what this is yet. Too large for a cow or anything like that. Probably an elephant, from a circus.'

The Thames is a time warp into which Ron has opened a little door. Its muddy waters are churning up hints of the past, competing to be found. They are offered to the keen-eyed, who conjecture their infinitely insignificant associations. A low tide and a skidding boat hull will reveal for a moment, for a day, for the sharp eyes of Ron a tangible proof that Higgs existed (medal awarded by the London County Council for punctual attendance in 1905).

There are coins from Nero and Hadrian. A Julia Maesa Augusta denarius. 'Very low content of silver with tin. The grandmother of two emperors,' explains the card.

Here is a coin from the reign of Yan Huan. What is a Chinese coin doing in the Thames? Ron did hear that some were lost overboard. He will wait for low tide to see if the river can spare any more where he found these.

Marbles, toys, knives, items of crime, a flea comb, Jews harps, buttons off clothing, coins out of pockets, clay pipes thrown away (Thames as rubbish dump), badges from the Rotherhithe, Surrey, 23rd Rifle Volunteers, 1861; the US Military; the RAF; ARP, Air Raid Patrol.

'You say how did the ARP get in there. These buttons came from the same place. There was a jetty next to a ARP row of cottages at Trinty Wharf. They used to dash out to a boat, fiddling with their jackets, when there was a fire.'

Musket balls. A river skirmish? 'No, lead works up the river. It makes sense when you find the clues.'

But the Thames defies the conventional archaeologist, used to uncovering remains in proper order, late over early. In the river mud George II snuggles next to an Anglo-Saxon coin. All jumbled together in temporal anarchy.

Love tokens, defaced and bent in the proper fashion, (does that mean requited or unrequited love?) Emperor Napoleon; Charles II in sharp detail; William and Mary, gaunt heads gazing resolutely right; George III. He has Queen Anne buttons but none of her coins yet.

Some finds hint at painful loss on the boat above. 'I turned over a stone and there was this George III halfpenny. I turned over one almost next to it and there was another, same date. The person lost both together. Probably a week's wages.'

The tide is as low as it can go. Ron, hatted indoors, is not out there seeking his tribute because the wind was stinging his eyes. I chat to him over the suspicious jowls of his huge wolfhound, masticating at my chest height.

He worked in Gerry Cottles circus, then did the markets; he was a docker, but he didn't like the unions. He went self employed because 'I didn't want anyone to tell me what to do.'

He has been walking the mud for seven years, since he gave up work to look after his daughter. 'Only on this side of the river up by Chambers Wharf, as far as the Spiller's building.'

On the other side is someone with a metal detector. Recently a silver collar valued at £27,000 (slight drawing in of breath by Ron) was found there. But Ron doesn't recognise a competitor. He never goes to the north bank. It might as well be France. The Londoner's loyalties are narrowly drawn.

'I'm only interested in this side. And I want to find what belongs to this area.' (Example: medallion from the Brunel Tunnel, 1843.) 'Its just like walking down the street. You get to know it.

'I could go down there one day and find nothing and in the same spot next day find a gold ring. Depends on how rough the weather is and if the river is stirring things up. The river is washing the cover way with the decline in shipping. A chap spent three days digging and I found more than he did on top.' He doesn't use a metal detector. 'There is so much iron there, and I might miss other things, such as bottles and clay pipes.'

Next week he hopes to find things on the edge of an exceptionally low tide. He wonders at the harvest even further out. A few months ago he found an Anglo-Saxon coin in perfect condition. 'Where those tyres are. Probably an original from Fresia which is modern 'Olland, or Denmark.'

Sometimes the master is outwitted by the pupil. He took some schoolchildren down to the mud. There was nothing about. Then a child found a seal in the shape of an upright figure, seventeenth century or medieval.

He shows me pottery, which may have come from the Delft factory up by the Angel, the site of Edward III's palace. Military buckles, clay pipes still tobacco stained. One has a goat's head with a salaciously upward pointing beard, the work of Edward Bellis of Elephant Lane. Others were crafted by Joseph Andrews, William Williams and Joseph Grout.

'I'm not in it for value. The only satisfaction is when I find something I haven't got. I've given a hell of a lot away.'

He did sell for £2,500, through Sothebys, a seventeenth century engagement ring. It carried this secret, enduring message on the inside rim: 'In Christ and thee my comfort be'. He sold a little pewter axe to the London Museum. 'I could have got eighty pounds but I took forty. I'm quite happy because I can see it and they gave me a couple of colour slides.'

Ron sees me politely out. We are in Docklands where nothing old is scheduled to last more than a few years. Ron expects to be displaced soon, like a coin, scuttling along the river floor. He is not even sure he wants to stay.

'When I was young, it was just like one big family around here. You could go into anybody's house; there was parties. These days people just break into your van, pinching things, breaking things. Just up the road here someone with a pellet gun shot a swan, which is out of order.'

I walk for a time through a strange, quiet land, where South London projects a firm, square shoulder into the Thames. Looking for something real by which to celebrate this empty stretch, I find what could be a timber warehouse but turns out to be the film studio where the acclaimed film of Dickens' *Little Dorrit* was made.

Further on, outside the Lavender Pond Nature Trust, is a perennial cornflower growing fine and tall and blue out of the pavement – the books have it growing in waste places and roadsides. I feel like a sailor spying land after many weeks at sea, in my case after a long walk through the metropolis: there are coots again, and reeds and a large pond where there was once a channel through which water used be pumped in from the river to maintain the levels into Lavender Dock.

The best photograph Bob Faller-Fritsch can find to show me the original spread of the old Surrey Commercial Docks on the South Bank was taken from a German Heinkel, on a bombing raid in 1940. Bob, in the company of crawling eighteen-month-old Katy, conducts a hundred school groups a year around this urban nature reserve. The visitors have left their creations, a giant cardboard bat and fly, hovering in the converted pump house.

The park, which, says Bob, caught 'the conscience of the developers', is the antidote to luxury apartments and slick business. 'Living proof that the two can get on.' This marsh, entirely man made since the docks closed, recreates a habitat that existed here about the time of the Romans. There are reed buntings, lesser and greater reed mace and the great hairy willow herb, known in this part of the country, even if it has never before been found in Docklands, as codlins and cream.

The reeds grow more vigorously than in the wild, an inch a day, because the imported soil on which they were planted was too rich. The pond is topped up with tap water, which is also too rich, and promotes too much weed growth. Left to itself, this ecological park would soon become Dockland's first jungle. Local people have absorbed it into their community. The vandals are bored with it. They accept it as part of the environment.

'The charm of this place is the answer Louis Armstrong gave when he was asked to describe the appeal of jazz,' says Bob. ' "If you don't know, I can't tell you." People come and work here on community work schemes for very little pay and become intensely loyal.'

Past a dozen apartment building sites, at Lavender Pier on the point of this shoulder of land, I meet an agitated man. He is just about to make the seventh or eighth recent attempt to start a passenger service on London's river – the sceptical old watermen are not sure how many failed attempts there have been. All along the river, ferries have closed and their boathouses have been washed away, yet Roger Mabbott of Thames Line is approaching the starting line with high hopes.

The trial service has already produced a rich library of traveller's tales. The conventional London commuter's story concerns breakdown, congestion or interference by spiteful weather. But those who come to work by water can relate to their wondering workmates the source material of rollicking salty yarns.

Journalists bound for the Isle of Dogs from Waterloo on one of the first river ferries in 1987 tantalised their landbound colleagues with reports of a close brush with a Brazilian destroyer. They speak, too, of the efficacy of the river for clearing the head: a brisk off-sea wind makes the Thames one of the most inherently refreshing commuter routes.

Roger, deputy managing director of Thames Line, dressed in a smart suit, is a businessman selling a brisk twenty minutes by hydrofoil, as he might canned drinks or hamburgers.

They are selling the river by plastic card. Business and estate agents will dispense cards, which carry electronic units of opportunity to ride on the Thames, as they might once have handed out cigars. There was to be a lot of giving away for the grand opening. Some of the boats are already named after banks and big newspapers, which treat the craft as a floating advertisement.

In selling its service, the company proclaims a bigger difference in quality between it and the competition – between travelling on land and on water – than those famous washing powder advertisements contrasting garments in shining white and dingy grey. Absolute metal-locked congestion on one side and unrestricted open river on the other.

The river, swept clear of commerce, is already attaining Max Hobb's dream by making London a little more like Venice and Hamburg. 'We are going back to where we were several centuries ago when the river was used as an artery of transport, across or down,' says Roger. 'Even until the 1950's there were vast numbers of passengers, before the world moved on. There has been a quiet period and we are trying to liven it up again.'

People were first carried about in large numbers on the rivers in wherries, which probably evolved in the fifteenth century. By about 1600 they were commonplace, used for short journeys on the London Thames just as taxis are today. 'The typical craft was clench-built with a high pointed bow ending in a sharp iron nose' notes a catalogue by Richmond Library. The disreputable rule of wherrymen who would rob or eject customers mid-stream if they argued over the fare, was ended by an 1555 act which led to the formation of the Company of Watermen. The skiff, introduced in the seventeenth century was a more graceful successor.

Thames Line chose an Incat, Australian design, built in Britain under licence. 'A much lower risk than many other more sophisticated craft. It came off the slipway, straight into the water and went down the river at twenty-five knots.' The cautious old Thames waterman, who alone is licenced to navigate the river, approves.

Thames Line may succeed, because London is becoming more like

Hong Kong than the planners ever imagined. The roads are full, public transport is bursting with passengers, yet I have walked through London along the side of a river more or less empty.

There is no impediment between Richmond and the river Barrier. The benefits of being conducted by fast boat between these two points, and anywhere within, are clear. Roger, a former seaman with a cruise company, sees markets isolated from and badly served by existing public transport. But he believes the great London public will not tolerate a waterways restatement of what he calls the bus-stop effect, where several buses arrive together, followed by a long gap.

I walk on along Rotherhithe Street to what might be the most expensive farmland in Britain, worth about £7 million for the two acres. The Surrey Docks Farm is another planned interruption of the sweep of exclusive residential and office accommodation.

There is rosebay willow herb, ox eye daisy and meadow sweet, Toggenbourg goats, Beulah Speckleface sheep, and bees. We are fast inside the city, yet this urban area has an unlikely reputation for agricultural achievement: the world record yield by a goat was once held by a Bermondsey animal.

Yachts tack across Greenland Dock, where once watermen stored acres of floating wood. The long open views are broken up by newly planted trees inside smart metal guards. A heavy shower bears down from an epicentre around St Paul's and, as I was once at Cricklade, I am caught without defence on the huge empty entrance to the dock. However, on this occasion I have remembered waterproof trousers. The torrent beats down unavailingly on my back as I curl up in the manner of a hedgehog. Within five minutes the sun is shining and I am dry.

The bleak flats of the Pepys Estate in Deptford is graced by sound of the distant countryside, the chattering of house martins sweeping through the air. The playwright Marlowe, murdered as political victim, or killed in a dispute over a tavern bill, is buried in the St Nicholas's Church. The pub names around me invoke the growing call of the sea – The Lone Sailor, Navy Arms, Norway Street.

And so to Greenwich, whose name is now as firmly linked with a single ship, the Cutty Sark, as any village on the Thames. Once it was esteemed for its fish dinner, 'perhaps the most curious repast ever invented by the ingenuity of the most imaginative hotel keeper,' wrote Dickens, junior. 'Many courses of fish prepared in every conceivable way, followed by ducks and peas, beans and bacon, cutlets and other viands.'

His father wrote: 'What a dinner! Specimens of all the fishes that swam in the sea . . . and the dishes being seasoned with bliss . . . were of perfect flavour, and the golden drinks had been bottled in the golden age and hoarded up their sparkles ever since.' It was said there was no morning-after headache like that which followed a Greenwich dinner.

> AT evening we may sometimes hear some vast splash, or a snort
> that only science could attribute to a fish, and we know that the wild
> beasts of the water underworld are out and playing.
> *– The Thames in June*, Anonymous.

I cross under the river in the Greenwich Tunnel, to the north bank, to the Isle of Dogs. On the front page of today's *Independent* is a picture, composed by a computer, depicting the Isle of Dogs from an imaginary viewpoint, fifteen thousand feet up and half a mile due west.

The isle, dewdrop-shaped and a mile across, is an ideal object for such contemplation. The river loops around it in one of the tightest bends on the river. It is the easiest area in all London to isolate and put into a picture.

It shows a proposed empire of offices, vaguely recalling the vast space cities science fiction writers used to favour. But this is no futurologist's fancy: this chummy, intense little neighbourhood where my maternal grandparents were born, played and lived in Ferry Street, will be overseen by Britain's largest skyscraper to date, and one of the most massive office developments in Europe.

From Eve Hostettler's crowded office on the tip of the isle, the birth pangs of the commercial leviathan at Canary Wharf, a mile or so north west, are inaudible above the pounding of heavy lorries on Manchester Road which runs along the dewdrop's base.

In this office the Island History Trust holds more than three thousand photographs. This is an essential reference point in any taking stock of the Island. When a community is challenged, as the Lilliputian islanders are as if by a giant's boot in a children's story, they may take strength by examining their own beginnings.

Few communities can call up such a wealth of pictorial recollections. The SS France at anchor off the isle in the 1920s; 1960s mill workers at McDougalls Flour Mill; Manchester Road in the 1900s; a 1956 Sunday School outing from Alpha Grove Methodist chapel, Millwall; Mr Raynor of Cubbitt Town, with grandchildren; an island wedding reception in the canteen of Sam Cutler's steelworks, Westferry Road, Millwall; a street peace party in 1919.

The power of these photographs works even on me. I am not an islander but this is the first place on the Thames where I feel a personal connection. Eve sustains it as if I am a local by looking up various Parrotts and Oakes, my grandfather and grandmother's names, in her file of three thousand named pictures.

I greet possible ancient members of the family, long forgotten since that dramatic day in 1904 when my grandparents hauled across to Paddington, with my late aunt, for a departure as complete and final as if they were bound for America.

The island has perhaps the most distinct identity of any part of London. It is cradled by the river on three sides. (It is an island only in the sense that it is an entirely distinct community, not in the geographical sense.)

My grandparents recalled the huge prows of ships overhanging Ferry Street. The Thames has shaped the island's history. They built an embankment round it to keep the river out. They ran ditches across it. It once contained the pastures where the best beef in London was raised.

Then came the docks. There was easy access on both sides, with a long foreshore for shipyards. Factories were built on its edge, with easy access for heavy goods. 'Now those newcomers pay an awful lot to look out on all that mud and those bodies floating past, so it is still shaping our lives,' says Eve. 'Our story is all about the Thames. We are made by the river. I can't imagine six hundred acres in Croydon with the same things happening.'

The isle's first big trauma came in the 1860s when ship-building collapsed. Between ten thousand and fifteen thousand people lost their jobs. Many people left the island. Then the docks were built. Evacuations in the 1939-45 war reduced the island's population from twenty-one thousand to nine thousand. Many islanders never returned. When the docks closed in the 1970s the traditional life of the island passed for ever.

It was a cold, bleak exposed place, with poor public transport. It is no longer isolated. Now, in the automated Docklands Light Railway, opened by the Queen in 1987, it has one of the best urban transport systems in Britain.

Islanders, trans-shipped by the little driverless trains to outside jobs, look down from those long-legged viaducts upon gangs of workers who will build up Canary Wharf a little higher before they return in the evening. This hugeness will be accepted as a natural part of their landscape by the young islanders, just as my grandparents accepted those magical, sculpted prows.

'Traditional society understood that a knowledge of where they came from was very important,' says Eve. 'This archive gives that knowledge to the islanders. People are happy to reconstitute the past. Whether they wallow in the past or face the future with more confidence, depends on the individual.'

It is the sort of project I would have expected to find in self-celebrating Barnes or Richmond. Study of local history tends to devolve to people who have the time and money to practise it. Eve is a rarity, an urban historian paid to uncover the islanders' past and welcome them in to examine it. Now she is interested in more recent photographs. 'History is slipping through people's fingers, like sand. We tend to equate historical value with distance. But what about the island now?'

And so to the end. I return to the south bank and walk down to Charlton, by the remote waterside: down Ballast Quay, River Bank, past Blackwall Reach where the clogging traffic is tucked silently away in a tunnel; past Bugsby's Reach, where the river begins to shake off London and its hindering curves, and straightens out; and on to Woolwich where the river is full and wide and not yet sea. Here I meet a happy riverman.

Bill Sargent, seventy, is still working on the river as a pilot, a job he loves. He was the last of ten children. His father died when he was six months in the 1918 influenza epidemic. His mother ran the famous Anchor and Hope, on Riverside, the pub taken over by his grandfather in 1878 after the river disaster when the *Bywell Castle* ran into the pleasure steamer *Princess Alice*.

He corrects what seems to be a common mistake in these parts. The landlord and wife were not both drowned on the Alice. His wife was drowned and by the next year the landlord had left the pub.

There was a second disaster outside the pub on June 8th, 1914, when the *Auriol* and the *Corinthian* collided. The *Auriol* sank and members of the Sargent family picked up fifteen crew members. 'It happened right there. We still have the *Daily Mirror* cutting.

'I was apprenticed to my older brother Harry. We were all freemen. If you were an apprentice lighterman, all you needed to know was how to pump water out of a barge, or sweep the hold out for cargo or make a rope fast to a tug. There was no comparison to the waterman's job. Some watermen were also lightermen. They were treated with respect.'

The family began as mud pilots. They would position barges on the wharf to unload or discharge them. Later they branched out into mooring ships on buoys, and moving them about on the river. I've taken boats in on the tide, discharged 1,200 tonnes of steel coils and taken them out again on the same tide. We would swing the vessels round when the crew were at tea break to point them out again.'

The Sargents, as pilots, are still one of the busiest families on the river. We watch the remnants of the river's trade – ships with scrap metal from Battersea, and sea-dredged aggregate for Millwall. 'The river was busiest in the 1950s and 1960s. On the Friday night sailing they would come down nose to tail, all trying to get past one another.

'There were regular weekly boats from the Clyde Shipping Company, between Dundee, Perth and London. You could set your watch by them, and General Steam Ships running out to the near-continent or Mediterranean.

215

'And the colliers. There used to be four sets of buoys here, with three ships on each, serving the gas works, power stations and coal wharves. We used to take them up to meet the pilot who took them under the bridges.'

He recalls outstanding feats. During the last war Bill and his brother piloted the ships carrying sixty thousand tons of sugar for the Ministry of Food from Tate & Lyle's warehouses to be dispersed to safer sites in the north. 'We would have fourteen ships lying around on buoys. I was the only one who knew what was the next one to turn. It was a fantastic situation. We were working night and day. It was just before Normandy.

'We cleared up sixty-five jobs in one day. That's a record for any family. In four months we quadrupled our earnings.' He could go for weeks without seeing a bus or tram, living in the pub, out of the pub, along the bank, into the boat to do what had to be done, intimately involved with the river.

Fog was the waterman's torment. 'After a few days of fog there would be ships littered all over the place.' One night he had been ordered to pilot a German ship from Surrey Docks down to Becton gas works. The dock master made him wait. His was the last ship out.

'It was getting dark. The fog was looming up. We went down to Greenwich safely. All of sudden we were lost. It was absolutely thick. We couldn't see the mast. It was like a blanket. We proceeded dead slow, on the high water. I told the master we couldn't stop. We had to keep going as far as we could.

'There were ships lying at anchor off the Isle of Dogs. Then I could see this one right across the river. I told him to look for the ship's stern close on the port side. "Yes, I can see it." We shot through down to Blackwell Point and it got slightly better. We turned the corner and reached Charlton Buoys. I said "Sod it, I'll keep going." Then we ran into the fog again. There were ships all over the shop, dotted about at anchor, down to the Royals in Woolwich Reach, dozens of them.

'I saw a bit of a gap. The master was flummoxed by then. I said "Let go." Down went the anchor. I saw her swing round. "Now up." The captain, he didn't even see the ruddy berth as we went alongside.

'After we berthed, the master said "Come with me." The bottles came out of the bonded locker. He said "Have anything you like." The mate came off the forecastle. He said "Pilot, never before have I seen anything like that." But it was ninety per cent good luck, one of those times when you push your luck and get away with it.'

Bill has had one accident in his long and distinguished career on the river. He was piloting a ship with wool for Goole. 'The skipper had been on the bottle. When we left the berth below the naval college, I saw this empty tug running up across my bow. I tried to pass him green to green.

'All of a sudden he changed course and came straight at me. By the time she hit us, we were all stopped. She hit us on the starboard bow, and pushed us round across the river into a tug and tow running up. The mate said "She's sinking. There's water running out." I said "We can't be sinking. If water's running out, it can't be running in." I never did hear how that case was settled.'

He admires a passing German barge from Hamburg. 'Wonderful thing to handle. She has a bow thrust that can turn her round in circles.'

His boat is filling with returning visitors from the Barrier. Even in the soft, undemanding duties of the tripping boat trade, Sargents try to be ahead of the river. 'One New Year's Eve we were around Big Ben waiting for midnight. There were a good few boats lying by Westminster Bridge. The bridge was chock-a-block, all cheering like mad.

'We went down under the bridge on the ebb tide and back up and level with the bridge when it started chiming and we were the only boat moving at midnight. There were four Australian girls in the cabin with us. I bet they talk about it even now.'

I walk on. The houses in Derrick Gardens, Charlton, have mock classical façades and pointed roofs. An address in River View sports a plaque depicting a Thames sailing barge. It is legitimate: the river is in view with some neck straining, and restored barges, like large brown butterflies, do occasionally flutter past to assist in another Sherlock Holmes film in which the artful camera work is required to exclude falsifying detail.

Some Japanese men have come to wonder at the Barrier. It is a long way from their West End hotel and they are impressed. How appropriate to meet Japanese here. After passing the Anchor and Hope and Vaizey Wharf, I walked along Nagasaki and Hiroshima Promenade, some of the most evocative place names on Earth appropriated for the cool, open approaches to this strange spot. Of course no name is sacred. Somebody has slashed through the 'H' in Hiroshima with a black paint gun.

The barrier reposes in the departing river like a shining, indented finishing line. It attracts a lot of civil engineers. The oriental visitors may have been impressed with this plaudit from wise observers, on a plaque: 'Concrete Society award for outstanding merit in the use of concrete, 1982. Also the Structural Steel Design Award 1983 for the steelwork design of the river barrier rising sector gates.'

The judges said this: 'The design, concept, structural analysis and attention to detail of these gates is worthy of the highest praise. The formidable task of fabricating and erecting the steelwork undertaken to extremely accurate tolerances, played no small part in the success of this unique project.'

Since the mid nineteenth century there had been talk of damming the river at Woolwich and turning it into a fresh water lake. That formidable champion of the river, Sir Alan Herbert, favoured blocking the river off and turning the foaming torrent into a tranquil stream. No more unsavoury mudflats.

At the peak of man's adulation of the motor car, there were proposals to do away with the Thames altogether, divert it down some massive culvert near Chiswick and convert this dry, looping valley into a ten-lane motorway between Woolwich and Kew.

As it became more difficult to build roads above ground in London, the construction company Costain tactfully suggested reversing the priorities. Leave the Thames where it was but build the combined road and railway under it. History will judge the merits of this proposal.

The Barrier – *The Times* saw it as a row of drowned Sydney Opera houses – seems to have settled the matter of the dam. A leading article noted at the time of the opening in 1984: 'In its spectacular overruns in price and delivery dates it was an emblem of the industrial history of the 1970s and 1980s. London is now protected against anything other than an astronomically remote threat for a century.'

Its construction was troubled by flooding and awful industrial action. 'A bit of a saga, to be honest with you.' says Stephen Gleeson, who manages the Barrier visitor centre, and used to be a theatre manager. The barrier cost £480 million; raising the riverbank, another £50 million. The rivers and rivulets entering the Thames in London have been similarly protected with gates, mini barriers and barrages. People along the river side have glass walls like an acquarium in place of privet hedges.

This was the best of five sites, with the firmest foundations, of tough chalk. For shipping coming up river it is the only place with a straight approach. But it has been hit by the occasional ship whose master lacks the skill to negotiatate a gap sixty-two metres wide. 'Recently one took a piece of roof off one side. Unbelieveable. There have been some classics. One hit the barrier so badly it broke up. It was towed over the side to a convenient scrap yard.'

I became aware of what sounds like a thunderstorm, set to music. It turns out to be a film show with loud percussion. I walk into this continuously repeating show at the point where massive flood gates, four thousand tonnes of steel are being towed the length of the East Coast in one operation. A gate is shown being manoeuvred into a slot, by computer controlled cranes, on a river smooth as glass after a blizzard. The gates were first successfully operated in October 1982.

It was an enormous civil engineering triumph carried out in a dreadful environment. Consider the divers who fixed its foundations. 'Forget the

North Sea oil rigs, those divers were working blind in this water. There was always mud and sediment in suspension.

I am looking for a twentieth century Brunel behind this wonder, while not expecting to find one. It is the way with great constructions these days. Authorship is democratically apportioned to a team, and a computer.

But, lo and behold, there is a single brilliant idea, easy enough for a primary schoolchild to grasp. It can be pinned on the grave of the late Charles Draper, who with Victorian sense of unreward died shortly before the royal opening in 1984.

Mr Draper, who happened to look at his gas tap, noted how it is partly solid, containing a valve which slides round to seal off the gas. And so it is with the barrier. Gates are retracted into concrete sills under the water and swing up into position to shut out the water. But it is not Draper's barrier, as it might have been Brunel's barrier 100 years ago. It is The Team's Barrier.

The Barrier is a guarantor of a safe night's sleep anywhere on the riverside, from here to Chiswick. As far away as Northern Scotland computers taste the weather thirty-six hours ahead of the sort of storm which activates the barrier. Typical barrier-closing conditions would involve a combination of storm around the north of Scotland, a very high tide and a wind blowing down the Channel, with a large mass of water splitting off into the river.

Such a tide might have devastated the entire city of London, most of Westminster and smothered communications in the City. Pepys recorded such an inundation: 'Last night there was a great flood in Westminster and men in wherries did row.' Stephen offers me a new theory – that King Canute was at Westminster and not at the seaside when he uttered his futile command to the waves.

'Don't get the impression London would have been flooded with a bloody big tidal wave like Krakatoa,' says Stephen, who has absorbed the theatricality of his former calling. 'It would just have been an abnormally high tide. I've actually stood on the side here with that sort of high tide, a ship has gone by and the wave of that ship has sploshed over the top of the wall.'

To date the barrier has been used four times to block a potential flood. Because it works nobody asleep in low Central London would know it has been deployed. It takes fifteen minutes to test. 'We try to raise the barrier two hours before low tide, leaving a damn great hole to take that extra water.'

This essential procedure is normally as unmoveable as a twenty-one gun salute for a ruling monarch. However a big ship at the Tate and Lyle sugar refinery, opposite and downstream, could stop it. 'If a large vessel came in

219

very deeply laden and we shut the gates, it might go wallop on the bottom. Closures have been cancelled for that.'

The Ark Royal is the only boat that makes the barrier look small. 'Band playing and Harriers on the front. Marvellous. It always goes through on the high tide so they don't scrape the bottom.'

The barrier is designed to stop flooding from the sea. But it is so big and important it is blamed for things it doesn't do: it does not cause flooding upstream by stopping the escape of river water, although people think so.

Stephen sounds like an umbrella salesman rejoicing in the prospect of rain as he outlines the barrier's growing justification. 'Weather conditions are damn well getting worse. South-east England is slowly sinking. The Polar icecap is melting. There is more water in the sea. So the barrier will be closed more frequently.'

The official opening, on a cold May morning, was a great river event, *The Times* noted. The Queen arrived in the barge Royal Nore, passing down under bridges sparingly decorated with bunting only on the side facing her progress. It tied up at Unity Pier, renamed Barrier Gardens Pier. She wore a lime green outfit by Norman Hartnell. Mrs Ethel Livingstone, mother of the leader of Greater London Council wore a two-piece pink suit from Marks and Spencer.

The Newham Borough band, playing a selection from the Water Music, was drowned by the sound of klaxons and hooters. One hundred and thirty-three dignitaries of greater or lesser connection with the barrier were on hand. The Queen expressed her pleasure that the barrier was finally open. In reality it had been open for eighteen months and the silver was already tarnished.

Is it the Eighth Wonder? 'I think so, in terms of its engineering and what it does. The Dutch have barrages, but there is no other structure like this in the world that allows things to go through at all times, except when it is closed for a flood or to be tested.

The Barrier has lots of imitators. The Chinese are interested in applying the principle to the tragically flooding Yangtse. Venice might build something like this. The theory is sound for any kind of waterway where passing space for big ships is needed.

Stephen's job is to demonstrate its value as tourist attraction. 'It is the cheapest paid London attraction. But it gets very little casual trade. People have to be 100 per cent determined to get here. They could reduce it to a teahut and still make a few bob.'

I descend into what is probably the river's most secret crossing. The walk across the third of a mile of water, along by tunnel and up by 485 stairs takes me half an hour.

On the other side, I am near the end of the river, standing on the edge of the empty Victoria Docks opposite Millenium Mills. The dismantling of Docklands has not yet touched these H. G. Wells, *War of the Worlds* cranes, which stand here still, huge and irrelevant on the edge of vast deserts of concrete.

'The flags of every nation fly from those tapering spars on the ships, in the great argosies of commerce that from every port in the world have congregated to do honour to the monarch of marts, London, and pour out the riches of the universe at her proud feet,' exulted the Victorian writer Aaron Watson.

The argosies have all gone. There are ducks in their place on the gale-whipped waters that extend for hundreds of yards in both directions. The windows of the Artful Dodger pub are shattered.

I am weary, exuberant and dazzled. Even in the slow evolution on the river over three weeks, the transition is remarkable. And so, my walk ends, next to a line of silver walnut shells, pressed into the river bed through which the river I first met as a damp line in a Gloucestershire meadow, is strained twice a day out into the North Sea.

In *Little Dorrit* Clennan symbolically releases the roses he has accepted from Minnie, who is pledged to marry, and does marry, someone else.

'When he had walked on the river's brink in the peaceful moonlight for some half an hour, he put his hand in his breast and tenderly took out the handful of roses. Perhaps he put them to his heart, perhaps he put them to his lips, but certainly he bent down on the shore and gently launched them on the flowing river. Pale and unreal in the moonlight, the river floated them away.

'. . . floated away upon the river. And thus do greater things that once were in our breasts, and near our hearts, flow from us to the eternal seas.'

Index

Windsor Castle, from Albert Bridge.

'The home of everyone is to him his castle and fortress.'

– Edward Coke.